THE COINAGE AND MINTS OF PHOENICIA

HARVARD SEMITIC MONOGRAPHS

edited by
Frank Moore Cross

Number 26

THE COINAGE AND MINTS OF PHOENICIA
The Pre-Alexandrine Period
by
John Wilson Betlyon

John Wilson Betlyon

THE COINAGE AND MINTS OF PHOENICIA
The Pre-Alexandrine Period

Scholars Press
Chico, California

THE COINAGE AND MINTS OF PHOENICIA
The Pre-Alexandrine Period

by
John Wilson Betlyon

C J
1379
.B47
1982

Copyright 1980
by
The President and Fellows of Harvard College

Scholars Press Edition, 1982

Library of Congress Cataloging in Publication Data
Betlyon, John Wilson.
   The coinage and mints of Phoenicia.

   (Harvard Semitic monographs ; no. 26)
   Revision of thesis (Ph.D.)—Harvard University, 1978.
   Bibliography : p.
   1. Coins, Phoenician. I. Title. II. Series.
CJ1379.B47 1980   737.4939'44   82–16897
ISBN 0–89130–588–2

Printed in the United States of America

Contents

Preface

This study is a revised version of a doctoral dissertation presented to the Department of Near Eastern Languages and Civilizations, Harvard University, in 1978. The project began at the suggestion of the late Professor G. Ernest Wright in the fall of 1974. Initial work with coins was undertaken in the summer of 1975 in the cabinets of the American Numismatic Society, New York City. At that time Dr. Margaret Thompson and Dr. Nancy Waggoner taught me the methodology of a numismatist, providing technical, stylistic, and inspirational advice ever since.

Throughout the various stages of this work's preparation, actual coins have been studied in various cabinets across the globe. I acknowledge the kind assistance of Dr. Martin Price (British Museum), Mme. Hélène Nicholet (Bibliothèque nationale), Professor Yigal Shiloh (Hebrew University, Jerusalem), Dr. Ya'akov Meshorer (Israel Museum), Dr. Joseph Elgavish (Museum of Ancient Art, Haifa), Dr. Joseph Ringel (Maritime Museum, Haifa), Dr. Arie Kindler (Kadman Numismatic Museum, Tel 'Aviv), Dr. Leo Mildenberg (Bank Leu, Zürich), and Frau Sylvia Hurter (Bank Leu, Zürich). Without the help of these people, work on the coins would have been impossible.

For financial assistance throughout the course of the preparation of this book, thanks are due to the American Numismatic Society, the Zion Research Foundation, the American Schools of Oriental Research, and the Johnson Research Fund of the American Philosophical Society.

Special thanks must go to the most influential of my mentors, Professor Frank Moore Cross. Through periods of discouragement his words of criticism and inspiration have enabled me to continue. I am deeply indebted to him.

I wish to thank Esther Finkelstein whose skill and expertise made possible the final preparation of the manuscript.

Finally, I would like to thank my wife, Stephanie, for her help in sorting through pages and pages of notes, stacks of bibliography, and her talent with pen and ink.

vii

Of course any mistakes found herein are solely the responsibility of the writer.

This study is dedicated to my parents and my parents-in-law, without whose support and understanding it would not have been possible.

Summer, 1980   Lycoming College
                                Williamsport, Pennsylvania

List of Abbreviations

AASOR	*Annual of the American Schools of Oriental Research*
AJA	*American Journal of Archaeology*
ANEP	*The Ancient Near East in Pictures,* ed. James B. Pritchard (Princeton: Princeton University Press, 1954)
ANS	American Numismatic Society
ANSMN	*American Numismatic Society Museum Notes*
ANSNNM	*American Numismatic Society Numismatic Notes and Monographs*
ASOR	American Schools of Oriental Research
BA	*The Biblical Archaeologist*
BASOR	*Bulletin of the American Schools of Oriental Research*
BMB	*Bulletin of the Musée du Beyrouth*
BMC Arabia, Mesopotamia, Persia, etc.	*Catalogue of the Greek Coins of Arabia, Mesopotamia, Persia, etc.,* by G.F. Hill (London: British Museum, 1922)
BMC Cyprus	*Catalogue of the Greek Coins of Cyprus,* by G.F. Hill (London: British Museum, 1904)
BMC Galatia, Cappadocia, and Syria	*Catalogue of the Greek Coins of Galatia, Cappadocia, and Syria,* by Warwick Wroth (London: British Museum, 1899)
BMC Lycaonia, Isauria, and Cilicia	*Catalogue of the Greek Coins of Lycaonia, Isauria, and Cilicia,* by G.F. Hill (London: British Museum, 1900)
BMC Palestine	*Catalogue of the Greek Coins of Palestine,* by G.F. Hill (London: British Museum, 1914)
BMC Phoenicia	*Catalogue of the Greek Coins of Phoenicia,* by G.F. Hill (London: British Museum, 1910)
CAH³	*Cambridge Ancient History,* 3rd ediion
CBQ	*Catholic Biblical Quarterly*
CIL	*Corpus inscriptionum latinarum* (Berlin, 1869-)
CIS	*Corpus inscriptionum semiticarum* (Paris, 1881-)

CMHE	*Canaanite Myth and Hebrew Epic*, by Frank Moore Cross (Cambridge, MA: Harvard University Press, 1973)
CTA	*Corpus des tablettes en cunéiformes alphabétiques*, by A. Herdner (Paris: Imprimerie nationale, 1963)
DLPS	*The Development of the Late Phoenician Scripts*, by J.B. Peckham (Cambridge, MA: Harvard University Press, 1968)
EI	*Eretz Israel* (Jerusalem)
Harden, *The Phoenicians*	Donald Harden, *The Phoenicians*, 2nd rev. ed. (Baltimore: Penguin Books, 1971)
HTR	*The Harvard Theological Review*
IEJ	*Israel Exploration Journal*
IES	Israel Exploration Society
IGCH	*Inventory of Greek Coin Hoards*, eds. Margaret Thompson, Otto Mørkholm, and Colin M. Kraay (New York: American Numismatic Society, 1973)
INCJ	*Proceedings. International Numismatic Convention, Jerusalem, 27-31 December, 1963* (Tel Aviv: Schocken, 1967)
INJ	*Israel Numismatic Journal*
JAOS	*Journal of the American Oriental Society*
JBL	*Journal of Biblical Literature*
JIAN	*Journal international d'archéologie numismatique*
JNES	*Journal of Near Eastern Studies*
KAI	*Kanaanäische und aramäische Inschriften*, by H. Donner and W. Röllig (Wiesbaden: Harrassowitz, 1962-1964)
Les Perses achéménides	*Catalogue des monnaies grecques: Les Perses achéménides, les satrapes et les dynastes de leur empire; Chypre et Phénicie*, by E. Babelon (Paris: Rollin et Feuardent, 1893)
MUSJ	*Mélanges de l'université Saint-Joseph* (Beirut)
NC	*Numismatic Chronicle*
NZ	*Numismatische Zeitschrift*

OIP	*Oriental Institute Publications*
PEQ	*Palestine Exploration Quarterly*
PNPPI	*Personal Names in the Phoenician and Punic Inscriptions,* by F.L. Benz (Rome: Pontifical Biblical Institute, 1972)
QDAP	*Quarterly of the Department of Antiquities of Palestine*
RB	*Revue Biblique*
RBN	*Revue belge de numismatique*
Traité, II, 2	*Traité des monnaies grecques et romaines,* Vol. II, Part 2, by E. Babelon (Paris: E. Leroux, 1910)
VT	*Vetus Testamentum*
YGC	*Yahweh and the Gods of Canaan,* by W. F. Albright (Garden City, NY: Doubleday, 1968)
ZAW	*Zeitschrift für die alttestamentliche Wissenschaft*
ZDMG	*Zeitschrift der Deutschen Morgenländischen Gesellschaft*

Introduction

In the late nineteenth and early twentieth centuries,
the first systematic attempts were made to study the earliest
coins of Phoenicia. J.P. Six, working in the last quarter
of the nineteenth century, sought to synthesize the available
data regarding coins from Sidon, Tyre, Aradus, and Byblos.
J. Rouvier built upon Six's work some twenty years later.
Efforts to publish the major collections in Paris and London
evolved in the same period. By 1920, G.F. Hill and E. Babelon
had completed the standard catalogues of the pre-Alexandrine
Phoenician coinages.

Classical scholars traditionally were called upon to
deal with the Phoenician coins, even though their ethnics
were written in the Phoenician or Aramaic languages — and not
Greek. Archaeological discoveries in the last two decades
have made it imperative that these coins be reexamined. M.
Dunand's excavations at Sidon, for example, have greatly
increased the precision with which the fifth and fourth
century B.C.E. Sidonian king list may be delineated. Consequently a new analysis and chronological survey of the coins
has been warranted.

During the fourth century, Sidon led the Phoenician city-
states in two revolts. Evidence purports that the Phoenician
cities of Tyre and Byblos were allied with the Sidonians.
Aradus, located much further north, was apparently kept from
joining the other three major cities through strict Persian
controls. The loose coalition of city-states which resulted,
however, manifested itself politically, militarily, economically, and monetarily.

Sidon, the largest and most important of the Persian
period Phoenician cities, will serve as the basis for this
study. The coins of the Sidonian mint are well known from
this period, beginning ca. 450 B.C.E. and continuing through
the conquests of Alexander the Great. Using evidence from
the coins themselves and from various archaeological sources,
the coins will be arranged in their chronological order of

1

issue by mint. Only extant types will be listed, with descriptions of obverse, reverse, metal, denomination, and the location of the specimen studied for this monograph. The collections of the American Numismatic Society form the core of the material used in the preparation of this study. Motifs on the obverse and reverse types will be discussed in some detail. The mints of Aradus, Byblos, and Tyre will be discussed in like manner as Sidon. The predominance of the Sidonian mint in the early years of the Phoenician mints' operations necessitates this order.

Plates, made possible by a grant from the American Philosophical Society, appear at the end of the text and depict the coins on a scale of 1 :: 1.

Chapter 1

SIDON

Classical sources have made it plain that Sidon was the most prominent of the cities in Persian period Phoenicia.[1] In wealth and resources, it surpassed by far all the other Phoenician cities, according to Diodorus.[2] Indeed, its coinage is one of the better known pre-Alexandrine series in the Levant. Studies of the coinage had been published by scholars such as Six, Head, Rouvier, Babelon, and Hill; but many problems of chronology and attribution remained.[3] With the recent resumption of excavations at Sidon by M. Dunand, however, new data have come to light.[4] Foremost among his discoveries was an inscription written in the lapidary Phoenician script of the early fourth century B.C.E. The new inscription contains the names of four previously unknown Sidonian kings.[5] This new information has made it possible for us to reexamine the pre-Alexandrine Sidonian coinage and to propose a revised chronological scheme for these issues.[6]

The Earliest Coinage
ca. 450-435 B.C.E.

1. OBV: Galley with mast and unfurled triangular sail to l. Border of dots.

   REV: Persian king standing to r., shooting bow held in l. hand; in incuse. Border of dots.

   AR 1/2 Šeqel, Vienna.[7] Plate 1.

2. OBV: Same as 1.

   REV: Three-tiered podium of the temple of 'Ešmun; in incuse. Border of dots.

   AR 1/32 Šeqel, New York.[8] Plate 1.

The galley appeared on almost all of the coins which Sidon minted before the coming of Alexander the Great in 332 B.C.E. Typologically, the depiction of the galley's sail is of the utmost importance, for on these earliest coins it is unfurled and triangular in shape. On later issues the sail is partially furled and eventually lost, being replaced by a bank of oars.

The half šeqel has an obverse depicting the galley and
its sail; the reverse type is the well-known engraving of the
Persian king shooting the bow. The obverse type is a very
early one; however, the reverse type has a number of later
parallels in the coin series. The thirty-second šeqel has
the same rendering of the galley on the obverse, but with a
completely new reverse.[9] This reverse type is unparalleled
in later issues; and when coupled with the early obverse type,
it definitely antedates the other coins with the king shooting
the bow or slaying the lion.

The unique design on the reverse type of the thirty-
second šeqel is a stepped pyramid, resembling a Mesopotamian
ziggurat. Fortunately, Dunand's recent excavations have
unearthed just such a structure.[10] Dunand described it as a
podium of ziggurat-like construction from Babylonian times
(early to mid-sixth century B.C.E.), which followed the plan
of the typical Babylonian temple. It was clearly built by
the Sidonians, however, and was subsequently altered by them
in the Persian period.[11] The method of construction is
clearly Phoenician, with parallels in Byblos and in the
temple of Jerusalem.[12] The Sidonian structure was the podium
of the temple of 'Ešmun,[13] which may have served as the focal
point of the Sidonian cult. This coin and the half šeqel
with the same obverse type are the only extant examples of
this early Sidonian coinage. Although the coins fit well into
a relative chronology, no attempt at an absolute dating is
possible. Consequently, it remains difficult to attribute
these coins to a specific ruler. Our problem is compounded
by the lack of names or abbreviations of names on these coins.
From the relative position in the coin series, however, we
may postulate that they came from the period ca. 450-435
B.C.E., and may be associated with either of the last two
kings of the dynasty of 'Ešmun ʿazor — Bôd ʿaštart or Yatonmilk
(Sidqyaton).[14]

The Second Sidonian Series
ca. 435-420 B.C.E.

3. OBV: Galley with mast and partially furled sail to l.,
          over two lines of waves.

REV: Chariot pulled by pacing horses to l., with driver
      holding reins in hands; King of Persia rides in
      chariot; figure of goat at l. above; in incuse
      square.

AR Double S̆eqel, Paris. Plate 1.

4. OBV: Same as 3.

    REV: King of Persia, wearing crown, with quiver at
          shoulder, shooting bow to r.; head of goat incuse
          to r.; head of satyr incuse to l. facing; incuse
          square.

    AR 1/2 S̆eqel, Paris. Plate 1.

5. OBV: Same as 3.

    REV: King of Persia, wearing crown, with quiver at
          shoulder, in running (kneeling ?) attitude to r.;
          king is shooting bow held in l. hand to r.; in
          incuse square.

    AR 1/16 S̆eqel, New York. Plate 1.

6. OBV: Same as 3.

    REV: Head of Satyr, facing.

    AR 1/64 S̆eqel, New York. Plate 1.

    The obverse types of this second series show a develop-
ment from those of the earliest Sidonian coins. The sail on
the galley is partially furled rather than totally unfurled.
Furthermore, the galley is depicted as riding the crests of
two rows of waves.[15] The reverse type of the double s̆eqel
has a chariot pulled by pacing horses, with a driver and a
rider in the chariot. A goat is at the top left of the
reverse. The figure riding in the chariot has been thought
to be the King of Persia since the earliest work on these
coins was completed.[16] More recently, however, H. Seyrig
has mistakenly argued that this figure is the statue of the
baʿl of Sidon.[17] He cited evidence to support this claim
from the terracottas published by Chéhab, which were found
at Kharayeb, near Sidon.[18] The evidence, however, is
inconclusive at best. The standing figure behind the
chariot driver is best described as the King of Persia, in a
pose identical to that of many glyptic examples of the same
scene.[19] As we shall see below, the King is depicted in his
role as suzerain over Sidon and god of the royal cult.

    The smaller denominations use the same type on their
obverses, but introduce new reverse types showing Persian

influence. On the half šeqel, the Persian king is shown
wearing the royal crown, with a quiver at his shoulder and
shooting a bow;[20] the head of a goat and the head of a satyr
appear on either side of the king.[21] The larger fraction
has a similar reverse type, without the goat and satyr's
heads, and with the king in a slightly altered position. The
smaller fraction has the usual obverse, but simply the head of
a satyr on the reverse; this satyr's head is not intaglio.
Although there is a difference in the reverse types, the
smaller denominations are clearly linked to the double šeqels
in time. These coins may have been minted by Yatonmilk or
some unknown king who ruled after him in the mid- to late-
fifth century B.C.E. (ca. 435-420).

Ba‘lšallim I
ca. 420-410 B.C.E.

7. OBV: Galley, to 1., before battlemented wall of city
          with five towers; galley has row of shields along
          bulwark; two lions salient addorsed in exergue.
          Cable border.

    REV: Chariot drawn by galloping horses to 1., driver
          holds reins; King of Persia rides in chariot;
          below, in incuse, goat running 1. looking back over
          shoulder; in circular incuse. Border of dots.

    AR Double Šeqel, New York. Plate 1.

8. OBV: Same as 7.

    REV: Similar to 7, except ℧𝟿 (בב) above chariot.

    AR Double Šeqel, New York.[22] Plate 1.

    As the development of the Sidonian coin types continued,
the obverse type underwent a further alteration in which the
sails were lost altogether on the galley. The vessel reached
another stage in its portrayal with a row of shields along
its bulwark and a battering ram affixed to its bow (probably
indicating that we are definitely dealing with a warship).
The galley appears to be anchored before the city wall of
Sidon, which has several battlemented towers. The scene
recalls the descriptions of Sidon in the Classical sources.[23]
In the exergue are two Persian-style lions.[24] The reverse
type was also modified. The chariot in which the King of
Persia is riding is drawn by galloping rather than pacing
horses. The goat, which had been above the chariot, is now

shown below it in a running position with its head turned
looking over its shoulder; the pose is reminiscent of Syrian
hunting scenes.[25] These changes in the obverse and reverse
types of the double šeqel may best be explained by a change
in the moneying authority of the city, which was the king.
From the inscriptional data, we may reasonably attribute
these coins to King Ba‘lšallim I, who ruled before ‘Abd’ešmun,
whose reign ended ca. 400 B.C.E.

Ba‘lšallim I is the first Sidonian king to place his
initials on his coin types. The letters **ש ל** (בש) may be
read on the reverse type of his double šeqel.[26] What
prompted this king to place his initials on his coins is not
known. Perhaps it was the example of other coinages which
were circulating throughout the eastern Mediterranean which
employed various systems of identification. Whatever the
impetus, we are certain that it was Ba‘lšallim I who began
this practice at Sidon. His example was followed by
succeeding monarchs. The use of ethnic-type inscriptions was
also begun by the other Phoenician mints, probably following
this example.[27]

‘Abd’ešmun
ca. 410-400 B.C.E.

9.   OBV: Similar to 7, except city has four towers.

    REV: Persian king wearing crown, slaying lion standing
          before him on hind legs; he seizes it by forelock
          with l. hand and is about to strike with dagger in
          r. hand; in incuse square.

    AR   1/2 Šeqel, New York.

10. OBV: Similar to 7, except city with three towers; one
          lion in exergue.

    REV: Persian king wearing crown to r.; standing, shooting
          bow to r.; bow held in l. hand; incuse head of goat
          to r.; incuse head of satyr to l.; all in incuse
          square.

    AR   1/16 Šeqel, New York.   Plate 1.

11. OBV: Similar to 7, except city with two towers; one lion
          in exergue.

    REV: Same as 10.

    AR   1/32 Šeqel, Paris (unpublished).[28]

12. OBV: Same as 7.

REV: Similar to 7, except **ᒐO**(עב) above chariot.

AR Double Šeqel, New York. Plate 2.

13. OBV: Similar to 7, except **ᒐO**(עב) above.

      REV: Same as 12.

      AR Double Šeqel, New York. Plate 2.

14. OBV: Similar to 7, except city has four towers and **ᒐ** (ב) above.

      REV: **ᒐO**(עב) between legs of Persian king (or hero?) and lion, which king is slaying; lion stands before king on hind legs to l.; king, to r., seizes lion by forelock in l. hand and is about to strike with dagger in r. hand; in incuse square.

      AR 1/2 Šeqel, London.

ʿAbdʾešmun placed the abbreviation of his name, **ᒐO**(עב),[29] on the same coin types used by Baʿ lšallim I. Except for these new abbreviations, he did not further alter the types which he inherited from his predecessor.

Issued probably under Baʿlšallim I and ʿAbdʾešmun were some fractional denominations (nos. 9-11) without nominal abbreviations. The half šeqel differs from the double šeqel on the obverse by deleting one tower from the representation of the city wall; on the reverse, however, is the Persian king slaying the lion. This is a common scene known from Achaemenid art at Persepolis[30] and from numerous Persian pyramidal stamp seals.[31] This half šeqel was followed by another with identical types and the added abbreviation **ᒐO** on the reverse. We have this coin only in an extant example which also has a **ᒐ** (ב) on the obverse. This is a transitional coin, probably from the early months of the reign of Baʿ naʾ, who followed ʿAbdʾešmun, and who used a *bet* to abbreviate his name. The reverse die of the earlier coin of ʿAbdʾešmun was still in use and had not yet been changed when Baʿ naʾ issued his first coins (no. 14).

A sixteenth šeqel, with a similar obverse type, but with only three towers and one lion in the exergue, and the reverse depicting the king shooting the bow, with the goat's head and the satyr's head, is probably of Baʿ lšallim I; such fractions may have also been issued by ʿAbdʾešmun without his initials.

Ba'na'
ca. 400-386/385 B.C.E.

15. OBV: Same as 7.
    REV: Similar to 7, except 𐤁 (ב) above.
    AR Double Šeqel, New York.

16. OBV: Same as 9.
    REV: Similar to 14, except 𐤏𐤁 (בע) between legs of king
         (or hero?) and lion.
    AR 1/2 Šeqel, New York. Plate 2.

A double šeqel is extant with 𐤁 (ב) above the chariot of
the reverse. A half šeqel was struck like the others with
these same types, but with 𐤏𐤁 (בע) on the reverse and no
letters on the obverse. These abbreviations are clearly
representative of the next king on the list, Ba'na'.[32] From
the evidence now available, his reign was probably from
ca. 400 until 386/385 B.C.E. It is not surprising that this
king did nothing to change the types of the coins, considering
the precedents set by his predecessors.

Ba'lšallim II
386/385-372 B.C.E.

17. OBV: Same as 7.
    REV: Chariot drawn by galloping horses to l., driver
         holds reins in hands; King of Persia rides in
         chariot; King of Sidon, in Egyptian-style garments
         carrying cultic scepter and votive vase following;
         below, in incuse, a goat running l. looking back
         over shoulder; in circular incuse. Border of dots.
    AR Double Šeqel, New York.

18. OBV: 𐤁 (ב) above; war galley to l., with oars, row of
         shields along bulwark; small figure as figurehead
         on bow; ornament over stern; rudder; below, two
         zigzag lines of waves. Cable border. Date:
         undated and 14.
    REV: Chariot drawn by pacing horses to l.; driver leans
         forward holding reins; King of Persia in chariot;
         King of Sidon in Egyptian-style garments carrying
         cultic scepter and votive vase follows chariot;
         double exergual line; all in incuse circle. Cable
         border.
    AR Double Šeqel, London.[33] Plate 2.

19. OBV: Similar to 18, except no date.
    REV: Similar to 18, except no King of Sidon.

AR 1/2 Šeqel, New York. Plate 2.

20. OBV: Same as 18.

    REV: Persian king wearing crown, slaying lion standing
before him on hind legs; he seizes it by forelock
with l. hand and is about to strike with dagger in
r. hand; in incuse square.

AR 1/16 Šeqel, New York. Plate 2.

21. OBV: Same as 19.

    REV: Persian king wearing crown to r.; standing,
shooting bow to r.; bow held in l. hand; incuse
head of goat to r.; incuse head of satyr to l.;
all in incuse square.

AR 1/32 Šeqel, New York.

22. OBV: Same as 19.

    REV: Head of satyr, facing; in incuse. Border of dots.

AR 1/64 Šeqel, New York.

    The crown prince listed in Dunand's inscription,
Ba'lšallim II, became King of Sidon after Ba'na'. He first
issued a transitional double šeqel which contained no inscription, but changed the reverse type to include a follower
behind the chariot of the Persian king. The "follower" is
the King of Sidon in his role as chief priest of the city's
cults of Ba'l, 'Aštart, 'Ešmun, and the royal cult of the
Persian king.[34] This is the first representation of a living
king on Sidon's coinage, and it must be considered a personal
innovation of Ba'lšallim II.[35]

    He also introduced a new obverse type throughout all
denominations while he continued changes in the reverse types.
Early in his reign (probably in his first year), coins were
struck with obverse types lacking the battlemented walls and
towers of the city and the lions of Persia. The obverse
type bore only the war galley of the Sidonian navy, with
shields along the bulwark, a small figurehead (pataecus) on
the bow, and a symbol associated with 'Ašerah-'Ēlat (the
mother goddess) on the stern with the rudder (aphlaston),
oars, waves below, and the letter 𐤁 (ב) above. Three aspects
of this new obverse type are of special interest: the war
galley is no longer depicted in port, but at sea;[36] the
standard is displayed on the galley's stern;[37] and the letter

ϟ (ב) is used as an abbreviation for Baʿlšallim II. This is
the same abbreviation which Baʿ na' used on occasion, but the
types have been so thoroughly changed that no confusion
between the two kings is possible.

The reverse type was also changed. The horses were
returned to their pacing attitude, and the goat was lost.
The Persian king, the Sidonian king, and the driver appear
as before. Baʿlšallim II went to great lengths to issue
coins peculiar to himself. Perhaps this was in response to
the growing power of Sidon on the Mediterranean, both militarily and commercially. His reign lasted fourteen years,
from 386/385 to 372 B.C.E. His coins are undated except for
one late double šeqel, with the date of regnal year 14 on the
reverse.[38]

Baʿlšallim II's half šeqel had the obverse type of the
double šeqel, but lacked the King of Sidon on the reverse
(probably for lack of space). His sixteenth šeqel, thirty-
second šeqel, and sixty-fourth šeqel had the same obverses
with reverse scenes familiar from earlier issues, including
the Persian king slaying the lion and the representation of a
satyr's head (facing) on the sixty-fourth.[39]

ʿAbdʿaštart I
372-362/361 B.C.E.

23. OBV: War galley to l., with oars, row of shields along
           bulwark; small figure as figurehead on bow; ornament
           over stern; rudder; above, dates, 1-9;[40] below, four
           zigzag lines of waves. Cable border.

     REV: Similar to 18, except ϟO(עב) in field above, and no
           incuse square.

     AR Double Šeqel, London and Rouvier.[41] Plate 2.

24. OBV: Similar to 23, except dates.
     REV: Similar to 23, except no King of Sidon to l.
     AR 1/2 Šeqel, London, Rouvier, and New York. Plate 2.

25. OBV: Similar to 23, except zigzag line of waves.
     REV: Same as 24.
     AR 1/4 Šeqel, New York.

26. OBV: Similar to 25, except border of dots.
     REV: Same as 14.
     AR 1/16 Šeqel, New York.

27. OBV: Similar to 26, except no dates and ᒐ (ב) above
          galley.

     REV: Similar to 14, except O (ע) between legs of king
          and lion.

     AR 1/16 Šeqel, New York. Plates 2 and 3.

28. OBV: War galley to l., with oars, row of shields along
          bulwark; ornament over stern; rudder; below, one
          zigzag line of waves.

     REV: King of Persia in kneeling attitude, with bow in l.
          hand and spear (lance) in r. hand held transversely
          over shoulder; in incuse square.

     AR 1/32 Šeqel, New York.

    Ba'lšallim II was followed in 372 (using the dated
double šeqel as a guide) by 'Abd'aštart I, known in the
Greek sources as Straton, the Philhellene.[42] 'Abd'aštart
made only minor changes in the Sidonian coin types. On the
obverse types, the initial of Ba'lšallim II was replaced by
the date — the year of the coin's issue, according to the
years of the king's reign. Some dies appear to have been
altered rather than scrapped entirely.[43] Where the date
appeared on the late double šeqel of Ba'lšallim II,
'Abd'aštart I placed an abbreviation of his name, ᒐO (עב).
Other than this, the only change he made was to increase
the number of lines of waves under the galley on the obverse
type from two to four on the double šeqel. In effect, the
types had been standardized.

    'Abd'aštart I's fractional issues included a half šeqel,
a quarter šeqel, a sixteenth šeqel, and a thirty-second šeqel.
The half šeqel lacks the King of Sidon following the chariot;
the quarter šeqel had only two lines of waves, instead of the
usual four on the obverse; the sixteenth šeqel has the
reverse type of the Persian king slaying the lion, with the
ᒐO inscription between the two figures' legs. An early
sixteenth šeqel of his reign retained the old obverse of
Ba'lšallim II with the ᒐ (ב), adding the O (ע) for
'Abd'aštart between the lion and king on the reverse. This
issue was quickly replaced with the new king's own obverse
type. The thirty-second šeqel has a new reverse type, seen at
Sidon again only on a bronze coin from this same period,
which depicts the Persian king with both bow and spear (lance)

held over his shoulder.

29. OBV: Same as 25.
    REV: Similar to 24, except border of dots; no inscription.
    AE 6.63 g., London and New York. Plate 3.

30. OBV: Similar to 25, except galley to r.
    REV: Similar to 29, except chariot drawn to r.
    AE 3.98 g., New York.

31. OBV: Similar to 25, except dates 3-10.
    REV: Similar to 28, except no incuse square.
    AE 3.49 g., New York. Plate 3.

32. OBV: Bearded, crowned head of ʽAbdʽaštart, to r.; **ϑο**
         (עב) on l.
    REV: War galley, with oars, row of shields along bulwark, to l.; rudder; date, 8, above; no waves below.
    AR Attic Tetradrachm, Israel Museum.[44] Figure 1.

33. OBV: Same as 32.
    REV: Similar to 32, except dates, 11-12, above.
    AE 3.00 g., London and New York. Plate 3.

Three groupings of bronze coins were issued by
ʽAbdʽaštart I, also: a coin weighing 6.63 g. with obverse
and reverse types similar to those of the silver half and
quarter šeqels, lacking an inscription on the reverse (a
variant of this coin [no. 30] has both types reversed); a
small coin, weighing only approximately 3.50 g. with obverse
similar to that of the silver quarter šeqel, and dated from
years 3 to 10, with reverse type showing the Persian king in
a kneeling (running ?) attitude, holding spear and bow; and a
small group of coins of the same weight as the previous group,
but with the bearded, crowned head of the local king on the
obverse and a galley with dates 11 and 12 on the reverse.
This group is coupled with the unique silver tetradrachm
bearing the same types and the year 8. These last two
groups provide an historical annal of the reign of ʽAbdʽaštart
I, in whose eighth year a revolt began against Persian
hegemony in which Sidon participated. This is recorded in the
silver tetradrachm and in the dated bronze coins, on which the
Persian king's likeness was replaced by that of the local king

in 365/364 B.C.E. This was the precise time when Sidon
sheltered the Egyptian king, Tachos, until his unconditional
surrender to the Persian armies.[45]

'Abd 'aštart I is remembered as a wealthy, powerful
monarch. Among other things, he received an Athenian embassy
on its way to the Persian court and consequently was "granted
the honor of proxenia by the Athenians."[46] He was clearly
pro-Greek in his politics, and his eventual participation in
a revolt is not surprising. The political use of his coinage
as a vehicle for propagandizing led to the eventual loss of
Sidon's minting privileges for a while. The change from the
Phoenician weight standard to the Attic standard for the
silver coins is exceptional. Small denominations appear to
have continued being struck on the Phoenician standard.[47]
The common denominator of trade, however, the double šeqel,
was replaced for a brief time by the tetradrachm, which must
have facilitated commerce for the few years that it was in
use.[48] Persian military operations against Egypt and those
allied with it led to the fall of the Sidonian government of
'Abd 'aštart I in 362/361 B.C.E. In an effort to maintain the
volume of trade established by the Sidonians, Persia
authorized the satrap of Cilicia and the satrapy "Across the
River," which included Phoenicia, to strike coins on the
types of Sidon. This series followed on the failure of
'Abd 'aštart I to lead Phoenicia to independence.

Mazday
362/361-358 B.C.E.

34. OBV: Similar to 23, except above, dates 1-4.

　REV: **ᐟ4ᐟᐟ**(מזדי) in field above; chariot drawn by pacing
　　　horses to l.; driver leans forward holding reins;
　　　King of Persia in chariot; King of Sidon in Asian-
　　　style costume carrying cultic scepter and votive
　　　vase following; double exergual line; incuse circle.
　　　Border of dots.

　AR Double šeqel, New York. Plate 3.

35. OBV: War galley to l., with oars, row of shields along
　　　bulwark; small figure as figurehead on bow; ornament
　　　over stern; rudder; above, dates; below, two zigzag
　　　lines of waves.

　REV: As 14, except **ᐟᐟ**(מד) between legs of king and lion.

　AR 1/16 Šeqel, New York. Plate 3.

Struck from dies cut by the same craftsmen who made
the dies for the local kings, Mazday's coins were minted to
fill the gap created by the lack of a minting authority over
Sidon. The satrap's name appears on the reverses in Aramaic,
rather than the usual Phoenician. Mazday's coinage is dated
according to the year of his reign, as satrap over Cilicia
and the province (or satrapy) "Beyond the River."[49] The
dating formula included the year of his reign, prefaced with
an Aramaic **ל** (ב), which is an abbreviation for the Aramaic
בשנת, "in the year...."[50] The coins are extant in the double
šeqel and the sixteenth šeqel. Their types are identical with
those of the Sidonian kings who followed his period of control with the exceptions of his Aramaic name and the unusual
dating system.[51] A half šeqel with a "Phoenician *mem* **(ツ)**"is
listed in the catalogue of the Fitzwilliam Museum, Cambridge.
It is supposedly on the obverse rather than on the usual
reverse. However, the coin is not an issue of Mazday.[52]

The proper placement of the issues of Mazday within
the scope of the Sidonian series has been the topic for much
discussion in the past. Hill reviewed the conflicting positions of Rouvier and Babelon,[53] arguing that the coins were
issued contemporaneously with those of ʿAbd ʿaštart III. He
viewed these issues as pay for soldiers and sailors of the
Sidonian fleet as preparations were made to do battle with
the advancing Macedonians.[54] To be sure, the types issued by
Mazday were the royal Sidonian ones, and not those which he
used in Cilicia. The style of the coins indicates that the
same workshops struck them which struck the coins of Tennes
and the later rulers of Sidon. To argue that they were
issued at the same time as coins of local rulers, given the
use of the same shops, would lead one to expect die linkage
between the series. No such links are known, however, even
though the engraving is definitely from the same hands.[55]

The four years indicated by the dating system used on
these coins correspond with the first four years of Mazday's
reign as satrap over this area — ca. 362/361 to 359/358 B.C.E.
He had received this region's rule for services rendered the
Persian king in suppressing the revolt in which ʿAbd ʿaštart I
had taken part.[56] No coins seem to have been issued from

the Sidonian mint in 358/357, a period in which the
government of the city-state was turned over to local kings
once again, after four years of military rule. The hand-
picked king, chosen by the Persians, was named Tennes.

Tennes
357/356-348/347 B.C.E.

36. OBV: Similar to 23, except above, dates 1-5.

    REV: **о𝈓**(עת) in the field above; chariot drawn by
            pacing horses to l., driver leans forward holding
            reins; King of Persia in chariot; King of Sidon,
            in Asian-style costume carrying cultic scepter and
            votive vase, following; double exergual line;
            incuse circle. Border of dots.

    AR Double Šeqel, New York. Plate 3.

37. OBV: Same as 35.

    REV: As 14, except **о𝈓** (עת) between legs of king and lion.
    AR 1/16 Šeqel, New York.

    Persian military forces occupied Sidon for a few years
under Mazday after ʿAbdʿaštart I's participation in the
revolt which ended in ca. 361 B.C.E.[57] When the Persians
felt secure enough to allow a new king to occupy Sidon's
throne, the historical and numismatic evidence indicate
that a man named Tennes was chosen.[58] His coinage is dated
to a five-year period, from 357/356 to 352 B.C.E. Hill saw
only coins dated to a four-year period; however, the collection of the ANS contains a double šeqel of year five, which
is one of only two known examples of this date in the
series.[59]

    The reinstitution of the kingship occurred in 357/356
B.C.E., which is a period well known from the Classical
sources.[60] Tennes resumed the silver coinage of the city
with the blessing of the Persian rulers, using the same types
which ʿAbdʿaštart I had used before his revolt and which
Mazday had also used. He apparently issued no bronze coins.[61]
Two denominations are extant from his reign, the double šeqel
and the sixteenth šeqel. Probably he also issued half and
quarter šeqels, although none are presently known. His coins
are identical to those of his predecessor, except for the
abbreviation **о𝈓** (עת) in Phoenician, the new dates, and the
border decoration. A minor development seen here, as on the

coinage of Mazday, is the garment worn by the King of Sidon
as he followed the chariot on the reverse of the double
šeqel. The Egyptian-style costume has been replaced by a
purely Asian one; Sidon's friendship with Egypt — the sector
of the Persian realm which began the revolt of ca. 365 — was
clearly under scrutiny. The quality of the workmanship in
the die cutting is inferior to earlier coin series also.
The lack of definition and the poor execution of minute
details which once were perfectly clear is proof of this:
the aphlaston — the standard of 'Ašerah-'Ēlat — above the
stern of the galley is a good example, for the moon and bull's
horns have degenerated into a crude starlike design. Less
detail appears also on the sixteenth šeqel's types.

Tennes stopped issuing coins in 352 B.C.E., when he
joined a general rebellion which had originated in Cyprus
and Egypt. The Persian king, Artaxerxes III,[62] tried
unsuccessfully to put down the revolt with a great military
campaign in 351/350 B.C.E.[63] Sidon fell either during this
first campaign or just before the conclusion of the second
one in 345 which finally crushed all Egyptian resistance.
The evidence of the coins would suggest the latter option,
for it was the failure of Artaxerxes' first campaign against
Egypt which gave Tennes the impulse to join the fray, leading
Palestine down with him.[64]

It is not surprising that no coins were struck in Sidon's
mint during the insurrection. The magnitude of the war was
great, unlike the minor revolt of ʿAbdʿaštart I's time,[65]
and a number of cities in the Levant suffered total devastation. Indeed by 345 B.C.E., Hazor, Megiddo, ʿAtlit, Lachiš,
and Jericho had all been destroyed.[66] The fate of Sidon —
betrayed by its own king into Persian hands — is well
documented in Diodorus. The Sidonians were particularly
hateful toward the Persians, since Sidon was a place where
Persian officials lived. These people may have been connected
with the fleet. Whatever their function, Diodorus (16. 41.
2ff.) tells us that they misbehaved, angering the Sidonians
and further straining relations between the conqueror and
the conquered. Behind the example of Sidon, all Phoenicia
rebelled this time. The entire Sidonian economy was converted

into a war machine as preparations were made to meet the
Persians' next foray into the Phoenician heartland.[67]   When
finally Artaxerxes III had again outfitted his mercenary
army, he marched on Egypt via Sidon, with forces under
Mazday, the Cilician satrap, and Euagoras II, a deposed
monarch from Salamis, Cyprus. There followed the defection
of Tennes, resulting in his own death and the deaths of
40,000 Sidonians who died in their own burning of the city.[68]
These events occurred in 348/347 B.C.E.[69]

    With the fall of the city and the probable re-institution
of martial law, Mazday again took control of the city's mint.

Mazday
347/346-342/341 B.C.E.

38. OBV: Same as 34, except dates 16-21.
     REV: Same as 34.
     AR Double Šeqel, New York. Plates 3 and 4.

39. OBV: Same as 35.
     REV: Same as 35.
     AR 1/16 Šeqel, New York.

    Using the same dating system and abbreviations which he
used previously, Mazday issued coins of the Sidonian types
for a period of 5½ to 6 years, from ca. 347/346 until
342/341, when the kingship of Sidon was restored to a local
monarch whom the Persians trusted. These coins may have
been intended to carry the damaged economy of Sidon through
the period of reconstruction after the devastation of the
war. As a central part of the empire's commerce, the
Sidonian silver was needed to maintain the monetary flow.[70]

    With the restoration of kingship, authority to mint
coins passed on to ʿAbd ʿaštart II in 342/341 B.C.E.

ʿAbd ʿaštart II
342/341-340/339 B.C.E.

40. OBV: Similar to 22, except dates 1-3.
     REV: Similar to 22, except OO (𐤏𐤏) in field above.
     AR Double Šeqel, New York. Plate 4.

41. OBV: War galley to l., with oars, row of shields along
          bulwark; above, dates; below, two zigzag lines of
          waves. Border of dots.

REV: Similar to 13, except **OO** (עע) between legs of king
      and˷lion.

AR 1/16 Seqel, New York. Plate 4.

    Babelon has conjectured that the ἡγεμόνια which
Euagoras II received from Artaxerxes III for his services
rendered in suppressing the revolt of Tennes was the governor-
ship of Sidon. He has argued this conclusion from the coins,
since Diodorus merely says that this hegemony was in Asia.[71]
Babelon believed that this series of coins bearing the
abbreviation **O O** (עע) was struck under the authority of
Euagoras II (עעגורא in Babelon's theoretical Phoenician
form).[72] Since these coins are dated 1 to 3, it was further
postulated that Euagoras II ruled Sidon following an
interregnum, with no account made for the coins of Mazday.

    The abbreviation which appears on the reverse types of
the double šeqel and sixteenth šeqels cannot refer to
Euagoras II. The Phoenician spelling offered by Babelon
עעגורא is impossible, because two ʿayins just did not appear
successively in Semitic. ʿAyin was still pronounced in
Phoenicia during this period; however, the repetition of
two laryngeal spirants would have been most unusual.[73]
Given the Greek spelling of Euagoras, and the use of א for
initial vocalic sounds, we would expect אוגורא in Phoenician,
or the like. The waw is necessary following the ʾalep.[74]
Needless to say, **OO** (עע) is not an acceptable abbreviation
for Euagoras according to the accepted conventions for
abbreviating names in Phoenician usage.[75] The **OO** (עע)
must refer to someone else.

    If Euagoras II of Salamis was given hegemony over Sidon,
he could not have struck coins, since Mazday filled this
function. He may have aided in the rule; his failure,
however, to administer control of his assigned areas led
to his downfall and eventual death.[76] If he ruled in place
of a Persian military government, or if some general was
actually in command (as appears to have been the case), the
period in question must have been between 347 and 342/341
B.C.E. In all events, the Persians restored the throne in
342/341 to a local ruler whose name was abbreviated **OO** (עע).
We believe this to have been another ruler named ʿAbd ʿaštart,

who ruled for only three years (342/341 to 340/339). The
abbreviation is a perfectly good one for this name, and it
differentiates this ruler from ʿAbdʿaštart I who used 𐤏𐤏 on
his coins.[77] When yet another ʿAbdʿaštart (III) ascended
to the throne in 340/339, the old abreviation was used
again; there were slight differences in these coin types.

Only two denominations are now known to have been
minted by our proposed ʿAbdʿaštart II: the double šeqel and
the sixteenth šeqel. The types are identical to those used
by Tennes and Mazday, with the usual exceptions of the dates,
abbreviations, and borders. Wear on the dies used by the
mint in these years was great, especially on the obverse
dies of the double šeqels. Die breaks and general disinte-
gration indicate that the dies were probably used well beyond
their normal life.[78] Perhaps this is an indication that
there were few skilled craftsmen to make the coins and the
dies needed to strike them as Sidon rebuilt after its
destruction in 348/347. Mazday had workmen of his own to
continue minting operations; but the municipality of Sidon
seems to have been forced to operate its mint without the
necessary manpower to keep it functioning efficiently and
well.

ʿAbdʿaštart III
340/339-332 B.C.E.

42. OBV: Similar to 23, except for dates, 1-9.
     REV: Similar to 34, except 𐤏𐤏 (עב) in field above.
     AR Double Šeqel, New York. Plate 4.

43. OBV: Same as 25.

     REV: 𐤏𐤏(עב) in field above; chariot drawn by pacing
           horses to l., with driver leaning forward holding
           reins; King of Persia in chariot; in incuse circle.
           Border of dots.

     AR 1/2 Šeqel, New York.

ʿAbdʿastart II was followed in 340/339 B.C.E. by
ʿAbdʿastart III. His double šeqels bear dates from 1 to 9,[79]
and the new abbreviation 𐤏𐤏 for OO. His half šeqels are
identical to the double šeqels, but lack the king's likeness
following the chariot on the reverse. This typical scene
depicting obeisance to the Persian crown was re-instituted

following ʿAbdʿaštart I's brief changes on the coin types.

It was ʿAbdʿaštart III who was ruling Sidon when Alexander III conquered the Levant in 332 B.C.E. Alexander replaced him with Abdalonymos (ʿbdʾ lnm) even though he capitulated without a fight.[80] He was called Straton in the Greek sources without reference to which ruler of that name he was. It has been assumed that he was Straton II although no mention was made in the Classical sources (see Diodorus, 17.46.6-47.1) of two Stratons ruling successively in this time period.[81] Several modern commentators have suggested the existence of three ʿAbdʿaštarts, although none applied their theories to the coin system.[82] If our theory is correct, the kings maintained their differentiation on their coinage by using different abbreviations for the same name; both abbreviations are acceptable within the rules of Phoenician grammar.

An unusual coin minted on the Sidonian types, with the abbreviation O (ע), and a different dating system on the obverse, is in the collection of the Bibliothèque nationale, Paris.[83] Reading ϟ𝄞 (ΒΣ or בש), with the year 10, we apparently have a new abbreviation for בשנת, "in the year...," with the script being Greek, although such a hypothesis is purely speculative. This coin was probably issued at the very beginning of ʿAbdʿaštart III's tenth year, when Alexander was on his doorstep, employing the dating system indicator adopted by Mazday. The coin, a sixteenth šeqel, may even have been minted by Abdalonymos, who merely continued the era of Sidon in his reckonings of the date.[84]

Regardless, Alexander the Great assumed full authority for the Sidonian mint, striking his own coins on his own types following ʿAbdʿaštart III's surrender of the city.[85]

In summation, we have seen that Sidon's first minted coinage was issued under an unknown king's authority in the mid-fifth century B.C.E. The types of the obverse and reverse remained rather conservative, with only minor variations until inscriptions were added to the coins' reverses. These inscriptions consisted of abbreviations of various kings' names, enabling us to attribute the coins to

minting authorities. Beginning with Ba'lšallim I, in the
period ca. 420-410 B.C.E., kings of Sidon struck coins with
identifying letters, abbreviating their names. The coinage
was standardized in the period of Ba'lšallim II, 386/385-372
B.C.E. Revolts interrupted the issues of the mint, with
the Cilician satrap, Mazday, striking coins for Sidon during
two interregnal periods. The mint's final coins before
the Alexandrine destruction of the city were struck by
'Abd'aštart III, in the year 333/332 B.C.E. Thereafter,
when the Sidonian mint was reestablished, it was under
Alexandrine authority and issued Hellenistic types.

Notes

1. F.C. Eiselen, *Sidon: A Study in Oriental History*
(New York: Macmillan, 1907), p. 61, n. 5.

2. Cf. Diodorus, 16.41.

3. The basic works on the Sidonian coinage include
the following: J. P. Six, "Observations sur les monnaies
phéniciennes," *NC* 17 (1877) 177-239, especially pp. 195-
221; and "Le satrape Mazaïos," *NC* 4, 2nd ser. (1884) 97-
159, especially 144-151 and pl. 4, no. 11f.; B.V. Head,
·*Historia nummorum*, pp. 794-796; J. Rouvier, "Numismatique
des villes de la Phénicie: Sidon," *JIAN* (1902) 99-116,
pl. 5f; E. Babelon, *Catalogue des monnaies grecques: les
Perses achéménides, les satrapes et les dynastes de leur
empire: Chypre et Phénicie*, pp. 228-236; and *Traité*, II,
2, pp. 543-608; and G.F. Hill, *BMC Phoenicia* (London:
British Museum, 1910), lxxxvii-cii and pp. 139-154. This
chapter does not purport to be a catalogue of the pre-
Alexandrine Sidonian coins. For information relating to
hoards of these coins, see *IGCH* and P. Naster, "Le developpement des monnayages phéniciens avant Alexandre, d'après les
trésors," *Proceedings. International Numismatic Convention,
Jerusalem, 27-31 December, 1963* (Tel Aviv: Schocken, 1967),
pp. 3-24.

4. Excavations resumed at Sidon in 1963 after a
hiatus of more than 53 years. Preliminary reports have
been published by M. Dunand as follows: *Bulletin du
Musée de Beyrouth* (hereafter *BMB*) 18 (1965) 105-109; 19
(1966) 103-105; 20 (1967) 27-44; 22 (1969) 101-107; and
his "Sondages archéologiques affectués à Bostan-Ech-Cheikh,
près Saïda," *Syria* 7 (1926) 1-8. See also W. Röllig,
"Beiträge zur norsemitischen Epigraphik (1-4)," *Die Welt
des Orients* 5 (1969) 121, no. 51.

5. The inscription was first published by Dunand in
"Nouvelles inscriptions phéniciennes du temple d'Echmoun à
Bostan ech-Cheikh, près Sidon," *BMB* 18 (1965) 105-109, esp.
106-109. Dunand chose to date the inscription in the third
quarter of the fifth century (pp. 107-108), following the
probable dating of the reign of Ba'lšallim II. A recent
photograph of the inscription, however, has allowed epi-
graphists to date the script with more precision (J. Teixidor,
"Bulletin d'épigraphie sémitique," *Syria* 49 [1972] 433).
E.T. Mullen, Jr., has argued that the script is to be dated
to ca. 400 B.C.E. ("A New Royal Sidonian Inscription,"
BASOR 216 [1974] 27-28). Mullen's dating of the inscription
is feasible, but a date closer to 380 B.C.E. is even better.
Some letter forms, such as *dalet* and *šin* are clearly
paralleled with forms from the Tabnit inscription of the
mid-fifth century; other letters, such as *yod, kap, mem* (with
its nearly vertical stance), and *ṣadeh* (which has been

rotated nearly 90° to the left from the forms known from
'Ešmun'azōr of the mid-fifth century to forms closer to
those of 'Umm el-'Amed of the late fourth or early third
centuries) are later in style. The first quarter of the
fourth century is a safer date for the inscription. See
DLPS, pp. 66-69, pls. 5-6 and p. 76, n. 25. The text of the
inscription reads as follows: הסמל ז אש יתן בעלשלם בן
מלך בענא מלך צדנם בן מלך עבדא\ש\מן מלך צדנם בן מלך בעלשלם
מלך צדנם לאדני לאשמן בען ידל יברך. "This is the image
which Ba'lšallim, son of King Ba'na', king of the Sidonians,
son of King 'Abd'ešmun, king of the Sidonians, son of King
Ba'lšallim, king of the Sidonians, gave to his lord, to
'Ešmun, at the spring Yidlal, (that) he may be blessed."
See Mullen, *BASOR* 216 (1974) 25f. for the detailed discussion
of the inscription's translation. The new kings are
Ba'lšallim I, 'Abd'ešmun, Ba'na', and Ba'lšallim II.
Following Mullen, we have emended the reading *'bd'mn* to
'bd'šmn, as the result of a haplography. Note, however,
that the name could well be *'bdhmn* — 'Abdhammōn; see *PNPPI*,
pp. 154, 312-313. It will be shown below how these names
appeared on the coinage of Sidon in their abbreviated forms.
The problem of dating the dynasty of 'Ešmun'azor has been
well treated by Peckham in *DLPS*, pp. 84ff. For a review of
the appropriate inscriptions, see H. Donner and K. Röllig,
KAI 13-16.

6. The original version of this chapter appeared as
"A New Chronology for the Pre-Alexandrine Coinage of Sidon,"
ANS Museum Notes 21 (1976) 11-35, pls. 2-4. The present
version is considerably revised.

7. Babelon, *Traité*, II 2, pp. 549-550, no. 888, pl.
118.4; see also *BMC Phoenicia*, xc, pl. 42,12.
N.B. All of the coins of pre-Alexandrine Sidon,
except one, were minted on the Phoenician standard of approx.
13.90 grams per šeqel. With the reign of 'Abd'aštart I,
however, the weight was reduced to about 12.90 grams per
šeqel. This adjustment of the standard was made to enhance
trade with Athens, for one reduced-weight Sidonian double
šeqel then equalled 1½ Attic tetradrachms — an easier
exchange ratio for commercial purposes.
For the reader's reference, the following chart is
appended to summarize the weights of the Sidonian issues.
Weights are averages.

A. Ca. 450-372 B.C.E. (before devaluation)

Double šeqel	27.80 g.
Šeqel	13.90 g.
1/2 šeqel	6.95 g.
1/4 šeqel	3.95 g.
1/16 šeqel	0.90 g.
1/32 šeqel	0.39 g.
1/64 šeqel	0.19 g.

B. 372-332 B.C.E. (after devaluation)

Double šeqel	25.80 g.
1/2 šeqel	6.40 g.
1/4 šeqel	3.25 g.
1/16 šeqel	0.85 g.

1/32 šeqel	0.40 g.
1/64 šeqel	0.19 g.

All of these denominational markings are for silver coins only. We have continued to use the traditional denominational labels. C.M. Kraay has pointed out, however, that given the weight of a mina, the largest Sidonian coins should be termed a four-šeqel piece rather than a double šeqel. See his *Archaic and Classical Greek Coins* (Berkeley and Los Angeles, CA: University of California press, 1976), p. 288, n. 4.

8. This coin was published for the first time in *ANS Museum Notes* 21 (1976) 13.

9. No other examples are extant with the portrayal of the podium of the temple of 'Ešmun.

10. M. Dunand, "Rapport sur les fouilles de Sidon en 1967-1968," *BMB* 22 (1969) 105-106; see also *Syria* 7 (1926) 7-8; and Dunand, "La défence du front méditerranéen de l'empire achéménide," *The Role of the Phoenicians in the Interaction of Mediterranean Civilizations*, ed. W.A. Ward (Beirut: American University of Beirut, 1968), pp. 43-51, esp. pp. 43-44 and pl. 13a.

11. Dunand, "La piscine du trône d'Astarté dans le temple d'Echmoun à Sidon," *BMB* 24 (1971) 19-25, especially 25, where he calls the battlement "pyramidal"; see also *BMB* 22 (1969) 105-106, and Dunand, "Le temple d'Echmoun à Sidon. Essai de chronologie," *BMB* 26 (1973) 7-25.

12. Cf. M. Dunand, "Byblos, Sidon, Jerusalem. Monuments apparentés des temps achéménides," in *Congress Volume, Rome,* Supplement to *VT* 17 (Leiden: E.J. Brill, 1969), pp. 64-70.

13. The coin was acquired by the ANS in 1922 from the P. Lederer collection. See Dunand's plates in *BMB* 18 (1965) pls. 1a, 1b.

14. *KAI* 15-16; *PNPPI*, pp. 82-88, 130, 177, 283-285, and 328-329.

15. As the use of the galley continued at Sidon, the ship ceased to represent the mercantile and naval power of the city alone, and became a symbol for the city and Phoenicia itself. It continued in use at Sidon well into Roman times. Cf. Schmidt, *Persepolis II* (n. 30 below), pl. 9, seal no. 32: galley with similar sail.

16. See Six, *NC* 14, 2nd ser. (1894) 335ff., for example; Babelon, *Traité,* II, 2, nos. 889ff.

17. H. Seyrig, "Antiquités syriennes: 70. Divinités de Sidon," *Syria* 36 (1959) 52-56. Ba'l is often depicted as a rider on a chariot, except that a conical hat and his thunder bolt are missing; see also Moshe Weinfeld, "'Rider of the Clouds' and 'Gatherer of the Clouds,'" *Journal of the*

Ancient Near Eastern Society of Columbia University 5 (1973)
421-426; see also P. Naster, "Le ba'al de Sidon," *Anadolu
Araştirmalari* (Istanbul: 'Edebiyat Fäkultesi Basimevi,
1965), pp. 327-332. Reliefs from Persepolis, for example,
depict this same scene: see the cylinder sealing of the
royal hunt in Frankfort, *Cylinder Seals*, pl. 37d, p. 221.
Without question these scenes with the king in the chariot
are identical to the one depicted on the coins. Seyrig's
argument cannot stand.

18. M. Chéhab, *Terres cuites de Kharayeb* (*BMB* 10-11
[1954]), p. 4, nos. 2-4, pl. 3.2. This evidence does not
prove Seyrig's conclusion, however. The figure in the
chariot is in the dress and attitude of the king of Persia
as seen on many reliefs and seals. The king is here depicted as the deified suzerain of the city. When the
figure of the King of Sidon is added to the reverse type,
it is understood that the Sidonian king's role is that of
priest of the royal cult and vassal of the deified Persian
ruler. The chariot scene is well known; see J.A.H. Potratz,
Die Pferdetrensen des alten Orient, Analecta orientalia 41
(Rome: Pontifical Biblical Institute, 1966), pl. 5.9.

19. Seyrig, "Divinités de Sidon," p. 54; on the cult
of the Persian king, see G. Widengren, *Die Religionen Irans*
(Stuttgart: Kohlhammer, 1965), pp. 151-155; and "The
Sacral Kingship of Iran," *Numen*, Suppl. 4 (Leiden: E.J.
Brill, 1959), pp. 242-257. The Persians worshipped their
king as an image of god; see also Plutarch, *Themistocles*,
27. Thanks are due to D.S. Whitcomb for this suggestion.
Similar scenes are known from Ugarit; cf. Dussaud, *L'art
phénicien du IIe millénaire*, pp. 59-61.

20. The identification has traditionally been on
analogy with the Persian darics and sigloi. See H.H.
Howorth, "The History and Coinage of Artaxerxes III, His
Satraps and Dependents," *NC* 3, 4th series (1923) 1-46,
esp. 33.

21. The satyr's head has usually been identified with
Bes, a deity known from Egyptian folk religion, who may
have been equated with 'Esmun at Sidon, according to W.
Culican, "The Iconography of Some Phoenician Seals and Seal
Impressions," *Australian Journal of Biblical Archaeology* 1
(1968-1971) 93. In contact with the Hellenic world, Bes
took on the attributes of Pan, including his satyr-like
features, as well as those of the goat. These symbols
probably appeared on the coins due to the presence in
Sidon of some cult in which Bes, Pan, or some related deity,
played a role. Satyr-sileni figures, closely allied with
nature and the god of wine and rejuvenation, Dionysus, may
have been part of the old Canaanite institution called the
marzih. That people participated in the *marzih*'s revelry
and party-making is well known (see especially text RS 1957.
702, published by L.R. Fisher, *The Claremont Ras Shamra
Tablets* [Rome: Pontifical Biblical Institute, 1971], pp.
37-54, pls. 9-11; C. Virolleaud, "Les nouveaux textes
mythologiques et liturgiques de Ras Shamra," *Ugaritica V*

[Paris: Imprimerie nationale, 1965], pp. 545-551; and
J.C. deMoor, "Studies in the New Alphabetic Texts from Ras
Shamra, I," *Ugarit-Forschungen* 1 [1969] 167-175). Whether
the *marziḥ*'s association with death rites is indicative
of a coalescence of it with the worship of 'Ešmun, as
healer, and Dionysus-Bes-Pan is unclear. That 'Ešmun was
linked with the fertility deity for animals is well known;
and thus, his identification with some of the aspects of
Ba'l and the notion of rejuvenation associated with both
Ba'l and Dionysus is crystallized. See J. Gray, "The
Canaanite God Horon," *JNES* 8 (1949) 27-34; and RS 24.643
in M.C. Astour, "Some New Divine Names from Ugarit," *JAOS*
86 (1966) 277-284, especially 281-282, notes 46-56. One of
Pan's chief duties was to make the flocks fertile, which is
parallel with 'Ešmun as fertility god and as shepherd of
the flocks (Gray, "The Canaanite God Horon," pp. 30-31).
The close association of satyrs and sileni with Dionysus
leads us to question the use of "Bes" here at all. The
figure is merely a satyr associated with the cult tied to
the *marziḥ*. We know from the Marseilles tariff (*KAI*, no. 69,
l. 16) that there were different *marziḥ*s of the gods (*kl
mrzḥ 'lm*). By the first century B.C.E., the *marziḥ* of
Sidon was a periodic festival, lasting a number of days
(cf. *KAI*, no. 60, l. 1). See also Fisher, *The Claremont
Ras Shamra Tablets*, pp. 46-47. In any case, the cult at
Sidon must have been syncretistic with the cults of Pan
and/or Dionysus. W.H. Roscher, in his *Ausführliches
Lexicon der griechischen und römischen Mythologie*, III, 1,
illustrates the close relationship Pan had with goats
(pp. 1409, 1414, 1465-1471) and with Dionysus (pp. 1439-
1452). Satyrs and Pan regularly appeared in art together
(vol. IV, pp. 519-520). Suffice it to say that this figure
is a satyr; its attribution as "Bes" only clouds the picture
with Egyptian problems which are unwarranted. On the
similarities between the Dionysiac rites and mythological/
liturgical rites from Ugarit, see C. Kerenyi, *Dionysus:
Archetypal Image of Indestructible Life* (Princeton:
Princeton University Press, 1976), R. Manheim, trans.,
pp. 255-256. The great popularity of the rites in Asia
Minor and Egypt is well known; cf. M.P. Nilsson, *The Dionysiac
Mysteries of the Hellenistic and Roman Age* (Lund: C.W.K.
Gleerup, 1957), Skrifter Utgivna av Svenska Institutet i
Athen, 8°, V, pp. 8-12. On the style of the goat's engraving,
see J. Boardman, *Intaglios and Rings* (London: Thames and
Hudson, 1975), ch. 3.

22. The same coin exists with the inscription reversed —
ꝑᴟ; this was an engraver's perceptual error. Babelon cites a
coin of Imhoof with ᴟᴊ on both obverse and reverse; *Traité*,
II, 2, no. 893.

23. Cf. K. Galling, "Die syrisch-palästinische Küste
nach der Beschreibung bei Pseudo-Skylax," pp. 193-194. "Bei
Sidon wird uns der λιμήν κλειστός, d.h. der in die Stadtmauer
einbezogene Hafen genannt-...." See also R. Naumann,
*Architektur Kleinasiens von ihren Anfängen bis zum Ende der
hethitischen Zeit* (Tübingen: Verlag Ernst Wasmuth, 1971),
2nd ed., pp. 311-319. Clearly, the conventions for the

depiction of battlemented walls predate these Sidonian
coins. Our thanks to D.G. Mitten for this suggestion.

24. See E.F. Schmidt, *Persepolis I: Structures,
Reliefs, Inscriptions* (Chicago: University of Chicago
Press, 1953), pl. 19, the E. stairway of the Apadama; pl.
115, the Hero's combat with a lion on the S. doorway in the
W. wall of the throne room; pl. 146, the E. doorway of the
main hall of the Palace of Darius; and pl. 195, the W.
doorway of the main hall of the Harem of Xerxes. For a
parallel to the reverse with the chariot, see M.F. von Oppen-
heim, *et al.*, *Tell Halaf III: Die Bildwerke* (Berlin: de
Gruyter, 1955), pl. 41; the standing figure of the King of
Persia may be seen in Schmidt, *Persepolis III: The Royal
Tombs and Other Monuments* (Chicago: University of Chicago
Press, 1970), pls. 41 and 42a. See also O.W. Muscarella,
Ancient Art: The Norbert Schimmel Collection (Mainz:
Verlag Philipp von Zabern, 1974), no. 154, an Achaemenid
relief mirror with lions.

25. Reliefs showing similar scenes, with the hunter's
prey below the chariot, even looking back toward the hunter
(or king in this example) are known from Carchemish. See
C.L. Woolley, *Carchemish, Part III: The Excavations in the
Inner Town*, pl. B.41.a-b; B.42.a-b; and pl. B.60.a-b. Cf.
H. Frankfort, *Cylinder Seals* (London: Macmillan, 1939),
pl. 37d: this cylinder sealing depicts our scene, except
with the king hunting from the chariot; also p. 221. Note
the Persian scene from a cylinder seal, on which the king
rides while shooting his bow and arrow at an attacking
lion-griffin; similar scenes appear on the coins. See G.F.
Hill, "Alexander the Great and the Persian Lion-Gryphon,"
Journal of Hellenic Studies 43 (1923) 159, fig. 2. The
king is in the traditional pose; see J.F.X. McKeon,
"Achaemenian Cloisonné-Inlay Jewelry: An Important New
Example," *Orient and Occident*, H.A. Koffner, Jr., ed.
(Kevelaer: Butzon and Bercker, 1973), p. 116,m fig. 6, a
gold medallion from the Vidal collection.

26. Babelon, *Traité*, II, 2, no. 894; *PNPPI*, pp. 100,
288-289, 417. The letters which appear on these coins and
those which follow, with the exception of the Mazday coinage,
are written in a generally conservative Phoenician lapidary
script. It has been studied in detail by Peckham in *DLPS*,
chap. 3, "Tyre, Sidon, and Vicinity."

27. At Aradus, for example, inscriptions began on
coins at this time. Whereas at Byblos, they were not used
until ca. 385 B.C.E. The familiar ethnic of Athens, AΘE,
as well as the common Cilician ethnic 𐤕𐤓𐤆 (*Tarz* in Aramaic),
were influential from the fifth century onwards.

28. The coin was excavated at Susa, and was part of
hoard #1; the coin is numbered 504.1 and 504.2.

29. See note 5 above; *PNPPI*, pp. 149-153. This
reading, as suggested by Mullen, may have been caused by
homoioteleuton and homoioarchton when *'mn* was read for the

intended ʾšmn. The latter is a more common name, and is well known from Sidon. Babelon mistakenly attributed these coins to ʿAbdʿaštart I (*Traité*, II, 2, nos. 903ff.)

30. See E.F. Schmidt, *Persepolis II: Contents of the Treasury and Other Discoveries* (Chicago: University of Chicago Press, 1957), pl. 10: PT4 385, and PT4 784; pl. 11; PT3 383 (seal no. 37), PT4 857, and PT4 704 (seal no. 38).

31. Cf. J. Boardman, "Pyramidal Stamp Seals in the Persian Empire," nos. 82, 84, 86, 87, 93, 97, 98, and 115 (from plates 4-5); and H.H. von der Osten, *Ancient Oriental Seals in the Collection of Mr. Edward T. Newell* (Chicago: University of Chicago Press, 1934), pl. 31, no. 467. This limestone seal is a perfect match for the coin type and measures 17 x 16 x 6 mm. (p. 67). G.M.A. Richter has theorized that Greek or East Greek workmen were responsible for many of these seals; see "The Late 'Achaemenian' or 'Greco-Persian' Gems," *Hesperia*, Supplement 8 (1949) 295-298, and pl. 31.3. See also F.M. Cross, "The Papyri and their Historical Importance," *Discoveries in the Wâdî ed-Dâliyeh*, p. 28, seal no. 4, pl. 62c. The seal is probably contemporaneous with the coins depicting the same scene of Royal combat. Note the bibliography cited by Cross.

32. Mullen has noted that the name Baʿnaʾ occurs in 1 Kings 4:12, 16, and in Nehemiah 3:4, besides being known from an unusual coin series which he would like to place in Sidon (see *BMC Phoenicia*, p. cxliv, pl. 42.2). The name is probably a hypocoristicon for a longer name. The coins are clearly, however, not Sidonian. Their types are either Cilician or Cypriote in origin, and are not related to Sidon in any way. This is a different Baʿnaʾ from the King of Sidon; he is probably from Cyrpus, and seems the best candidate for the minting authority. Babelon attributed these coins to Bôdʿaštart (*Traité*, II, 2, no. 906). Cf. Mullen, p. 29, n. 12.

33. The inscription parallels that of the previous king; our attribution is based on typology and not simply the *bet* which abbreviated Baʿlšallim or Baʿnaʾ.

34. Seyrig, "Divinités de Sidon," pp. 55-56; P. Naster, "Le suivant du char royal sur les doubles statères de Sidon," *RBN* 103 (1957) 1-20. See also N. Aimé-Giron, "Un naos phénicien de Sidon," *Bulletin de l'Institut français d'archéologie orientale* 34 (1933) 31-42; and the review of this article by R. Dussaud in *Syria* 14 (1933) 335-336, wherein the cultic significance of this personnage was first recognized. The costume and the hat of the Sidonian king might better be described as "Syrian"; see von Oppenheim, *Tell Halaf III: Die Bildwerke*, pl. 16, 25.

35. Naster, "Le suivant du char royal," p.11, pls. 2-3 and 17-19. Henri Seyrig, "Antiquites syriennes: 69. Deux reliquaires," *Syria* 36 (1959) 43-48, pl. 8. The example in Seyrig's pl. 8, shows the storm god — Baʿl — with various

iconographic symbols of his cult, including the sun and the
so-called "Hathor" moon disk set in the horns of a bull.
See also the ancient witness of Sakkunyaton, as recorded in
Eusebius, *Praep. evang.*, I 10, 31, where Astarte, to show
her royalty, crowned her head with the head of a bull.
Astarte, or 'Aštart, with her epithet *šem ba'l* ("name of
Ba'l") known from Ugarit of the fourteenth century B.C.E.
and Sidon of the fifth century is semantically equivalent
to the epithet *panē ba'l* used of Tannit at Carthage (*CTA*,
16.6.56 and *KAI* 14 and 18), according to Cross (*CMHE*, p.
30, n. 101). In fact, Cross has shown (pp. 33ff.) that
Astarte, 'Anat, and 'Ašerah are all confused at times,
as can be seen in the Winchester relief published by Edwards.
The Hathor iconography may be applied to all three of these
goddesses (*CMHE*, pp. 34f.).

On the follower, G. Contenu has noted an Assyrian
relief from the Louvre which depicts this same scene; see
La civilisation phénicienne (Paris: Payot, 1926), p. 215.
The goat in incuse made its last appearance in the earliest
coins of this king's reign; on that technique, see P. Naster,
"La technique des revers partiellement incus de monnaies
phéniciennes," p. 507.

36.   The ship is the symbol of Sidon and of its powerful grip upon the waters of the eastern Mediterranean. We
do not think it too highly speculative to term Ba'lšallim's
representation of the ship as propagandistic. The Sidonians,
as the leaders of the Phoenician city-states, had lost face
to the Athenian navy in the fifth century, and this may
have been part of a campaign to restore some of that image.
A commercially circulating coinage bearing a representation
of a military vessel is not to be discounted merely as a
monetary token of fixed value; its psychological values
with respect to potential enemies are clear.

37.   The symbolism on the aphlaston has been discussed above (note 35). 'Ašerah-'Ēlat is here invoked in
her role as protectress of ships at sea. The victory of
Ba'l over Yamm is recalled from the myths of Ugarit in this
iconography. On later coins, such as those issued under
Mazday, Tennes, 'Abd'aštart II, and 'Abd'aštart III, the
symbol is lost in the inferior die cutting. The symbolism
is confused, through the syncretism of the three deities.
The confusion is the strongest with 'Ašerah, as the conqueror
of sea — '*atiratu yammi*, "she who treads on the sea" — as
known from Ūgarit (*CMHE*, p. 31). In the treaty of
Asarhaddon of Assyria with Ba'l of Tyre — a treaty dating
from the eighth century B.C.E. — Milqart, 'Ešmun, and
'Aštart were all called upon in the curse formulae to punish
any violators by sending storms against ships at sea, tearing
up mooringposts, and causing ships to be swamped by mighty
seas (Albright, *YGC*, pp. 226-227). The relationships between
'Ešmun and Astarte in regard to ships and the sea are clear:
'Ešmun, 'Aštart, and Ba'l, the three principal deities of
Sidon, were all understood as protectors of ships at sea.
The figurehead on the bow of the Sidonian galley is repre-
sentative of a deity also (probably 'Astart, as the warrior).

See N. Jidejian, *Sidon Through the Ages* (Beirut: Dar el-
Machreq, 1971), p. 55; Herodotus 3.37. Such symbolism, as
this insignia of the mother goddess, is also known from
Ugarit; see C.F.A. Schaeffer, "Nouveaux témoignages de culte
de El et de Baal à Ras Shamra-Ugarit et ailleurs en Syrie-
Palestine," *Syria* 43 (1966) 17, fig. 11. In this case,
the arm rests and supports for a throne are bulls, with
elongated horns and the lunar discs inside them. See also
R. Petai, *The Hebrew Goddess* (Jerusalem and New York: Ktav
Publishing, 1967), pp. 32-34 and 54-56. As the 'Ēlat of
Sidon, 'Ašerah (in the role as mistress and consort of
Ba'l Samēm) was the protectress of ships at sea. The
aphlaston and pataecus are discussed in more detail elsewhere; see, however, L. Casson, *Ships and Seamanship in
the Ancient World* (Princeton: Princeton University Press,
1971), pp. 64, 66, 94-96; and Cecil Torr, *Ancient Ships*
(Chicago: Argonaut, 1964; reprint of 1894 ed.), A.J.
Podlecki, ed., pp. 64-69, for a discussion of these
physical features of the Phoenician ships.

38. *BMC Phoenicia*, p. 144, no. 25. The coin is late
in date with its reverse being cut similarly to those
of 'Abd'aštart I. The engraving of the dies of this coin
shows a decline from the skill exhibited in the earlier
coins of Ba'lšallim II.

39. Schmidt, *Persepolis I*, pls. 19, 115, 146, 195;
also, see n. 30-31 above.

40. No examples have dates in excess of "year 9."
Examples from London and Paris which have been read as
years 10 through 13 are actually years 1 to 3. The mark
read as "10" is not the mark used for the numeral on the
rest of the coins and must be an engraving error or a die
break. This is certainly the case with *BMC Phoenicia*, p.
146, no. 35, as pl. 19.10 shows. Also in Rouvier,
"Numismatique des villes de la Phénicie: Sidon," the half
šeqel (no. 1109) is not dated; the double šeqel of year 12
(no. 1111) is actually of year 2. The confusion has been
caused by the aphlaston, the intended rudder/ornament, over
the stern of the galley; see Babelon, *Catalogue de la
collection de Luynes*, vol. 3, pl. 115, no. 3184 — this
sixteenth šeqel does read year "10." This was issued
during the revolt.

41. The important sign for this series, as varying
from the series of 'Abd'aštart II and III, is the Egyptian-
style costume on the King of Sidon. Cf. *BMC Phoenicia*, p.
145, no. 29; and Rouvier, "Numismatique des villes de la
Phénicie: Sidon," nos. 1103, 1104, 1107, 1111.

42. The name of this king is a common one, especially
at Carthage (*PNPPI*, pp. 162-163 and 386-387); it means "the
servant of 'Aštart," using the very common root '-b-d in a
familiar construct-chain construction. Note that 'Aštart
has even been identified with Ba'l at Sidon (*Corpus inscriptionum semiticarum pars prima: Inscriptiones phoeniciae*
[Paris: Academie des inscriptions et belles lettres, 1881-],
nos. 3, 18.

43. This is a second cause for the misreading of dates 1 to 3, or so; on a number of coins, the *bet* used by Ba'lšallim was merely rubbed out, with the dating mechanism of 'Abd'aštart replacing it on the obverse types. *BMC Phoenicia*, p. 146, no. 35 is an example of this situation. On the new reverse type of the thirty-second šeqel, see G.A. Eisen, *Ancient Oriental Cylinder and Other Seals with a Description of the Collection of Mrs. William H. Moore* (Chicago: University of Chicago Press, 1940), no. 102; the scene is that of the Persian king killing a Greek soldier (p. 31). Our coin type lacks the Greek soldier, although clearly we have the same subject intended.

44. This coin was viewed, measured, and drawn by the writer on 12 January 1976 at the Israel Museum, Jerusalem, Israel. Two photographs of the obverse and a brief description have been published by Y. Meshorer in *Coins of the Ancient World* (with R.L. Currier) (Minneapolis: Lerner, 1975), pp. 49, 68-69.

45. Some of the smaller silver denominations continued to be struck during the rebellion; however, the larger coins, such as the double šeqel, were replaced with the tetradrachm. No double šeqels are known beyond year 9; in year 8 the tetradrachm which is extant was minted. The revolt coinage appears to have been a supplement to the usual issues on the Phoenician standard, or else an aborted attempt at changing to the Attic standard. The coins with the highest dates are the bronze coins dated year 9-10 and those with the types of the revolt dates to years 11-12. The Egyptians began the problem for the Persians, inciting Cyprus to join them. Sidon entered the revolt, it would appear, as an afterthought. Of Phoenicia, it alone sided with Egypt, if we may trust the scanty evidence which we have. See W. Judeich, *Kleinasiatische Studien*, pp. 166, 209.

46. See *CIS* no. 114; and O. Hamdy Bey and T. Reinach, *Une nécropole royale à Sidon* (Paris: E. Leroux, 1892-1896), Texte, p. 390.

47. Only the tetradrachm in Jerusalem is known to have been minted on a standard other than that of the Phoenician. The headdress of the king on these coins of the revolt is typically royal, being known from Persian sources. See G. Thompson, "Iranian Dress in the Achaemenian Period," *Iran* 3 (1965) 125. The weight of the coin is 17.0 grams, which is almost exactly that of four Attic drachms.

48. Undoubtedly the shift to the tetradrachm would have made trade between the Greek world and Sidon easier, at least in terms of monetary exchange. However, the military problems which harassed the Levant in these troubled years spelled an end for active trade. As always happened during times of war, trade fell victim to the necessities of the conflict. Silver was not in great enough supply to continue the issuance of coinage, so small bronze coins acted as replacements and small change. The craftsmanship of some of these coins is inferior to earlier issues;

see, for example, the bronze coin illustrated in T.E.
Mionnet, *Description de médailles antiques, grecques et
romaines* (Paris: Imprimerie nationale, 1808), Supplement,
Planches 10, pl. 19.7. The real effects of the change in
standard were not felt because of the ensuing war; the
immediate result of the Persian victory and deposing of
'Abd'aŝtart I was the re-establishment of the Phoenician
standard. For a fleeting moment, Sidon had reached its
pinnacle of power and dominance over the eastern Mediterranean. The Sidonian participation, at least as evidenced
in its attempted monetary reform, in the revolt may have
signalled the end of the Persians' use of Sidon as their
Phoenician base. See I. Kleemann, *Der Satrapen-Sarkophag
aus Sidon* (Berlin: Gebr. Mann, 1958), p. 161: "Die
Stadt war in dieser Zeit ein Hauptquartier der Perser."

49. His reign appears to have begun in ca. 362/361
B.C.E. It was, as a result of his help in putting down the
revolt of the period 364-361, his reward by the Persian
king to rule over the region of Cilicia, Phoenicia, and
Cyprus. Cf. G.F. Hill, *BMC Lycaonia, Isauria, and Cilicia*,
p. lxxxii; and A.F. Rainey, "The Satrapy 'Beyond the River,'"
pp. 70-71. We disagree with Rainey concerning the moment
in which Belesys lost his job as satrap of "Beyond the
River." Rainey (p. 71) argues that it was after the revolt
of Tennes. The coins indicate, however, that Mazday took
over control of Phoenicia as early as 362/361 B.C.E., when
the revolt was just over and Tachos was in Persian custody.
Perhaps Belesys ruled inland regions, and Phoenicia was
attached to Cyprus and Cilicia. This may account for the
apparent problem in the account of Diodorus (16.42.1) in
which Belesys is called satrap of Syria in the period of
Tennes, unless Diodorus, himself, was confusing the two
revolts which were in such close proximity to each other.

50. Babelon, *Traité*, II, 2, p. 582; J. Halevy, *Mélanges
d'épigraphie et d'archéologie sémitiques* (Paris: Maisonneuve,
1874), pp. 64ff. On the Aramaic script used on this coin,
see J. Naveh, *The Development of the Aramaic Script*. Proceedings of the Israel Academy of Sciences and Humanities,
vol. 5, no. 1 (Jerusalem: Ahva Press, 1970), pp. 51-54,
pl. 11.1-2. The script is conservative, as is the script
on most of these coins. The exception to this rule is the
ŝin used on the Phoenician script coins, which is late when
compared to the other forms.

51. The abbreviation is **ʒʃ**(מז).

52. This coin is no. 9496 of the McClean Collection
of the Fitzwilliam Museum. See S.W. Grose, *Catalogue of the
McClean Collection of Greek Coins*, vol. 3 (Cambridge:
Cambridge University Press, 1929), p. 372, pl. 351.6. The
inscription is better read **ʒ**, than **ψ**; it is a coin of
Ba'lŝallim II.

53. *BMC Phoenicia*, pp. xcvi-xcix; Bableon, *Traité*, II,
2, nos. 934ff. A critique of Hill's proposal is in Peckham,
DLPS, p. 74, no. 18. See Diodorus, 17.5.3-6.

54. *BMC Phoenicia*, p. xcviii. Cf. G. Hern, *The Phoenicians: The Purple Empire of Ancient World*, trans. C. Hilher (London: Gollancz, 1975), pp. 159-160.

55. A study of these coins to find die links resulted merely in links between coins of the same year and the same ruler. New dies appear to have been made each year. No conceivable reason can be advanced for the argument that two parallel, identical issues were struck by local king and regional satrap in the same city in the same year from the same workshops. Our present reconstruction of the coinage of Sidon's mint issued in this period eliminates most, if not all, of the problems which formerly clouded the mint's record.

56. The issuance of these coins established Sidon's monetary backing so that trade could continue. Obviously Mazday minted his coins on the Phoenician standard. The aim of the Persian government was to maintain the status quo in the western provinces at all costs. This included having the satrap fund the striking of coins even while military forces were standing at the ready, in case trouble flared again.

57. Babelon was undoubtedly correct in attributing the coins with the abbreviation **ᴐʌ** to this new king. Although we do not have his name in Phoenician, the abbreviation is entirely possible and may correspond to any number of names. It could be a verbal sentence name including elements such as Tannit, plus one of the verbs like *ᶜnn, ᶜmš, ᶜmš, ᶜz, ᶜzr*, and the like. Forms of these verbs and others could have led to the abbreviation and the Greek form "Tennes." Another possibility is a hypocoristicon, such as *Tinnāy*, from a form like *Tinnitᶜamos*, on analogy with the name *Pumay*, which is known from Nora (see Cross, *CMHE*, p. 220, n. 5). The name may also have been derived from *Tabnit-ᶜAštart*, for example. Our thanks to F.M. Cross for these suggestions.

58. Tennes came to the throne following a period of military rule under Mazday. The new king was certainly a pawn of the Persian king, or his satrap, and was expected to "toe the line" as dictated to him from Persepolis. There may have been a year or so in which no coins were struck by the mint while power was again turned over to the local people and the city tried to regain its peacetime footing.

59. The second example was excavated by Dunand at Byblos; see his *Fouilles de Byblos*, vol. 1, p. 409, no. 6309.

60. Diodorus, 15.40ff. Mentioned in the Oxyrhynchus Papyri is a Sidonian named Akton, who is thought by some to have been a king of Sidon. See also B.P. Grenfell and A.S. Hunt, eds., *The Oxyrhynchus Papyri* (London: Egypt Exploration Fund, 1908), vol. 5, pp. 149, 214, P. Oxy. 842, col. iii, l. 26. The reading of Akton as a king is not clear; such a person, if he existed (the text is broken), appears to have been a leader of the fleet, it anything at all. The word

"king" is lacking, and therefore, the inclusion of this name
on the king list is most inadvisable.

61. See R.N. Frye, *The Heritage of Persia* (Cleveland:
World Publishing, 1963), p. 119.

62. See R. Ghirshman, *Iran* (Baltimore: Penguin Books,
1954), p. 201. Note that the typical pose of the Persian
king remained in use on the double šeqel which had been
used for years. Kleemann speaks of the Greek influence on
this image which was one of the official seals of the
Persian kings; see *Der Satrapen-Sarkophag aus Sidon*, pp.
164-165.

63. We agree with F.K. Kienitz, in his *Die politische
Geschichte Ägyptens vom 7. bis 4. Jahrhundert vor der
Zeitwende* (Berlin: Academie-Verlag, 1953); see J. Vandier's
review of Kienitz' arguments in *Bibliotheca orientalis*, 11
(1954) 189-190.

64. No coins were struck in Sidon from 352/351 until
Mazday again issued coins for Sidon, on his own authority
as Satrap. Our dating differs slightly from that of
Kienitz (pp. 182-184).

65. This may account for Diodorus' not elaborating
upon the first revolt, since it was insignificant in
comparison with the carnage of the Tennes rebellion.

66. D. Barag, "The Effects of the Tennes Rebellion on
Palestine," *BASOR* 183 (1966) 7. See also Isocrates, *To
Philip*, 101-102, in which he urged Philip (in 347/346 B.C.E.)
to make war on Persia, since its satrapies were able to
hold out so long against the weak central government.
Isocrates wrote that Cilicia, Phoenicia, and Cyprus revolted
only after Artaxerxes III failed to subdue Egypt early in
the struggle (ca. 351/350 B.C.E.).

67. Diodorus, 16.41.4-6.

68. Diodorus, 16.45.4-6.

69. Judeich, *Kleinasiatische Studien*, p. 175.

70. No differences in the types used by Mazday are
worthy of note. The dates which appear on the coins
correspond to the years of his reign as satrap in the Levant,
dating from 362/361 B.C.E. Sidon's importance as a center
for Phoenician trade is obvious from the exposure which the
city's coins received. Sidonian coins, even in this period
of military problems and the overall decay of the Persian
system, were circulating far and wide, as hoard evidence
corroborates: cf. *IGCH*, Sidonian coins of this period have
been found in hoards from the Phoenician coast into Palestine
(hoard 1492) and Syria (hoard 1493), to the inland (Baalbek,
hoard 1506) and coastal (Gezer, hoard 1507) trade routes, to
Egypt (Giza, hoard 1653), and even into Persia (Media, hoard
1790; Susa, hoard 1792). The silver of the Sidonian mint

was clearly an important part of the Persian monetary
system.

71. Diodorus, 16.46.2; *DLPS*, p. 73; *BMC Cyrpus*, pp.
cix-cx, in which Hill expresses doubts concerning Euagoras'
"satrap" coinage in Cyprus. F. Imhoof-Blumer also argued
against such a narrow attribution in his *Kleinasiatische
Münzen* (Vienna: A. Hölder Verlag, 1901-1902), vol. 2,
pp. 519-520. See also O. Hamdy Bey and T. Reinach, *Une
nécropole royale à Sidon*, p. 391, n. 3. Reinach's general
assertions concerning the coinage of Sidon are wrong,
although his suspicions concerning Euagoras are well founded.

72. Babelon, *Traité*, II, 2, pp. 589-590. Hill
accepted this notion (*BMC Phoenicia*, xcvi). The name is
from Greek, meaning "good market"; see A. Fick, *Die
griechischen Personennamen* (Göttingen: Vandenhoeck und
Ruprecht, 1874), pp. 31, 97.

73. Z.S. Harris, *A Grammar of the Phoenician Language*,
pp. 16, 27. It was not until Neo-Punic times that *'ayin*
lost its pronunciation as a laryngeal spirant. Note the
Latin attempt to render the earlier Punic name עזרבעל as
Hasdrubal.

74. Note the spelling of the name *Severus*, שאוארא
(Harris, p. 19); or *Faustus*, פעוסתא (Harris, p. 16). Per-
haps אוגורא was the proper Phoenician form of the name.
The ending א- stood for -ος, -ας, or -ης (J. Friedrich,
"Griechisches und römisches in phönizischen und punischen
Gewande," *Festschrift Otto Eissfeldt zum 60. Geburtstage*,
ed. J. Fück [Halle an der Salle: N. Niemeyer, 1947], p.
110).

75. *PNPPI*, pp. 235-237. One- and two-letter abbreviations are derived in three ways: (1) the first two
letters of the name; (2) the first letters of the two
components of a compound name; and (3) the first and last
letter of the name. Such conventions rule out OO for
Euagoras.

76. Diodorus, 16.46.3. This must have been after 346
according to Judeich, *Kleinasiatische Studien*, pp. 135-136.
Indeed, the use of the word ἡγεμόνια in Classical and
Patristic Greek does not imply the authority to strike
coins; it is merely preeminence or command during war.

77. The abbreviation is composed of the first letters
of the two elements of the compound name, עע; this differs
from 'Abd'aštart I's use of the first two letters of the
first element of his name.

78. The obverse dies were very badly worn, showing
die breaks and general aging. Coins in the collection of
the ANS have shown these breaks. See the illustrations of
coin No. 39 in my article in *ANS Museum Notes*, no. 33 in
that version of this paper.

79. The existence of three 'Abd'aštarts at Sidon is
not new in scholars' attempts to unravel the history of
Sidon in the fourth century B.C.E. Babelon proposed such
a reconstruction, although his dating and reconstruction
were incorrect. Also, Joseph Ringel has proposed such
a reconstruction, although he too did not recognize the
problem with Euagoras' nominal abbreviation; see *Cesarée
de Palestine: Étude historique et archéologique* (Paris:
Ophrys, 1975), pp. 20-21. Whether an 'Abd'aštart reigned
in the fifth or even the sixth centuries we do not know.
If so, then our sequence would have to be revised in number.
We have no evidence to support such a possibility, however.

With regard to the dates known on the coins, Babelon,
in his *Traité*, II, 2, p. 602, lists a number of coins with
dates from 10 through 13, which he attributes to 'Abd'aštart
III. However, these coins are all issues of 'Abd'aštart I,
given the use of bronze and the appropriate abbreviation of
the king's name. The only problem coin is Babelon's no. 973,
a double šeqel of year 12 of 'Abd'aštart I, since the costume
of the follower is "Egyptian." This coin is one of those
which we discussed above, on which the *bet* of Ba'lšallim II
had been erased from the obverse, and the year "2" added;
the reading is not year "12."

80. *DLPS*, pp. 72-75; Justin, 11.10.8-11; Curtius,
4.1.15-26; and A.T. Olmstead, *History of the Persian Empire*,
p. 506.

81. Diodorus confused Sidon with Tyre at this point.

82. See n. 79 above. Babelon, of course, applied his
efforts to the coin system, but he did not know about
'Abd'ešmun or any of the other kings of the inscription
which Dunand published in the *BMB*.

83. The coin is numbered "M.6479" and was viewed by
the writer in July 1976. The coin's script is apparently
Greek: certainly we do have a good *sigma*, although for
the period, *beta* is archaic and reminiscent of a Phoenician
bet. Cf. K. McCarter, *The Antiquity of the Greek Alphabet*
(Missoula: Scholars Press, 1975), pls. 4-6, for the *sigma*.
The *beta* may have been a local variant. This is probably a
coin struck by Abdalonymos, on which the Aramaic phrase
"In the year..." was put into a Greek transcription in
abbreviation (the first two letters only). This is quite
speculative, but it is the only answer available from the
existing data. Abdalonymos may have been trying to make
a good impression upon Alexander; the letters are not
Aramaic or Phoenician (except for the possibility of the
beta).

84. The coin may have been struck just after the city's
capitulation, although this is doubtful. The unique specimen is not our only unanswered question within the Sidonian
mint. Another coin in Paris, no. "1966/258," is a sixteenth
šeqel, with the usual king vs. lion obverse but a reverse
with "une sorte de contre marque." The counter-mark, if it

is such, looks like this: 👞 . The coin may date with
any of the sixteenth šeqels with similar reverses, although
early series lacking inscriptions are the best bets:
'Abd'ešmun or Ba'na', for example.

85. On the Alexandrine issues, see E.T. Newell, *The
Dated Alexander Coinage of Sidon and Ake* (New Haven: Yale
University Press, 1916), pp. 21ff. The review of this book
by Hill in *NC* 16, 4th ser. (1916) 407-409, is helpful. See
also Arrian's *Anabasis*, 2.15.6, in which the Sidonian's
loathings for Persia and Darius were discussed; and I.L.
Merker, "Notes on Abdalonymos and the Dated Alexander
Coinage of Sidon and Ake," *ANS Museum Notes* 11 (1964) 13-20.

Chapter 2

TYRE

Tyre was one of the leading Phoenician ports during the Persian period, surpassed only by Sidon in its importance. Located south of Sidon on the mainland and two small offshore islands, the city played an important role in Persian naval operations throughout the eastern Mediterranean in the fifth and fourth centuries, B.C.E. The Tyrian admiral ranked second to the Sidonian.[1] As with the other Phoenician cities, little or nothing is known of Tyre's history after about 500 B.C.E. until nearer the conquest of Alexander the Great.[2] Along with Sidon, numerous cities along the Levantine coast and elsewhere in the eastern Mediterranean were populated by Phoenician colonists in this period.[3] This much appears certain from the Classical sources and the archaeological data which are extant. Specifics, such as the possibility of Euagoras I of Salamis having controlled this part of the coast ca. 386 B.C.E.,[4] are extremely difficult to prove. Unquestionably, however, the city took part in the general revolt against Persia in the time of Tennes, ca. 351 B.C.E.[5] Most noted by the historians was the resistance which Tyre raised against Alexander in 332 B.C.E. Unlike the other Phoenician cities, Tyre fought the Macedonian advances, forcing a siege by land and by sea.[6] Some of these events may be mirrored within the coinage.

The prevailing standard adopted by the Tyrian mint was the Phoenician.[7] Unlike Sidon, Tyre later changed to the Attic standard in the mid-fourth century B.C.E., setting a precedent among the Phoenician cities.[8] The precise circumstances surrounding this metrological deviation will become apparent below.

The Earliest Tyrian Series
ca. 435-410 B.C.E.

1. OBV: Dolphin, to r.; over three lines of zigzag waves; below, murex shell; cable border.

   REV: Owl standing to r., head *en face*; over l. shoulder

crook and flail; shallow incuse impression
surrounding type; all in shallow incuse square.
AR Šeqel, Paris and London.[9]

2. OBV: 𐤔𐤋𐤔𐤍(שלשן) above dolphin; otherwise, same as 1.
REV: Same as 1.
AR Šeqel, Jameson Collection.[10] Plate 4.

3. OBV: Same as 1.
REV: Same as 1.
AR 1/24 Šeqel, London.

4. OBV: 𐤌𐤇𐤑𐤕(מחצת), above dolphin; otherwise, same as 1.
REV: Same as 1.
AR 1/2 Šeqel, Paris (de Luynes).[11] Plate 4.

These four issues comprise what was probably the first
series issued by the Tyrian mint. If earlier issues were
minted, no evidence exists presently to corroborate this
fact. The standard in use at Tyre was the Phoenician, the
same one used at Sidon further north along the coast.[12]

The dolphin is used consistently on the obverse types
of this series. We will see the dolphin elsewhere, in its
function as a member of the entourage of marine deities.[13]
Likewise, the waves and the murex shell are known from
other types. The murex shell, in the case of Tyre, is certainly representative of Tyre's role in the production of
the much coveted purple dye, for which the Levantine coast
was so well known.[14] The scene with the dolphin above the
waves and the shell is repeated on all three of the extant
denominations.

The two inscriptions, found upon the šeqel of the
Jameson collection and the half šeqels from the Paris and
de Luynes collections, are difficult. Certain other coins
have traces of these same inscriptions, but few of them are
as complete or clear as the examples cited.[15] When coins
were first struck at Tyre, inscriptions were probably not
utilized. Given the similarity of types, however, these two
variations were probably incorporated soon thereafter into
the mint's repertoire. The inscriptions are: (1) from the
šeqel שלשן; and (2) from the half šeqel מחצת. Paleographically, the letter forms are clear examples of the lapidary

script of the late fifth century, B.C.E.[16] This is in
keeping with our projected dating for these issues. Inscriptions first appeared on the Sidonian coinage in this same
period.[17] The significance of the inscriptions is in the
labelling of certain denominational differences — an
inscriptional use not attested elsewhere in the Syro-
Palestinian region, save a problematic unique coin known
from Judah.[18] Our readings for the coin inscriptions are
as follows: (1) *šillašōn*, "thirtieth part of";[19] and (2)
maḥṣīt, "a half."[20] The first is based on the mina, and the
second on the standard šeqel weight. Both inscriptions
appeared only on the early series; later inscriptions were
limited to the typical abbreviations of kings' names and the
dating systems.[21]

On the reverse, the owl is somewhat reminiscent of the
Athenian owl which appeared on the Athenian coinage of the
mid- to late-fifth century B.C.E. Unquestionably Attic
coins were known in Tyre in this period, and probably circulated freely through the town's coffers. The method employed
to depict the owl is in the Syro-Phoenician style, after
that of the Egyptians. Similar stylistic considerations
were noted at Byblos.[22] The pose of the Egyptian hawk, so
well known from reliefs, statuary, and the like, is strikingly
similar.[23] Behind the owl are the crook and flail, which,
of course are traditional symbols of kingship in Egypt, and
were perhaps also known in this manner in Phoenicia.[24] The
incuse method of engraving is typical of the late fifth
century and has already been discussed for its use at the
other Phoenician mints.[25]

Our dating of this series stems partially from the
paleographical data: letter forms similar to those of the
Bôd 'aštart inscription from Sidon, dating to the second half
of the fifth century B.C.E. are found on the coins. Also,
we must take into consideration the use of inscriptions and
the incuse engraving method. The inscriptions continue in
use, in one form or another, into the next series, which
lacks the intaglio. The period between 435 and 410 B.C.E.
best fits the evidence.

No information is available as to the name or names
of the minting authorities behind the Tyrian mint in this
period. Certain influence from Sidon, the stronger of the
two cities at this time, may have been felt. It is
interesting that no larger denominations are known, although
perhaps the reason for this lies in the use of Sidonian
double šeqels along this section of the coast, since the
standards were identical and the currencies therefore inter-
changeable. Hoard evidence from around the eastern
Mediterranean and inland Syria, Palestine, and the surrounding
region indicates that the trade of the two cities were
dramatically linked.[26] To the south, Tyre was the Phoenician
trading leader; but Sidon held administrative and military
leadership of the unofficial league which appears to have
held the Phoenician cities together.

The Second Tyrian Series
ca. 410-390 B.C.E.

5. OBV: 𝗌𝘃𝗌𝘃(ששלן), above; dolphin to r., over three
          lines of zigzag waves; murex below; cable border.

    REV: Owl, standing to r., head *en face*; over left
          shoulder, crook and flail; shallow incuse square.

    AR Šeqel, Paris.

6. OBV: Similar to 5, except without inscription.

    REV: Same as 5.

    AR 1/2 Šeqel, Rouvier.

7. OBV: Dolphin, to l.; below, murex shell; dotted border.

    REV: Owl, standing to l., head *en face*; over r. shoulder,
          crook and flail; dotted border; slight incuse
          circle.

    AR 1/24 Šeqel, London. Plate 4.

8. OBV: Similar to 6, except without murex or waves.

    REV: Similar to 6, except slight incuse circle.

    AR 1/24 Šeqel, London. Plate 4.

9. OBV: Same as 8.

    REV: Same as 8.

    AR 1/48 Šeqel, Rouvier.

10. OBV: Same as 8.

    REV: Rosette with eight petals; concave type.

    AR 1/48 Šeqel, Rouvier. Plate 5.

11. OBV: Dolphin, to l.
     REV: Head of bull, horned, to l.; dotted border.
     AR 1/48 Šeqel, Paris.[27]

In the second series, only one coin of the largest
Tyrian denomination — the šeqel — is known. It preserves
part of the same inscription which we know from the
preceding series.[28]

The major difference between the šeqel of this series and
the seqel of the first grouping is the lack of intaglio around
the reverse type. This alteration indicates a later time of
minting, probably near the lower end of this period, ca.395 to
390 B.C.E. Few coins of this series are known; and as commerce
increased after 390 B.C.E., more and more currency was needed
to facilitate the cash flow within the economy. The most numerous coins of the city are from the third and later series.

The smaller denominations are similar to the šeqel in
most ways. The half šeqel is identical, except for its lack
of an inscription. The inscription on the half šeqel of
the first series is lacking here; the difference is the lack
of the intaglio in this coin.[29] On the twenty-fourths and
forty-eighths, no waves or murex shells are depicted.
Reversal of the types is not unknown, with the dolphin and
owl facing to the left, rather than to the right. On such
a variant, the murex was still used; these coins may have
been minted earlier than those which lack the murex. Indeed
this group may have been an engraver's mistake, in which a
mirror image of what had actually been intended was engraved
on the dies.[30] Similar practices are evidenced in later
series' small denominations, however, with similar types
being minted in both silver and bronze. These groupings
began sometime after 390 in all probability. The murex was
used on some types and omitted on others. Being a symbol
for Tyre, its omission is not easily explained; its longevity
as a symbol is clear, as was the use of the dolphin.[31]

In this period, especially from about 400 until 390
B.C.E., several variations upon the smaller denominations'
types were in use. The rosette from the reverse type of one
of the forty-eighths (no. 10) is a common motif in Greek and
East Greek art of the Persian period.[32] The bull's head,

with the large horns, is probably to be associated with the cult of Tyre, specifically concerning Ba‛l's manifestations there. The bull was a common symbol for the storm god, as an ample number of examples from Syro-Phoenician art have shown.[33] The bull is known from other coinages of the eastern Mediterranean, but not in the form seen here.[34] The representation on this coin is unique, differing from the other depictions of the bull fighting with an ibex, cow, or stag.

The dating of the series is based on the continuation of the inscription known from the preceding period coupled with the probable dating of the technology used in the manufacture of the coins. The lack of the intaglio method, specifically, is a significant factor. The disappearance of the murex on the larger denominations is also important, because it will never again appear on the larger coins; its appearance on the smaller denominations is representative of the practice of the Phoenician mints to use old types in later small denominations, both silver and bronze. We have noted this peculiarity in both the mints of Aradus and Sidon.[35] This series preceded the introduction of the new types which were to be in use in the first quarter of the fourth century, when the combined trade of Sidon and Tyre reached new heights. Therefore, for dating purposes, the twenty-fourths are important for they provide a transitional type which gives us a preview of the type to come, without the seahorse, but with the dolphin.

Once again, no data are available which provide any names of authorities which were in power in Tyre during the period when these coins were struck.

The Third Tyrian Series
ca. 390-377 B.C.E.

12. OBV: Deity, bearded, riding on seahorse with curled
          wing, to r.; deity holding reins in r.; in l.,
          he holds an arched bow; below, two lines of waves,
          and dolphin, to r.; cable border.

     REV: 𐤌 (ם), in field, to r.; owl standing to r., head
           en face; over l. shoulder crook and flail; cable
           border.

     AR   Šeqel, London and Paris.[36]

13. OBV: Seahorse, r., with curled wing; below, dolphin
           to r.; cable border.
     REV: Similar to 12, except without inscription; all in
           shallow incuse circle.
     AR   1/24 Šeqel, London.

14. OBV: Same as 12.
     REV: 𐤌 (מ), in field to r.; 𐤁 (ב) in field, to lower l.
           of owl; otherwise, same as 12.
     AR   Šeqel, London.

15. OBV: Dolphin, to r.; cable border.
     REV: Same as 13.
     AR   1/24 Šeqel, Lefkowitz Collection (ʿAkkō).[37]

All of these coins were minted with what has been
called a "thick fabric,"[38] which is a qualitative statement
regarding the thickness of the coins. Later series, as will
be seen, were struck using a more refined technology in
which the fabric was thinner. The resultant coinage maintained a much higher standard of quality in its production.

This series, as those previously discussed, was struck
on the Phoenician weight standard. However, an unusual
technique was employed in this case, for some of the coins
are plated. That is, they are bronze cores plated with
silver. This is a practice practically unknown in the
other mints,[39] and may be indicative of a poorly backed
currency on the international market. Coins in the fourth
century B.C.E. were constantly being tested for their
purity and precise weight.[40] Of the examples in the cabinet
of the British Museum, for instance, two of three šeqels are
plated.[41] If this is indicative of the series as a whole,
then 67% of the coins had to be plated for lack of the
necessary silver to sustain the minting operation. This was
probably due to gross devaluation, perhaps caused by such
fiscal innovations and the resulting inflation.[42] This
project may have been the work of a specific ruler or minting
authority, precipitating changes within the economic system
of the city-state. Phoenicia as a whole, of course, was
exceedingly strong, economically, at the time, and no data
exist which would suggest that Tyre's economy was facing
difficult times. Therefore, the possibility remains

that this plated coinage was part of a fraudulent operation aimed at someone's personal gain at the expense of the consumer and the city's commercial reputation. That the coinage was minted for such a short time may lend some proof to this suggestion. Definite proof is lacking.[43]

The obverse types (similar to no. 12) show an innovation, in the use of the winged seahorse, surmounted by the crowned, bearded figure of a deity. The iconography present in the scene is difficult, with apparent mixing. A certain syncretistic thread may be seen in this late period which may explain the apparent problems of a deity riding on a winged seahorse, over the sea, with a bow in one hand.[44] Certainly the age-old identification with Milqart must be avoided for there are no underworld images in the type.[45] The iconography of Baʿl Hadad is also problematic, even though the imagery of the storm god as a rider is well known.[46] In the Hellenistic period such a syncretism may have occurred, if we interpret the evidence from Syria correctly.[47] Unequivocal corroboration is impossible; our best conclusion is to term the deity "marine."

The deity's dominance over the sea and the maritime world is indicated by his riding over the waves and sea creatures. This is reminiscent of the rider (divine) of the clouds.[48] Stylistically, the waves are stereotypical of the Phoenician mints of the period. Note the similarity of the headdress on this depiction of the deity with that of the King of Persia on the Sidonian types. Both are typically Persian garb, familiar from a number of reliefs from Persia.[49] The dolphin's use is continued from earlier series.

On the reverses no variants on the basic type of the owl with the crook and flail occur: at least in the larger denominations, standardization to the right has taken place. These types and the new obverse types became the standard ones of the Tyrian mint throughout the fourth century, even though minor variations continued to take place.[50] The inscription on the reverse of this series is the only difference between this grouping and the last. The earliest coins of this series had on them a *mem*, which was

supplemented with a *bet* late in the period (probably ca.
380 B.C.E.). The *mem* appears to have been the abbreviation
for a king's name, perhaps a man named *Mattōn*, a name
known from Josephus, Herodotus, and other sources.[51] The
name is undoubtedly a hypocoristicon for a sentence name
such as MTN'LT, or MTNB'L, or others.[52] The appearance of
the *bet* signalled yet another change in the minting authority,
with a transitional type leading into the next series, which
lacks lettered abbreviations, but uses a slash system for
dating. The *bet* may have been an abbreviation for the
powerful Sidonian leader who ruled at this time and may have
had power over Tyre as the leader of the Phoenician league,
Ba'lšallim II.[53]

In the twenty-fourth (no. 13), variations caused by
spatial limitations are evident. Notably, the deity is
absent on the seahorse, leaving the animal much as it was
known at Aradus. The other twenty-fourth (no. 15) may be
merely a coin on which the seahorse was struck off flan;
however, the possibility exists that it is an intentional
omission.[54] In the next series, numerous small denominations
were struck to meet the need for large quantities of coins,
with such a type being used. However, this example has the
typical "thick fabric" while the others — coins struck in
both silver and bronze — have the thinner fabric typical of
later series.[55]

Our dating of this series is based upon the usage of
the abbreviated personal names on the reverse types, along
with the possible Sidonian ruler's nominal abbreviation.
The next series (being dated) enables us better to establish
the relative position of these coins in the chronological
scheme of the Tyrian mint's issues. Throughout the four
Phoenician mints, standardization of types occurred in the
period 390-380 B.C.E. From this point, within the principle
denominations, only dating systems and names or abbreviations
of names accounted for the variations from series to series.
This was an era of political stability, with little or no
interference from the Persian overlords. The types which
evolved were more nationalistic than earlier ones. Such
motifs as the galley at Sidon or the murex and owl of Tyre

exemplify this. Moreover, religious symbols abounded
within the coinage. Given the nationalistic surgings
apparent in the fourth century throughout the satrapies,
such symbols had a power beyond their literal denotation;[56]
they were not merely ornaments. The small coin with the
head of the horned bull from the previous series may have
been a precursor of this innovation; coinage honoring the
chief deity (or deities) of the city, in which temples had
been constructed for worship, became the norm throughout
the realm in which coinage was used in the fourth century.[57]
Babelon records a specimen on which he read the letters 𐤑𐤓
(צר), for Ṣur-Tyre.[58] The poor state of this coin, however,
makes such a reading impossible. His dating of this issue
to the end of the fifth century cannot be accepted either,
because it fits well into the scheme of this series.[59]
Hill's dating to a period of 400-332 B.C.E. clearly require
some refinement.[60]

The proposition that a king named *Mattōn* was ruling at
Tyre in this time is backed by what evidence may be gleaned
from the Classical sources.[61] Sidon and Tyre were closely
affiliated, with the Sidonian king taking precedence; we
may even note the numerous times when the Classical writers
confused the two cities.[62] Their might and power were
linked into a united Phoenician front, which set the stage
for still further growth, economically, in the second quarter
of the century.

The Fourth Tyrian Series
ca. 377-357 B.C.E.

16. OBV: Same as 12.

    REV: Similar to 12, but lacking the inscription, and
         adding the dates 1 to 13; for those coins with
         dates 11 to 13, a 𐤅(ז) is prefixed.

    AR Šeqel, New York. Plate 5.

17. OBV: Same as 12.

    REV: Similar to 12, but no date or inscription.

    AR Šeqel, Paris (de Luynes). Plate 5.

18. OBV: Similar to 12, but of a flat fabric.

    REV: Similar to 17, but of a flat fabric.

    AR Šeqel, New York. Plate 5.

19. OBV: Seahorse, to r., with curled wing; below, dolphin
           to r.; cable border.
     REV: Owl, as on the preceding šeqels; cable border;
           all in shallow incuse circle.
     AR 1/24 Šeqel, New York.

20. OBV: Similar to 19, except type to 1., with waves
           below seahorse, and no dolphin.
     REV: Similar to 19, except type to 1.; some examples
           are dated.
     AR 1/24 Šeqel, Paris and Tel 'Aviv.[63] Plate 5.

21. OBV: Winged sphinx, sitting, to 1.
     REV: Same as 20.
     AR 1/24 Šeqel, Paris.[64]

22. OBV: Bearded head of satyr, *en face*.
     REV: Dolphin to 1., over single line of waves.
     AE uncertain denomination, Jerusalem.[65]

23. OBV: Same as 22.
     REV: Murex shell, vertical on type; cable border (or
           dotted border).
     AE uncertain denomination, Jerusalem and the Lefkowitz
         Collection (Akkô).[66]

24. OBV: Head of satyr, *en face*.
     REV: Cedar tree.
     AE uncertain denomination, Jerusalem.[67]

25. OBV: Winged seahorse, to 1.
     REV: Bearded head of satyr, *en face*.
     AE uncertain denomination, Lefkowitz Collection.[68]

26. OBV: Dolphin to r.; murex to r., below; dotted border.
     REV: Satyr, *en face*.
     AR 1/48 Šeqel, Lefkowitz Collection.[69] Plate 5.

27. OBV: Dolphin, to 1., dotted border.
     REV: Ram's head, to 1., dotted border.
     AR 1/48 Šeqel, Lefkowitz Collection and Tel 'Aviv.[70]

28. OBV: Seahorse to r.
     REV: Dolphin to r.
     AR 1/48 Šeqel, Lefkowitz Collection.[71]

29. OBV: Same as 25.
     REV: Same as 25.

AR   1/24 Šeqel, Tel 'Aviv.[72]

The fourth Tyrian series follows the city through a rather troubled period in its history. The short-lived rebellion in which Sidon participated inevitably affected Tyre and its coinage.

The types of the larger denominations remained basically unchanged. The major variations were the deletion of the inscriptions and the use of a simple dating system, with a single slash representing one year and an arc (⌒) representing a decade.[73] The first sub-series included dated coins with regnal years up to thirteen, ca. 377-365/364 B.C.E. These years represent the reign of an unknown king who reigned side-by-side with Ba'lšallim II and 'Abd'aštart I of Sidon.[74] The small denominations used during this period reflect the types known from our specimen no. 18, which is the typical issue of the series. For the years 11 to 13, the date appears as | ⌒ ѡ or ||| ⌒ ѡ. These read 11 ᴛ and 13 ᴛ respectively, with the *zayin* being an abbreviation for the name of an unknown king. On analogy we have the use of '*ayin* on a later Tyrian series. The form of the letter is perfectly good for the mid-fourth century, although no king's name is known from Tyre at that time. The nationalistic zeal of the decade is clearly present in this *zayin* and the attempt of the local ruler to personalize his coinage; similar changes occurred in the coinage of the Sidonian mint in the mid-360's. Numerous new silver and bronze types came into use in this period, with no major variations in the types. All of the new types are known either from Tyre or Sidon,[75] with the increased output of the mint again being indicative of the growth of the regional economy.

In 365/364 a change occurred in the minting authority of Tyre, resulting in alterations to the coin types; specifically, the dating system was deleted although the types which were used remained the same. By 360/359 B.C.E., the Persians were forced to put down the insurrection within the Phoenician littoral. The coinage of Tyre appears to have been interrupted for several years pending the healing of relations with the Persian government. Whether coins were

imported from other mints is unclear. The evidence from
Sidon, for example, suggests that Persia placed its
Cilician satrap in overall charge of the rebellious area
for several years, pending the end of the hostilities and
the replacement of the local governments with hand-picked
persons who were friendly with Persepolis.[76]

With the resumption of minting privileges in ca. 357
B.C.E., a new technological advance in the actual striking
of a coin was instituted in the mint. Foreign technicians
may have been involved in this methodological change.[77]
Coins were struck with a much flatter fabric, making more
aesthetically pleasing coins, which were technically
superior to the former ones. Similar changes in the
Sidonian mint's methodology probably stem from similar
stimuli.[78]

Of special interest are the small denominations.
Examples 19 and 20 appear to have been the usual types.
However, in the nationalistic years of this phase of the
city's history, a number of new types were struck; whether
the nationalism of the time may be seen in these types or
not is purely speculative. For example, the change of the
type to the left, without the dolphin (no. 20), is not
surprising; nor is the use of this die with other reverse
types and on bronze coins. The winged sphinx, the satyr's
head, the ram, the dolphin, the murex shell, and the cedar
tree provide an interesting series of silver and bronze
types. The ram's head and the cedar tree are unique in
this series; the ram's head probably being indicative of
an animal specially dedicated within the Tyrian cult, while
the cedar tree remained a staple of the city's trade
complex.[79] The interchange of the types from bronze to
silver denominations is paralleled in this period at Sidon.
The value of the smallest denominations, especially those
struck in bronze, is impossible to fathom. From the prove-
nances of these smallest coins, their usage appears to have
been limited to local dealings rather than to international
commerce; the larger silver denominations were employed for
this, although not exclusively.

The relative independence of this 5 to 10 year period,
from about 367 to 357 B.C.E., may have enabled Tyre to
increase the production of its mint so dramatically.
Whether some of these small denominations continued to be
struck in the following years is impossible to ascertain.
Without doubt, however, restrictions were placed on the
Phoenician mints following Sidon's participation in the
revolt of ca. 365/364 B.C.E. The role played in this revolt
by Tyre, Byblos, and Aradus is not known. Most of the small
denominations discussed here are unique specimens, indicating
the small production of the mint. When minting rights were
re-established in ca. 357, Tyre was forced to fill a larger
role in the Phoenician economy, given the restrictions
placed upon Sidon and its difficulty in regaining its old
footing in the international marketplace.[80]

As noted previously, we have no name or names of the
rulers or minting authorities of Tyre in these decades. Our
dating of the series is heavily dependent upon typological
comparisons with the coinage of Sidon, which is more easily
dated.

The Fifth Tyrian Series
ca. 357-355 B.C.E.

30. OBV: Deity (marine ?), bearded, riding on seahorse, to
r.; seahorse has curved wing; in r. he holds reins;
in l. he holds a strung bow; below, two lines of
zigzag waves; below, dolphin, to r.; cable border.

   REV: | **9**(לב), in field above, to r.; **ש** (מ) in field
below to r.; owl standing to r., head *en face*;
over l. shoulder, crook and flail; cable border.

   AR Attic Didrachm, New York. Plate 5.

31. OBV: Same as 30.

   REV: **ש**(מ), in field to r., with varying dates from 1
to 3; otherwise, similar to 30.

   AR Attic Didrachm, New York.

32. OBV: Seahorse, to l., with curled wings; below, two
lines of waves; border of dots.

   REV: |**ש**(לב), above to l.; owl standing to l., head *en
face*; over r. shoulder, crook and flail; border
of dots.

   AR uncertain small denomination (approx. 1/8 Attic
drachm), Tel 'Aviv.[81]

33. OBV: Same as 32.
     REV: Similar to 32, except lacking the inscription.
     AR uncertain Attic small denomination, London.[82]

34. OBV: Same as 27.
     REV: Similar to 20, except no dates, and border of dots.
     AR uncertain Attic small denominations, Tel 'Aviv.[83]

35. OBV: Similar to 34, except type to r.
     REV: Similar to 34, except type to r.
     AR uncertain small denominations, Tel 'Aviv.[84]

With the issues described herein, the Tyrian mint
continued its changes from the older methodology, striking
coins not only on a wider, flatter fabric, but also on a
new standard — the Attic standard. En masse, these issues
are ascribed by the older catalogues to the period following
the conquest of Alexander in 332 and following.[85] The
difficulty with such a presupposition, however, is that we
know from the Classical sources that Tyre resisted the attack
of Alexander with force, causing him to lay siege to the
island fortress for at least six months.[86] To assume that
Alexander after militarily defeating this enemy in battle
then granted them the continued privilege of minting
independent coinage is absurd. No commander in history has
been so foolishly liberal with people who were fighting him
without an appropriate occupation period. As elsewhere, we
would have expected the first coinage after Alexander's
capture of the city to have been struck on Alexander's
types, with the Heraklian head in the lion skin.[87]

Not until the discovery of several groups of coins in
Palestine within the last twenty years has enough evidence
appeared to lend credence to the notion that Tyre had
already changed its standard before the coming of Alexander.
Certainly, to assume that the city was defeated in battle
and continued to mint its own independent types under the
authority of the new Macedonian rulers is difficult to
comprehend, at best. However, evidence was lacking which
could have proven that the coins were struck before
Alexander.

In his work on the discoveries from the Wâdī ed-Dâliyeh, F.M. Cross has suggested that a Tyrian didrachm, found with a number of other coins,[88] must be dated to the time just prior to the conquest of Alexander.[89] The other coins date from the decade or two just prior to the fall of the Levant, but never before had such a Tyrian issue been included in a group of coins dating to this period. The coin in question is part of our seventh series, although all of the coins of groups 5 through 7 were struck on the Attic standard. Cross has noted that, as late as 1957, Henri Seyrig argued that these Tyrian coins were post-Alexandrine.[90] His argument was that, since this coin was struck on the Attic standard rather than on the Phoenician standard, such a shift must have coincided with the coming of Alexander.[91] This is a change which is paralleled at other Phoenician mints, notably Aradus and Sidon, where post-Alexandrine issues were on the Attic standard.[92] However, these coins were minted under Alexander's authority, and were struck on his types; they were not independent issues such as these Tyrian coins. The two categories are quite different; and the latter became "excessively rare in Phoenicia, Syria, Palestine, and Cyprus."[93] Indeed, only a few coins struck by Mazday may be classed "independent" in this time, even though he had changed his loyalties to Alexander from Darius in 332.[94]

Cross correctly perceived that Seyrig's argument rested on the supposition that the Attic standard was introduced to Phoenicia and Palestine by Alexander.[95] This was not the case, however, as can be seen in the early coinage of the southern Palestinian mints, the mint of Jerusalem, and the earliest mint (or mints) from Syria.[96] For almost a century, coins were struck and circulating within the sphere of Phoenician influence which were of the Athenian standard, rather than the Persic or Phoenician standards.

Seyrig, however, did provide some helpful evidence for corroborating this argument, in that he recognized that certain marks on some of the Tyrian coins (such as **O**) were actually abbreviations for names of kings rather than

numbers.[97]   Seyrig, however, did not recognize the significance of the ʿayin for this period's history. When Tyre
fell in 332 the city was destroyed and colonized by
Macedonian soldiers, who fortified the city under Philotus,
who acted as the military governor.[98]   The Tyrian king was
spared because he took refuge in the temple of Herakles-
Milqart; it is excessive, however, to suppose that his
throne was spared also.[99]   The ʿayin is the abbreviation
of the name of the last king of Tyre, whose name was
ʿUzzimilk (see our seventh series).[100]   The coin which
Cross described from the Wâdî ed-Dâliyeh was from the
fifteenth year of ʿUzzimilk's reign, or ca. 335/334 B.C.E.,
coinciding with the reign of ʿAbd ʿaštart III of Sidon and
Mazday's reign as satrap of Cilicia.

Working simultaneously with Cross, A. Kindler published
an important article, "The Mint of Tyre — the Major Source
of Silver Coins in Ancient Israel."[101]   There, Kindler
discussed two hoards, one from Tell Abū Hawâm and the other
from Tell Fukkhâr. Both were found in definite pre-
Alexandrine contexts and contain Tyrian issues struck on
both the Phoenician and Attic standards. These data further
support the conclusion that Tyre shifted its standard from
the Phoenician to the Attic before the coming of Alexander
the Great. From the dating systems on the coins, a date
ca. 357 B.C.E. appears most plausible.

The types of the fifth series exhibit only minor
changes, such as the use of two lines of waves instead of
three. The dated didrachms came after the first didrachm
of these types, which was the transitional coin from the
previous issues. The small denominations, all struck in
silver following the problems of the late 360's, especially
the plainest types which lack abbreviations or dating
mechanisms, probably continued to be struck until 332 B.C.E.
No differentiation of one rule from the next was made on
these small types.

Some inscriptions appeared on coins of this series:
the first example had two letters, ב and מ, on the reverse.
The bet was made with the numeral "1," so that it was
probably the same bet which we have seen on the Mazday coins

from Sidon of the period 362/361 to 357 B.C.E. The letter
abbreviated the phrase בשנת, "in the year...."[102] Only
one example of this type is known.[103] The *bet* was not used
for a long duration because its usage was from the Aramaic,
not from the Phoenician. The ruler in 357, however, being
a crony of the Persians, apparently felt obliged to use
the system used by the satrapal government in dating his
coins. There may have been a quick change in minting
authority, or rather a return to Phoenician nationalistic
zeal following the retreat of the Persian armies. The *bet*
appears only with coins of the year "1"; other examples of
this same year and with years up to "3" are extant.[104]
The *bet* was deleted, and the simple slash system — formerly
used by the Tyrian mint — was re-instituted.

The *mem* on these issues probably represented the minting
authority's name in abbreviated form. Any number of
possibilities exist for such a name; sadly, we are lacking
in knowledge about the names of the Tyrian kings in this
period. Suffice it to say that king "M" ruled for a period
of three years, ca. 357-355 B.C.E., overseeing the introduction of the Attic standard into the Tyrian series.

Without doubt, the shift in standard was made only with
the blessing of the Persian government. After a damaging
revolt in the late 360's, a recovery of lost commercial
revenues necessitated the functioning of the economies of
Sidon and Tyre at their fullest potential. The introduction
of the Attic standard, which was already in use in Palestine,
the Arabian cities bordering on Egypt, and in Egypt itself,
facilitated the reopening of trade relations with these
areas — also affected by the revolt — where the silk and
spice routes terminated.

The small denominations, probably 1/8 drachms, were
used with the larger denominations throughout this period
and the next. The types of the small coins are known from
earlier series, and again we see the practice of reversing
the types.

An additional note on the artistic style of the
engraving of the owl on the reverse dies is necessary. More
and more, the style of the engraving less resembled that of

the Egyptian hawk and more resembled the Athenian owl.[105]
The presence of Greek or East Greek craftsmen in Tyre is
very possible. This influence is most marked in the later
series, in which the Attic standard had been fully adopted.

The Sixth Tyrian Series
ca. 355/354-352/351 B.C.E.

36. OBV: Same as 30.
    REV: Υ (צ), in field to r., with dates, 2 to 4 above;
         otherwise similar to 30.
    AR Attic Didrachm, New York. Plate 5.

This series was struck contemporaneously with the
coins of Tennes in Sidon, who led Phoenicia and much of
Palestine into a revolt with Cyprus and Egypt. The types
remained the same. The dating, to years 2 through 4,
corresponds to the years ca. 354/353-352/351 B.C.E. The
sadeh is an abbreviation for the name of the city Sur.[106]
The abbreviation persisted into the seventh series on only
one example.[107]

A poorly struck coin of this series, now in the
British Museum, provides some interesting data.[108] The
dolphin on the obverse is "blundered"; the type of the reverse
is reversed, facing to the left. In the left field is the
numeral "4," with no sadeh. Hill refers to the style as
"barbarous."[109] A similar coin in the Paris cabinet has
a thicker fabric and numerous indications of poorer workmanship in its design and production.[110] No doubt the
revolt of Tennes had already begun and, as the Phoenician
cities prepared for the military campaigns of this time,
the minting operations were drastically curtailed. Other
mints experienced the same problems.[111] Quality and quantity
of coinage was sacrificed as wartime needs arose. The
deletion of the sadeh is surprising, given the propagandistic
usage of coinage in wartime.

Tyre fell to the armies of Artaxerxes III very quickly.
The city did not resist the Persians so vehemently as did
Sidon. Consequently, Tyre had its privileges of minting
coinage restored earlier. These coins were the seventh series.

The Seventh Series: Coins of ʻUzzimilk
ca. 347-332 B.C.E.

37. OBV: Same as 30.
     REV: ♂ (ע), in field to r., with dates 3 to 17;[112]
           otherwise similar to 30.
     AR Attic Didrachm, New York.

The final series of pre-Alexandrine coins issued by
the Tyrian mint were all struck under the authority of King
ʻUzzimilk.[113] The name is well known in Phoenician and has
been discussed above.[114] On an early issue, of the year
"3," a *ṣadeh* appears, perhaps from a re-used die of the
pre-revolt days; this coin, moreover, is plated, as are a
number of the extant issues of ʻUzzimilk.[115] The period was
a poor one economically, as Phoenicia tried to recover
from the devastating onslaught of the Persian mercenaries.

The years indicated on the coins are 3 through 17.
ʻUzzimilk was not permitted to issue coins in the first two
years of his post-revolt reign over Tyre. The Persian
government restricted the resumption of liberties, such as
coinage, to control the region more successfully. It was
already clear that Phoenician naval forces would soon be
needed to thwart the Macedonian threat, which loomed darkly
on the western horizon.

The types of this series remained unchanged, except
for the new royal abbreviation and the dates, which were
correctly interpreted by F.M. Cross. The dating is on the
era of the local king, as was the usual Phoenician custom.
On only one example is there any differing data; and this
type has merely a substitution of a dotted border for a
cable border.[116]

In conclusion, the coinage of Tyre played an important
role in the development of the Phoenician commercial power
in the eastern Mediterranean. From the earliest issues,
when Tyre's place was second to that of Sidon, the city's
mercantile functions pulsed with those of all Phoenicia.
After the revolts of the fourth century, when Tyre shifted
to the Attic standard, it was left with the tenuous leadership of the Phoenician league. A decimated Sidon could no
longer function as the leader of the coalition. ʻUzzimilk's

coinage helped to restore some of the commerce lost to
Phoenicia because of the war. Consequently, until ʿUzzimilk
and his son did battle with Alexander in the first half of
332 B.C.E.,[117] the city's coinage formed the foundation of
the Phoenician economy in the decades following 347.

The next coins issued by a mint in Tyre were
authorized by Alexander's successors in the Seleucid period
(the late fourth/early third centuries B.C.E.).[118]

Notes

1. Cf. Herodotus 7.98 and 8.67. The name given by Herodotus for the Tyrian is Ματτὴν Σιρώμου. In Josephus, *Contra Appian*, 1.18, reference is made to a king of Tyre named Mattenos or Metenos; the reference is secondary via Menander of Ephesus. We may be dealing with the same person; it was customary for the local kings, as Persian vassals, to be placed in command of their own segments of the fleet.

2. Historical sources are lacking. Archaeological excavations have shed only a little light on Tyre's past; inferences from other sites in Phoenicia and in Palestine have been somewhat helpful, especially with regard to the Tennes rebellion. Epigraphically, only two Tyrian inscriptions are dated; both come from 'Umm el-'Amed, which is 19 km south of Tyre. Both inscriptions date from the Seleucid era, 100 and 200 years, respectively, after the fall of Tyre. Of the known Tyrian inscriptions, none is earlier than the end of the fourth century. Additional materials from the recent excavations at Sarepta may shed some additional light on this problem. See *DLPS*, pp. 76-77. We must work on the supposition that what befell Phoenicia also befell Tyre.

3. The two largest Phoenician cities had established a strong trading network along the Levantine coast and elsewhere. A number of cities were specifically under their control, if the Classical sources may be trusted; cf. Galling, "Die syrisch-palästinische Küste nach der Beschreibung bei Pseudo-Skylax," pp. 195-201.

4. Judeich, *Kleinasiatische Studien*, pp. 122f.

5. Barag, "The Effects of the Tennes Rebellion on Palestine," pp. 6-7; Judeich, p. 171; Wallace B. Fleming, *The History of Tyre* (New York: Columbia University Press, 1915), p. 53.

6. Cf. Arrian, 2.15.7; 24.5. The siege lasted from January of 332 until about August. Curtius and Diodorus record some of the particulars of the siege: cf. Fleming, *The History of Tyre*, pp. 55-57. See also Pietschmann, *Geschichte der Phönizier*, pp. 61-63: the writer recalled the use of former Tyrian allies' ships in the blockade and siege, by land and sea. "Die wesentlichsten Dienste bei der Belagerung der Stadt leisteten vielmehr die Schiffe, welche Alexanders Bundesgenossen, die Sidonier, Gerostratos, der König von Arados, Enylos, der König von Byblos, die Rhodier, das kilikische Soloi, die Städt Lykiens und die Könige von Cypern, unter ihnen die von Amathus und Kurion, und Pnytagoras von Salamis ihm zur Verfügung stellten. Diese Flotte, die aus mehr als 220 Schiffen bestand, war der tyrischen weit überlegen" (p. 63).

7. Two standards were used at Tyre, the Phoenician and its later replacement, the Attic. The standards may be summarized as follows:

I.   Phoenician Standard: Silver Stater (Tyrian double šeqel) = 12.53-13.90 g. (10.30-10.40 plated)

½ silver šeqel = approx. 3.20 g.

1/24 silver šeqel = 0.71-0.47 g.

II. Attic Standard: Silver šeqel = 8.11-8.83 g. (6.95 plated)

8. Recent evidence from Palestine has shown conclusively that Tyre made this change *before* the conquest of Alexander and not after, as was previously assumed.

9. Babelon, *Traité*, II, 2, pp. 609-612, no. 980.

10. Babelon, *Traité*, II, 2, pp. 611-612, no. 981. This is the best preserved example of the type. The coin is now in Paris; its inscription is minute but legible.

11. Two examples of these half šeqels are in Paris; a third — as yet unpublished — is in London. It was part of the Weber Collection and is numbered "1922 Hall, H.P." The inscription is very finely done; magnification is required to verify the reading, which is clear and legible. Note that the *taw* was mistakenly engraved upside down during the minting process.

12. We do not know if any earlier issues came from this mint. The types are developed and are not really typical of the earliest coinage of a Phoenician mint. The use of a common standard with Sidon, Tyre's commercial and military partner, is to have been expected.

13. Certainly the dolphin's use alludes to the maritime interests of Tyre, as Hill has argued (*BMC Phoenicia*, p. cxxvi).

14. On the purely zoological and chemical aspects of the dye, see L.B. Jensen, "Royal Purple of Tyre," *JNES* 22 (1963) 104-113. See also E.A. Speiser, "The Name Phoinikes," *Oriental and Biblical Studies*, eds. J.J. Finkelstein and M. Greenberg (Philadelphia: University of Pennsylvania Press, 1967), pp. 324-331; M.C. Astour, "The Origin of the Terms 'Canaan,' 'Phoenician,' and 'Purple,'" *JNES* 24 (1965) 346-350; and George Rawlinson, *History of Phoenicia* (London: Longmans, Green, and Co., 1889), pp. 245-250. Very clearly, trade in this dye went well back into antiquity.

15. Babelon's first publication of the coin from the Jameson collection was in the *Comptes rendus du Congrès international d'archéologie classique*, 2me session (Cairo, 1909), p. 274. This example is exceptional; the clarity of the inscription was attested by the writer in July 1976, in Paris. Before the publication of this coin, however, confusion was caused by several illegible coins of the same

type, resulting in erroneous readings: see Six, *NC* 17
(1877) 194, n. 82; Babelon, *Les Perses achéménides*, nos.
1980-1982; and Rouvier, no. 1775. On the De Luynes coins,
see Babelon, *Traité*, II, 2, pp. 611-612, no. 983. In the
British Museum, there is an additional unpublished example,
on which the *mem*, *ḥet*, and *ṣadeh* are clear, although the
taw is somewhat obscured. The denomination is the same;
each coin weighs approximately 3.20 grams. The readings
were first proposed by Babelon. Close readings of the
actual coins in Paris and the additional, unpublished
examples in London confirm Babelon's original readings.

        16. The *šin* on the *šeqel* is known from the Bôd'aštart
inscription of the second half of the fifth century B.C.E.
Lamed is developing a downward tick in this period; our form
is a rather developed form. The curving dropline of the
form is indistinguishable on these small coins. The more
rectangular *šin* was a later development. Some of the
triangular *šin*s are known from this period, although even
earlier forms persisted into the early fourth century in
inscriptions from Athens and the Piraeus (*DLPS*, pp. 66-67,
line 4; pp. 95-96, 99). *Mem* is reminiscent of the
Bôd'aštart inscription, also, with a curving baseline up to
the shoulder on the right; the stance is not so vertical
as in the Bôd'aštart text, but it is more vertical than in
'Ešmun'azor. *Ḥet*, although unknown from the mid-fifth
century until the third and second centuries, is closer in
form to those of 'Ešmun'azor than to those of the 'Ešmun
temple; it must date to ca. 450-400 B.C.E. (*DLPS*, p. 67,
line 3). The letter has no right shoulder, and the cross-
lines are complete, unlike the forms of the later period.
Ṣadeh has the usual z-shaped head, which was so typical of
the Tyrian series (*DLPS*, p. 99). *Taw* was similar in stance
and form to examples of third and second century inscriptions from the 'Ešmun temple of Sidon (*DLPS*, p. 67, lines
7-8). The head was not so accentuated in its downstroke,
however, and was probably a transitional form from the more
horizontal head known in Bôd'aštart. See n. 20 below.

        17. Ba'lšallim's (I) use of inscriptions at Sidon
dates to ca. 420-410 B.C.E.

        18. The coin was found in the vicinity of Hebron in
1943 and was published by A. Reifenberg in "A Hebrew Shekel
of the Fifth Century B.C.," *PEQ* (1943) 100-104, pl. 7; see
also S.B. Luce, "Archaeological News and Discussions," *AJA*
48 (1944) 185; and A. Reifenberg, *Ancient Jewish Coins*
(Jerusalem: Rubin Press, 1973), 6th ed., pp. 5-8, 39, pl. 1a.
The coin may be described as follows:
OBV: Male head, bearded, wearing fillet, to l.; eye full;
      hair partly shown by granulating lines and taken up
      in knot at back; border of dots.
REV: Female head, to r. wearing necklace; hair falls on
      back of neck; eye full; she wears an earring; below
      in field to r., *bq* ' (=½); in incuse square; chisel-
      marked.
The reading is Reifenberg's (pp. 101-102). Indeed, with the
earring belong the *'ayin*, and the letter forms unclear at

best, a better reading for the inscription may be simply
'z: an ethnic for the mint of Gaza. Reifenberg's insis-
tance that the earring was a letter was apparently based on
a misreading of M. Narkiss, *Coins of Palestine*, 2 (Jerusalem:
Jewish Palestine Exploration Society, 1938), pp. 87-88
(Hebrew); cf. Reifenberg's n. 8 (p. 101). Narkiss wrote
בלחי סמוך לאוזן האות, which merely notes that an *ʿayin* was
on the cheek near the ear of a *male* figure; this coin
simply has the earring on the ear of a female figure, where
we would expect it.

All of this, thus, lends little help in reading denominational indications on these Tyrian coins. They remain
unique for their day.

19. Gesenius, in his *Hebrew Grammar*, E. Kautzsch, ed.
(Oxford: Clarendon Press, 1970), trans. A.E. Cowley, p. 292,
discussed the use of the afformative with the feminine forms
of the ordinal numbers. This is the case in point here; the
example given is that of עֶשְׂרוֹן, "a tenth part." On analogy
with this *qittalōn* form, our vocalization is שְׁלֹשִׁן, "a
thirtieth part." See also Friedrich and Röllig, *Phönizische-
Punische Grammatik*, p. 243.

The reference to the thirtieth part of a standard mina,
however is a problem. The Phoenician šeqel is 1/50 of a
Phoenician mina, by normal definition. These coins weigh,
on the average, 13.50 to 13.60 grams. This weight x 30 ≠
a Phoenician mina; however, it does equal an Attic mina —
that is, the weight of 50 Attic staters. The precise ratio
is 427.4 grams (30 Phoenician šeqels) to 436.6 grams (an
Attic mina, or 100 drachms). See F. Hultsch, *Griechische
und Römische Metrologie* (Berlin: Weidmannsche Buchhandlung,
1882), pp. 134-135. The ratio between the Phoenician coins
and the Attic coins is not surprising, although the system
of marking Phoenician šeqels according to their equivalent
in the Attic standard is unique. It is characteristic only
of these early issues in Tyre; Attic commerce in the ports
was at an all-time high.

20. This inscription refers to "a half"; the weight
is about 3.25 grams and roughly corresponds to the weight
of a drachm (half a didrachm; 50 didrachms = 1 mina). It
may be that the examples which are extant of this rare
type are deficient by weight to the norm. Our vocalization
of *maḥṣit* is based on the Hebrew; see Exodus 30:13, 15,
where the phrase מחצית השקל is used: "half of the šeqel."
The *taw* was mistakenly reversed by the engraver. Having
the weights marked on the coins in such a manner is
unparalleled. This may have been an effort to facilitate
daily commerce in the marketplace where bilingual trans-
actions were in progress.

21. These inscriptions may have been explanatory only,
to increase the use of coins in a region where local issues
were new and conservative mercantile factions may have been
slow to accept foreign innovations.

22. Recall the Byblian depiction of the sphinx on
the early issue of the mint; in the words of R.D. Barnett,
"The Phoenicians used Egyptian symbolism for their own purposes and gave it meanings of their own. Their artistic
viewpoint was much the same as that of the Egyptians." See
Barnett's *A Catalogue of the Nimrud Ivories*, p. 62. Attic
coins were found with Tyrian owls at Daliyeh (n. 88 below).
Tyrian coins were important means of exchange as early as
the fifth century B.C.E.

23. The Phoenician owl almost looks like the hawk with
an owl's head. It is probably coincidental that the Athenian
coinage of the mid-fifth century used depictions of the owl
of Athena which also resemble quite closely this bird.

24. The crook, or *hq3t*, was the symbol of rule in
Heliopolis and was usually held in the left hand of Osirian
figures. The flail, or *h3h3*, is the royal scourge which was
carried in the right hand of Osiris and signified "rule"
or "dominion." See A.E. Knight, *Amentet* (London: Longmans,
Green, and Co., 1915), pp. 198 and 211; and *BMC Phoenicia*,
p. cxxvii. In a famous stele from the British Museum, 'Ēl
is seen holding the crook and flail over his l. shoulder,
also. The stele was erected in Egypt by Canaanites who
were apparently serving as mercenaries in Pharoah's army.
Cf. Dussaud, *L'art phénicien du IIe millénaire*, p. 52, fig.
17.

25. The whole type is in relief, surrounded by the
characteristic impression. The exact method in use at
Tyre differs slightly from that of Sidon, Aradus, and
Byblos; however, the same impression is attained stylistically.

26. Hoards where coins from Tyre and Sidon have been
found together are as follows (reference numbers are from
IGCH): 1256 from Cilicia (ca. 405 B.C.E.), 1483 from N.
Phoenicia (ca. 425-420 B.C.E.), 1490 from Aleppo (400-350
B.C.E.), 1500 from Beirut (ca. 332 B.C.E.), 1504 from
Nablus (ca. 332 B.C.E.), 1506 from Baalbek (ca. 332 B.C.E.),
1507 from Gezer (ca. 330 B.C.E.), 1510 from Galilee (ca.
319 B.C.E.), 1651 from Cairo (360 B.C.E.), 1747 from
Mesopotamia (390-385 B.C.E.), and 1790 from Media (ca. 375
B.C.E.). Hoards of Tyrian coins only have been found from
the Nile Delta (1649 of the fourth century) to Bactria
(1820 dating to ca. 385 B.C.E.). One of the trade routes
turned inland from near Tyre toward Damascus, providing a
link for Tyre and Sidon with the inland regions and the
products available from Syria and Mesopotamia. Kraay
(*Archaic and Classical Greek Coins*, p. 288) has suggested
that the coinages of the two cities were purposefully struck
in complimentary denominations, which is very probable.

27. Babelon, *Traité*, II, 2, no. 992.

28. Babelon, *Traité*, II, 2, no. 985; the first *šin* is
doubtful, but the rest of the inscription is legible.

29. The inscription is deleted permanently from the Tyrian issues.

30. Such reversals of types were most common when inexperienced die cutters began their work. These coins, however, may present us with a completely new set of dies, purposefully reversed with variable types. At Tyre this method was used for years by the mint.

31. The murex shell was used as late as the first and second centuries of the Christian era.

32. See Babelon, *Traité*, II, 2, no. 981, with drawing on pp. 613-614. The rosette was commonly used as a stamped impression upon black-painted Greek and East Greek pottery of the fourth century B.C.E. See the authoritative work of B.A. Sparkes and L. Talcott, *Black and Plain Pottery*, The Athenian Agora XII (Princeton: The American School of Classical Studies at Athens, 1970), *passim*. This type of pottery is known from all areas of the eastern Mediterranean from ca. 420 until Hellenistic times. More isolated use of the rosette as a motif is known from older contexts within Syria-Phoenicia: note, for example, the section of an ivory panelled box with incised designs of bulls and a rosette from Nimrud. The box is now in the Ashmolean Museum, Oxford (no. 1956.960). Cf. Harden, *The Phoenicians*, pl. 69, p. 285. A number of rosettes are also known from the art of Ugarit. A rosette decorated a stele depicting a priest offering oblations to 'Ēl; see Dussaud, *L'art phénicien du IIe millénaire*, pp. 59-60, fig. 23, and *Syria* 18 (1937), pp. 128f. and pl. 17. A bronze axe, laminated in iron, also from Ras Shamra, has a decorative design with a rosette dating from the 15th/14th centuries B.C.E. (Dussaud, pp. 69-70, 72, and fig. 39). The motif is purely decorative.

33. Albright (*YGC*, pp. 198-199) has documented a development in which Ba'l Hadad's cult is symbolised by the storm god throwing a thunderbolt while riding on the back of the bull, then to just the bull with the thunderbolt on its back, and finally to just the bull itself. Cf. T. Obbink, "Jahwebilder," *ZAW* 47 (1929) 264-274; and Albright in *From Stone Age to Christianity* (New York: Doubleday Anchor Books, 1957), 2nd ed., pp. 298-300.

34. Usually the bull is depicted attacking a stag or some other animal. From 'Aḥiram's tomb, ivory fragments depict a bull's head in just such a manner; see Dussaud, p.101, fig. 63, and also fig. 65 (from Tell ed-Duweir) and fig. 66 (from Megiddo).

35. The difference here is that these are silver coins; in Sidon and Aradus this practice was generally restricted to bronze issues.

36. Babelon, *Traité*, II, 2, no. 993; *BMC Phoenicia*, nos. 11-12. These coins are bronze plated with silver. The currency in Tyre in this time must have been poorly backed, for such coinage would not have circulated easily within the marketplace.

37. The coin is in the personal collection of M. Lefkowitz of ʿAkkô, and was viewed by the writer on 16 January 1977.

38. All of the commentators have noted the "thick fabric." This technique for striking a coin is older than the one in use when Alexander conquered Tyre, giving us a bit of evidence for our relative chronology.

39. One reason for the "thick fabric" may have been the need to approximate the weight standard of a purely silver coin with a core of bronze, which weighs a bit less. No coins are known from the other three Phoenician mints which were plated.

40. Numerous examples exist of coins which were cut or chiseled as tests for purity. Countermarks appeared attesting to the weight and metallic content of the coinage. Silver must have been scarce for the Tyrian mint to have exposed its coinage to such gross devaluation. The trade routes to the silver producing areas in Anatolia and the western Mediterranean may have been blocked at this time due to animosity between Persia and the Greeks, especially the Athenians whose navy ruled the waves.

41. The šeqel which is not plated is the later example, with the *bet* (our no. 14).

42. Without a solid basis, that is, without silver to back silver, Tyre's coinage must have been devalued by severe inflation and poor buying ability against other currencies. No reserve was needed to support the legal tender in this time; the coinage was the backing since the metals were as pure as possible.

43. This was a time when political and military problems may have entered into Tyre's minting processes. In the late 380's Euagoras I of Salamis (Cyprus) led an insurrection against Persian authority in Cyprus. The revolt spread into Egypt, Palestine, and southern Phoenicia. Euagoras seized Tyre; we do not know what fate befell Sidon and the more northern cities of the Phoenician league. It may have been the Euagoras who authorized these plated issues. As soon as the revolt was suppressed, Tyre resumed its usual silver coinage exclusively, with new denominational types and even a separate bronze series.

44. The iconographic problems associated with this type are numerous. Certainly Baʿl Šamēm is well known in the Phoenicia of the fourth century B.C.E. with which we are dealing. R.A. Qden has collected the data recently in an article, "Baʿal Šamēm and ʾĒl," *CBQ* 39 (1977) 457-473. Oden noted that this deity had a special regard for the earthly king: thus, the minting authority of Tyre may have had its patron in the chief deity of the city, Baʿl Šamēm. The seventh century treaty made between Baʿl of Tyre and Esarhaddon, the Assyrian king, listed a number of deities as witnesses from Assyria, Syria, and finally Tyre's own *dBa-al-ša-me-me dBa-al-ma-la-ge-e dBa-al-sa-pu-nu*

(Riekele Borger, *Die Inschriften Asarhaddons Königs von Assyrien* [Graz: E. Weidner, 1956], Archiv für Orient-forschung, 9, p. 109), along with Milqart, 'Esmun, and 'Astart. Oden notes that the deity is here placed at the head of the pantheon, just as he was in the Yaḥimilk and Zakir inscriptions (p. 463). From Sakkunyaton, we read that Ba'l Samēm was the deity to which the Phoenicians turned in time of drought, as they lifted their heads to the sun (πρὸς τὸν ἥλιον); this god, as Oden pointed out, they considered "the only Lord in Heaven" (μόνον οὐρανοῦ κύριον), Βεελσάμην; this was the equivalent, according to Sakkunyaton, of the Greek Zeus. The solar identification with 'El is not easily reconciled. Nowhere in the Ugaritic texts, for example, is such an identification made. 'El was not a rider, while Ba'l was a rider of his cloudy entourage. However, nowhere do we have Ba'l Hadad using a bow in battle, as did 'El. Cf. *CTA*, 23.44ff., in which 'El draws his bow and shoots a bird out of the sky. As Cross has noted (*CMHE*, p. 23) *ḥṭ* here means "bowstave"; we have it in parallelism with *qšt*, "bow," in text 19.1.14. Interestingly, the god Aššur, from the period of Tukulti-Ninurta II (ca. 890-884 B.C.E., seems to combine this imagery of rider and bowman. An emblem of the god from this period shows him with wings, driving in a chariot (with a driver) drawn by a horse, with a drawn bow (*ANEP*, 536). Sennacherib recorded having made an image of this deity in similar fashion: "(I made) an image of Aššur...holding a bow and riding in a chariot... the god of Amurru is a charioteer holding the reins" — *ṣalam Aššur...qaštu kî ša našû ina narkabti ša rakbu...Amurru ša ana mukil appāti ittišu rakbu* (*OIP* 2, 140:6-8); see also M. Weinfeld, "'Rider of the Clouds' and 'Gatherer of the Clouds,'" p. 424.

Aššur was a "god of the fathers" which was an Old Assyrian term for the personal god, like the Biblical "The Lord God of your fathers, the God of Abraham, the God of Isaac, and the God of Jacob" (Ex 3:15). Thorkild Jacobsen has drawn attention to this fact in his *The Treasures of Darkness* (New Haven: Yale University Press, 1976), p. 159. For Aššur, of course, this notion stands in apposition to his role as leader of the cult and the substitute for Marduk in the *Enūma eliš*. Aššur as divine patriarch was somehow combined with Aššur the divine warrior, the storm god. This may be the situation of the deity depicted upon these coins of Tyre. We have a strange composite, which is a peculiarly mid-first millennium problem, because we do not see any signs of this earlier. B. Mazar has argued further, for example, that Ba'l Samēm was held in honor by Phoenician seamen because of his being a deity of the sea and storms, as well as a patron of shipping. His argument is based on the treaty of Asarhaddon and Ba'l of Tyre. "It is for this reason that Ba'l Samēm was held in awe by Phoenician seamen, either under this name or under one of his other appellations. Little wonder that in a period of great maritime development, of flourishing international trade and negotiations which encompassed *orbis terrarum*, Ba'l Samēm should have assumed a cosmopolitan character." Cf. "The Philistines and the Rise of Israel and Tyre," *Proceedings of the Israel Academy of Sciences and Humanities*, 1.7 (Jerusalem, 1967), p. 19.

On the treaty curses, see W.F. Albright, "Baal-Zephon,"
Festschrift Alfred Bertholet zum 80. Geburtstag, W. Baumgartner, *et al.*, eds. (Tübingen: J.C.B. Mohr, 1950), p. 9.
Even so, no specific appellation of the divinity can safely
be made here. We do not know how Ba'l Šamēm was depicted
in this era.

45. A notion that Ba'l Šamēm may have been represented
upon these types, given the paucity of information we have
concerning this deity, came from F.M. Cross's discussion of
the coins excavated in the Wādī ed-Dâliyeh. He termed the
deity on these Tyrian types as "Milqart or Ba'l Šāmēm" (*AASOR*
41 [1974], p. 59). Milqart (*milk-qart*, "king of the city")
is a deity, in this period, who has merged with Rašap,
becoming a lord of the underworld city of the dead. Albright
has developed this point in *YGC*, pp. 145-146. J.M. Solá
Solé has shown that *ršp* was identified with *mlqrt* in Punic
Spain ("Miscelánea púnico-hispana. I.3. HGD, 'RŠF y el
pantheon fenico punico de España," *Sefarad* 16 [1956] 341-
355); H. Seyrig, furthermore, has shown that in Roman Syria,
Milqart was still identified with Nergal (*Syria* 24 [1947]
62-80). No evidence exists which would verify Dussaud's
notion that Milqart was a fusion of Ba'l Hadad and Yamm
(see "Melqart," *Syria* 25 [1946-1948] 205-206). Part of
his reasoning centered on the identification of Milqart/
Herakles and the association which Herakles had with aquatic
monsters. Cf. R. Flacelière and P. Devambez, *Héracles:
Images & Récits* (Paris: E. de Boccard, 1966), pp. 105-109,
pls. 16.1-2. Some of the arguments surrounding Milqart,
such as Dussaud's, are reviewed in M.C. Astour's *Helleno-
semitica* (Leiden: E.J. Brill, 1965), pp. 208-211. Certain
elements of the iconography of Milqart are known from the
stele dedicated to him which is in the Museum of Aleppo:
he wears an Aramaean hat and carries a fenestrated axe; he
has no bow, nor does he ride on anything (M. Dunand, "Stele
araméenne dédiée à Melqart," *BMB* 3 [1939] 65-76, esp. pl. 13).
This iconography does not match that of the deity riding the
seahorse on our coin. It does match the iconography of
Herakles' cult in Hellenistic and Roman times; see Wathiq
al-Salihi, "Hercules-Nergal at Hatra," *Iraq* 33 (1971) 113-
115, and 35 (1973) 65-68. Albright points out the composite
bow, however, held in the r. hand of the deity; cf. "A
Votive Stele Erected by Ben-Hadad I of Damascus to the God
Melcarth," *BASOR* 87 (1942) 29. The chthonic nature of this
deity is further discussed in Albright, *Archaeology and the
Religion of Israel* (Garden City, NY: Doubleday Anchor Books,
1968), 5th ed., pp. 78-79. See A. Hus, "Sculpture étrusque
archaïque: Le cavalier marin de la villa Giulia," *Mélanges
d'archéologie et d'histoire* 67 (1955) 71-126, pls. 1-2, esp.
126, where he argues for the "origine syro-anatolienne" of
the seahorse.

46. Ba'l, as known from the Ugaritic texts, went forth
taking with him "his clouds, his winds, his *mdl*, and his
rains"; *CTA* 5.5.6-8: *qh . ʿrptk . rhk . mdlk . mṭrtk. Mdl*
is most probably harnessing or rigging for a cart with horses;
it appears in parallel with *smd* in *CTA* 19:52-53. Ba'l went
forth, thus, with his entourage, including a chariot yoked

to a team. (Cf. J. Greenfield, "Ugaritic *mdl* and its
Cognates," *Biblica* 45 [1964] 527f.; A.A. Wieder, "Ugaritic
Hebrew Lexicographical Notes," 84 [1965] 164; Weinfeld,
"'Rider of the Clouds' and 'Gatherer of the Clouds,'" p. 424;
CMHE, p. 17.) An epithet of Zeus, ὑποζύγος (from the
Iliad 4:166; 7:69; and 11:544), meaning "high above the
yoke," is similar, paralleling the appellative "high-
throned" and "high in the clouds." Cf. Pindar, *Olymp.* 5:17;
Nem. 4:65; *Isthm.* 6:16; and Nonnus' *Dionysiaca*, 26:147.
The iconography of the riding weather god is well established
in Syria-Phoenicia, using motifs established in Ugarit and
earlier. This iconography may explain *part* of our coin type.
The types of statuary which depict the storm god as a rider
are reviewed and summarized in Wolfgang Helck, *Betrachtungen
zur grossen Göttin und den ihr verbundenen Gottheiten*
(Munich and Vienna: R. Oldenbourg, 1971), Religion und
Kultur der alten Mittelmeerwelt in Parallelforschungen,
C. Colpe and H. Dörrie, eds., Vol. 2, pp. 169-209, especially 189-191 and 206 (drawings). The types of Syrian
weather gods of the second millennium are fully discussed,
with some parallels there.

47. Oden has noted Eissfeldt's arguments concerning
several passages in Daniel, where conscious *Entstellungen*
of Ba'l Šamēm may have occurred; Eissfeldt went so far as
to hypothesize that a cult object may have been erected in
the Jerusalem temple dedicated to Ba'l Šamēm ("Ba'al-šamēm
und Jahwe," *ZAW* 16 [1939] 24; Oden, pp. 466-467). Oden
cites additional evidence from Palestine, Palmyra, Dura-
Europos, Hatra, and other sites. Only in Hellenistic and
Roman times can one approach Oden's claim that "Ba'al Šamēm
is characterized in ways that coincide with characterizations
of 'El because the former is an epithet of the latter"; p.
473. Such arguments, however interesting, remain purely
speculative, and defy corroboration in this early period.

48. See our arguments above.

49. See G. Thompson, "Iranian Dress in the Achaemenian
Period," p. 125.

50. These variations were primarily those of ethnic
abbreviations and dating systems, as well as minor changes
in the smallest denominations (silver only).

51. Cf. *PNPPI*, pp. 356-357; the name means "gift" and
is a hypocoristicon for a longer name. See Josephus,
Antiquities, 9.154 for Μαθάν; *Contra Apian*, 1.125 for
Μεττήνος or 1.157 for Μυττύνος; Herodotus, 7.98 reads
Ματτήν.

52. *PNPPI*, pp. 356-357.

53. This is speculative, at best. The Sidonian king
may have led the Phoenician league which met at Tripolis
(Greek) or 'Atar (Phoenician). Sidon, Tyre, and Aradus
each sent 100 delegates to serve on the supreme council; it
is only natural that the strongest city would provide the

chairman. Since this specific coin is plated (silver over bronze), the *bet* may be Ba'lšallim's guarantee that it is of full value as a Phoenician šeqel; when the plating stopped, so did the use of the *bet*. Of the several possibilities we have suggested for the *bet*'s use, no one theory has any more proof behind it than another; all are speculative. Cf. Olmstead, *History of the Persian Empire*, p. 434.

54. Variations within these small denominations make it impossible to be certain whether part of this type was struck off flan or not.

55. This suggests that the seahorse was probably still in use on the type, as was the case in the earlier series.

56. "A symbol is 'an image or design with a significance, to the one who uses it, quite beyond its manifest content,'...'a word or form which expresses more than it indicates, and so has power beyond its literal denotation'; 'symbols have a way of dying, of apparently losing their power, and becoming merely ornaments.' And they also have the power of coming to life again, as fresh associations and religious awakenings take old symbols for their own." Arthur Darby Nock, "Religious Symbols. I," *Essays on Religion and the Ancient World*, Vol. 2, Z. Stewart, ed. (Cambridge, MA: Harvard University Press, 1972), p. 879. Given the possibilities of Phoenician independence, as Persian power waned, such new life must have revitalized these symbols.

57. Cf. Philip Grierson, *Numismatics* (London: Oxford University Press, 1975), p. 13. The bull is well known for its associations with both Ba'l Hadad and with 'El. Oden has argued that Ba'l Šamēm by the second century was called "Olympios" when the merger with Zeus was complete; cf. Oden, pp. 466-467. Josephus, *Contra Apian*, 1.113, wrote that Hiram built a causeway to connect the city on the shore with the island's temple of Olympian Zeus. Josephus confused this temple with a temple to Ba'l Šamēm. Cult tools which bore the likeness of the bull are known from Ugarit; see Schaeffer, "Nouveaux témoignages du culte de El et de Baal à Ras Shamra-Ugarit et ailleurs en Syria-Palestine," pp. 10ff. No satisfactory explanation of this circumstantial evidence is possible, however, at Tyre in this early period.

58. Babelon, *Traité*, II, 2, pp. 617-618, no. 997.

59. The reading is impossible; the coin, in the cabinets of the Bibliothèque nationale, is in very poor condition and cannot be read. The letters alleged by Babelon are not legible. We are not able to make any other suggestion for a reading, except that *mem* is the usual reading on the reverse types, and this one may have been damaged by die breaks, resulting in Babelon's misreading.

60.   Babelon's dating was even further off the mark, "de 420 à 400 environ"; *Traité*, II, 2, pp. 615-616.   Cf. *BMC Phoenicia*, p. 229.

61.   There are no problems with the name; whether papponymy was in use or not, there could have been a ruler with this name in this century.   Cf. Cross, "Jar Inscriptions from Shiqmona," p. 227.

62.   Diodorus, for example, confused Sidon and Tyre several times in his histories.

63.   The Paris coin is no. 1965/751; it was unearthed at Byblos.   The Tel 'Aviv examples are all from 'Akkô: no. K-1315, dated "year 2"; no. K-1316, dated "year 10"; no. K-1313, dated "year 4"; and no. 1763, dated "year 1." These coins are in the collection of the Kadman Numismatic Museum of the Museum Ha'aretz, Tel'Aviv.

64.   The coin is no. 1965/753 and was found at Byblos.

65.   This coin is from the Israel Museum and was viewed by the writer on 12 January 1977.

66.   Examples of this coin are in the collections of the Israel Museum and of M. Lefkowitz of 'Akkô.   The coin with cabled border is in Jerusalem; the dotted border is in 'Akkô.

67.   The cedar tree is most unusual; the motif looks like this: ⚶ .

68.   The coin was found in the vicinity of Tel 'Akkô (*not* part of the Tell el-Fukkhâr hoard.)

69.   This is a reversal of the types of our no. 22 (bronze).

70.   This coin, in the Tel 'Aviv collection, is numbered K-1332 and is from the Tell el-Fukkhâr hoard.

71.   There is also an example of this type from the Tell el-Fukkhâr hoard, no. K-1337 from the Kadman Museum.

72.   The coin is numbered K-1319 and is from the Tell el-Fukkhâr hoard.

73.   The dating system is identical to that used at Sidon.

74.   Their reigns extended from 386/385 until 362/361 B.C.E.

75.   Space limitations may have dictated certain changes in the types.   *N.B.*: *Zayin* sometimes represents the numeral "20," although this seems not to apply in this case.

76. See Judeich, *Kleinasiatische Studien*, pp. 171, 175; and D. Barag, "The Effects of the Tennes Rebellion on Palestine," pp. 6-8.

77. Greek craftsmen may have lent their technological expertise to the mint. Greek workmanship may be seen in the magnificent, fourth century sarcophagi found at Sidon. The presence of so much Greek pottery, for example, in Phoenicia in the fifth and fourth centuries indicates the volume of the trade between the countries. Greek trading settlements, such as the one at Tell Sukas, may have been commonplace in this period. Cf. P.K. Hitti, *History of Syria* (New York: Macmillan Co., 1951), pp. 227-228.

78. Sidon's coinage used the "flat fabric" also; her friendship with Athens probably gained her access to Greek technicians.

79. Tyre's trade in cedar wood was still important at this time. A tree like this took on the same significance as the murex shell.

80. In 360 B.C.E. Sidon had harbored the Egyptian king Tachos, who had helped to instigate the revolt. Sidon paid more dearly than did Tyre.

81. The coin is numbered K-1318 and was found on Tell el-Fukkhâr, but not in the hoard.

82. *BMC Phoenicia*, p. 233, no. 43.

83. The coin is numbered K-1324 and is from the Tell el-Fukkhâr hoard.

84. The coin is from the Tell el-Fukkhâr hoard; it is unnumbered.

85. *BMC Phoenicia*, p. 231; Babelon, *Traité*, II, 2, pp. 621ff.

86. The seige lasted from January until July/August of 332; cf. W.W. Tarn, *Alexander the Great* (Cambridge: Cambridge University Press, 1948), vol. 1, p. 40.

87. Such were the usual Alexandrine coins which were struck after his take-over of a city's mint. See E.T. Newell, *The Dated Alexander Coinage of Sidon and Ake* (New Haven: Yale University Press, 1916), pp. 21ff. The head may have been a portrait of Alexander: see Bellinger, *Essays on the Coinage of Alexander the Great*, pp. 14-21.

88. See F.M. Cross, "Papyri from the Fourth Century B.C. from Dâliyeh," *New Directions in Biblical Archaeology*, D.N. Freedman and J.C. Greenfield, eds. (Garden City, NY: Doubleday Anchor Books, 1969), pp. 53-54. The other coins included an Attic tetradrachm of Philip II, Alexander's father; a silver šeqel of Mazday from Cilicia, which may date as late as Darius' reign (336-331 B.C.E.); and two small silver coins — one of the Philisto-Arabian grouping

and one from 'Abd'aštart III of Sidon, ca. 339-332 B.C.E.
Cf. Cross, "Coins," *Discoveries in the Wâdî ed-Dâliyeh*,
P.W. and N.L. Lapp, eds., *AASOR* 41 (1974), pp. 57-59.

89.   All of these coins date within a decade or two
prior to Alexander's conquest.

90.   H. Seyrig, "Antiquités syriennes: Sur une
prétendue ère tyrienne," *Syria* 34 (1957) 93-98.

91.   Seyrig, pp. 97-98; he believed that the coinage
was to be used strictly on a local basis. Hoard evidence,
however, has shown how far afield the coins circulated,
indicating that trade was in progress.

92.   Seyrig also mentions 'Akkô's mint; pp. 96-97.

93.   Cross, "Coins," p. 57.

94.   Mazday's coinage was officially sanctioned by
Alexander because he was serving as a satrap for his new
overlord. He had moved, however, from Cilicia to Mesopotamia,
changing his weight standard from the Persic to the Attic,
as the new government required. Mazday did not resist
Alexander; he, on the contrary, changed his allegiance and
aided the coming conqueror in defeating his enemies, such
as Tyre.

95.   Cross, "Coins," pp. 57-58.

96.   All of these mints — Gaza, 'Ašdôd, 'Ašqelon,
Jerusalem, Hierapolis, and probably Damascus — used the
Attic standard. There may also have been other mints.

97.   Cross, "Coins," p. 58; the letter is Phoenician
ayin.

98.   Cross, "Coins," p. 58, notes 25-26.

99.   The several passages within the Classical sources
which may have shed some light on this event are hopelessly
corrupt. "Straton" of Sidon is confused with the king of
Tyre in Diodorus and Justin; see Cross, "Coins," p. 58, n. 27.

100.   The name is a nominal sentence name, in which the
divine appellative is in the second position; the form of
the name is predicate-subject. It means "Milk ("King,"
probably Milqart) is my strength." Cf. *PNPPI*, pp. 222, 344-
345, and 374.

101.   The article was published in *Eretz-Israel, 8:
E.L. Sukenik Memorial Volume* (Jerusalem: Israel Exploration
Society, 1967), pp. 318-325, pl. 1A (Hebrew). Kindler noted
that M. Narkiss had argued a pre-Alexandrine date for these
coins as early as 1939. Cross, "Coins," p. 58, n. 28.

102.   The same usage has been noted at Sidon, with
Mazday's striking of coins following the city's participation
in the rebellion.

103. The construction is peculiar, because it is
Aramaic. If it was Phoenician, we would expect *bšt*, "in
the (one) year"; because *bšnt* would refer to "years," in
the plural. Since Sidon's coinage at this same time,
issued by Mazday, used this dating system, it is possible
that it was introduced into Tyre by Mazday, also. He was
in command of post-revolt Phoenicia. The usage was associated with the central government.

104. *BMC Phoenicia*, p. 231, no. 25. The coin, examined
personally by the writer in June 1976, has numerous die
breaks and is badly worn. In all probability, no new dies
were made following the revolt; old ones were merely altered
with the new dating system and coins were struck. The Paris
cabinet has an identical coin, numbered 2,007, and another
in the de Luynes collection: see Babelon, *Traité*, II, 2,
pp. 621-622, no. 1009, and pp. 623-624, nos. 1010-1012.

105. The earliest representation of the owl was very
similar to the bird of prey known from Minet el-Beida,
discussed by Dussaud in his *L'art phénicien du II*[e] *millénaire*,
p. 70, fig. 36. These later engravings, however, show a
marked change to a more Athenian style owl. Greek die cutters
were probably the reason for this alteration.

106. Harris, *A Grammar of the Phoenician Language*,
p. 142.

107. *BMC Phoenicia*, p. 232, no. 33. The coin may have
used an old, recut die from before the Tennes rebellion,
since it was from the first group of coins struck after the
revolt.

108. *BMC Phoenicia*, p. 231, no. 31.

109. This is a parenthetical notation on p. 231 (*BMC
Phoenicia*). Apparently, the die was not made well; the
workmanship was very crude.

110. The coin was personally examined by the writer
in July 1976; it is numbered 2,013 in the Tyrian trays of
the Bibliothèque nationale, Paris.

111. Sidon, for example, had difficulty in producing
high quality coins in the fourth century, with its political
and military problems.

112. The coins include the following inscriptions
and dates:

a.	⫼ o	(year 3)	g.	⫼⌒o	(year 12)
b.	⫼o/ᛦ	(year 3)	h.	⌒o	(year 13)
c.	⫼⫼ o	(year 4)	i.	⌒o	(year 14)
d.	⫼⫼⫼ o	(year 6)	j.	⌒ρ	(year 15)
e.	⫼⫼⫼o	(year 8)	k.	⌒o	(year 17)
f.	⌒o	(year 10)			

113. Cf. Arrian, 2.15.7; 24.5. The king ruled, with his son, when Alexander conquered Phoenicia.

114. The name has been discussed above in n. 100.

115. Coins of years 3, 13, and 17 are plated, as chisel cuts have shown: *BMC Phoenicia*, p. 232, nos. 33, 38, and 41.

116. *BMC Phoenicia*, p. 232, no. 42.

117. Rawlinson, *History of Phoenicia*, pp. 511-529. Rawlinson recounts all of the gruesome details as recorded in the Classical sources; attocities abounded on both sides in this six- to seven-month battle. Additional data on the siege of Tyre may be gleaned from Fleming's old history, *The History of Tyre*, pp. 56ff.

118. Cf. E.T. Newell, *The Coinage of the Western Seleucid Mints from Seleucus I to Antiochus III* (New York: ANS, 1941), p. 23; *IGCH*, p. 209.

Chapter 3

ARADUS

The seaport of Aradus was situated on a small island
off the northern coast of Phoenicia.[1] In antiquity, the
region was called the παραλία of the Aradians.[2] The city
was the central point of a small state which included a
number of smaller cities and villages located in the nearby
coastal and inland regions. Strabo and Pliny give the names
of these satellite cities, which depended upon Aradus.[3]

During the Persian period, the role of Aradus in the
commercial, political, and military life of the Phoenicians
is difficult to determine. The ancient sources are almost
completely mute regarding this city. A number of traditions
survive concerning the origin of the city. Strabo wrote
that Aradus was founded by Sidonians in the eighth century
B.C.E.[4] Mention of *Hā'ārwadî*, one of the sons of Canaan in
Genesis 10:18, would antedate Strabo's date by at least two
centuries.[5] Still another tradition attributes the founding
of the city to people of the island of Aradus in the Persian
Gulf.[6] Suffice it to say that Aradus was under Persian
hegemony in the fifth and fourth centuries B.C.E., when
coinage was first used in the Levant. The histories of the
Greeks from the Persian period tell us only of the situation
surrounding the surrender of the city to the armies of
Alexander the Great. Diodorus Siculus recounts the event
in which Gerostratus, a vassal of the Persian king, gives
up Aradus, Marathus, Sigon, Mariamme, and several other
cities of the πρόσοικοι of Aradus.[7] From this time on, the
city was under Greek control, and its mint issued coins
under the authority of Alexander the Great and later Seleucid
rulers.[8] Our interests predate these events, however.

Since the works of Six, Rouvier, Babelon, and Hill,[9]
little has been done to elucidate the complex history of
the early coinage of Aradus. Unfortunately, no systematic
archaeological excavations have occurred in the vicinity of
the ancient site which have maintained sufficient strati-

graphical control to make new data available. Problems of
attribution and dating remain unsolved. Comparison with the
coinages of the neighboring cities of Byblos, Sidon, and
Tyre, however, has made some progress possible in bringing
order to this quagmire. In this chapter we will present
the evidence of the extant coins of Aradus, with our reconstruction of the city's mint. Of special interest are the
functions and role of the pre-Alexandrine issues of Aradus.

The Earliest Coinage
ca. 430-410 B.C.E.

1.   OBV: Marine deity, to r., human to waist, bearded and
            with plaited hair; lower body that of a fish, with
            bifid tail and fins, covered with scales (consisting
            of dots); fish held by the tail in each hand; border
            of dots.

     REV: Galley to r., with rudder astern; row of shields
            along bulwark; ornament and standard above deck
            to l.; all in shallow incuse square.

     AR   Tetrobol, New York.

2.   OBV: Same as 1 above.

     REV: Similar to 1 above, except with canopy on deck
            and dolphin below to r.

     AR   Diobol, New York.   Plate 6.

The coinage of Aradus began during the last years of
the fifth century B.C.E., as did the coinages of the other
Phoenician cities. The major difference was that Aradus
used the Persic standard rather than the Phoenician standard
— the one adopted by the other Phoenician city-states.[10]
The Persic, or Babylonic, standard was lighter in weight
than the Phoenician standard, and was that which the Persian
kings used for the official coinage of the empire. The
reason for the use of this different weight system at Aradus
is unknown. Given the port's proximity to the trade routes
which led into the Euphrates River valley, it is possible
that the Persian government wished to maintain a stricter
control over Aradus. This sign of uniformity with the city's
overlords is unknown in Byblos, Sidon, or Tyre, and may
suggest that Aradus functioned as an official Mediterranean
port for the Persians.[11] However, the use of another standard may simply be due to Aradus' relative isolation from
the rest of Phoenicia.[12] More likely is the different

relationship which Aradus had to the Persian court, as
compared to the other Phoenician cities.[13]

    This earliest series of coins was issued in the late
fifth century. We know nothing of the rulers of Aradus at
the time, so no concrete attributions can be made.[14] Given
the small denominations of the extant coins, it is possible
that they were to serve merely as the "small change" in a
monetary system which employed larger coins, also. Hill
pointed out that five of the tetrobols weigh nearly the
same as the normal weight of an Athenian tetradrachm.[15]
These coins were certainly known all along the Levantine
coast, and it may be that the Athenian coinage was the
parent coinage of that of Aradus. Some later Aradian
issues appear to be more or less conscious imitations of
Athenian issues, with the predictable Phoenician variations.[16]

    There are no inscriptions on these earliest coins. No
inscriptions were used on Phoenician coins until the last
years of the fifth century or the early fourth century.[17]

    The primary reasons for placing these coins early in
the Aradian series are typological. First, the style of
the die-cutting is archaic.[18] The method used to represent
the deities shown upon the coin types developed over time
into a more "Hellenic" style; the shift is clear and unmis-
takable.

    Second, we have the problem of the identity of the
deity shown on the obverse types of the coins. Called by
Babelon the "type de Dagon ichthyomorphe,"[19] Hill chose to
refer to the figure merely as "a marine deity."[20] Clearly,
Hill's suggestion is safer than that of Babelon, but it
solved no problems. Beginning with an article by Alfred
Maury in 1848, the theory that there was a "Phoenician
Neptune" gained some prominence.[21] Maury brought up such
names as Derketo and Dagon, finally settling upon an identification of the deity as "Baal-Moloch dont Melkarth n'était
qu'une forme."[22] Both Dagon and Milqart, thus, became
candidates for the deity represented on these coins.

    The argument for Dagon was put forward by Maury, as
follows: "L'existence d'un dieu ayant la forme d'un poisson
marin monstrueux rapelle le *Dagon* des Philistins qui avait

la forme d'un poisson, ainsi que l'indique son nom...."[23]
Such an identification has also been argued by Babelon,[24]
Six,[25] and Rouvier.[26] Rouvier challenged Six and Babelon
on the designation of the later Aradian types, on which
only the head of the deity appears, as "Melqart"; Rouvier
maintained that the deity was "Dagon ichthyomorphe" but in
a Hellenized style.[27] Dagon, however, was not a "fish god."
He was, according to the Ugaritic texts, the father of the
storm god, Ba'l.[28] Despite the wealth of information
yielded by excavations all over the Near East, F.J.
Montalbano notes that "present-day archaeological knowledge
of the Canaanite divinity Dagon is, as it were, still
wrapped in swaddling clothes."[29] Although some have guessed
his name to be derived from the Phoenician/Hebrew word *dag*,
"fish," it seems clear now that the root is *d-g-n*, meaning
"corn, grain."[30] The half-man, half-sea monster deity of
Aradus cannot be this grain god.

The argument concerning Milqart meets with equal
difficulty and problems. Albright argues convincingly that
Milqart, "king of the city" (*milkqart*), refers to the
underworld city of the dead.[31] The chthonic nature of the
deity is reinforced by his later association exclusively
with Heracles.[32] However, the deity shown on these Aradian
coins is not a god of the underworld; he is a marine deity.

Arguments from French scholars concerning the identification of this deity have abounded. It is possible that
Aradus would incorporate the deity most revered by its
people onto its coin types. Being a city dependent upon the
sea for its well-being and defense, it is only logical that
a deity associated with these features of the Phoenician
world would be used. Unfortunately we do not know which
deity is depicted here. The Tyrian use of a marine deity
has provided little help in solving this Aradian problem.[33]
Dussaud, in an effort to establish a basis for the syncretism
of Yamm and Ba'l into Milqart, argued that this deity from
Aradus is Yamm — the deified sea.[34] There is no evidence
to suggest, however, that the cult of Yamm was still alive
in fifth/fourth century Phoenicia.[35] No positive identification of the deity is possible given our present data.[36]

Future discoveries may illuminate this problem for us.

The reverse types of these first coins show the typical galley. With Byblos, Sidon, and Tyre, Aradus used the galley as a standard for the Phoenician city-states. Each mint used the motif, emphasizing the political and military interests of the Phoenicians as leaders of the Persian naval forces in the eastern Mediterranean.[37] Although Aradus never led the navy in battle during the Persian period,[38] we know from Herodotus of a certain king, Merba'al of Aradus, who commanded the Aradian ships of the fleet in battle for Xerxes.[39]

The craftsmanship employed in the die cutting for these coins is archaic and not equal to the workmanship displayed on later issues. On the obol, detail is completely lacking; on the tetrobol, the close, detailed work is also early in date.[40] Comparing, for example, the quality of the die cutting exhibited on the Sidonian galleys to that of the Aradian workshops, Sidon clearly maintained a higher level of quality. The aphlaston on the galley's stern is not clearly done. The sign of 'Ašerah cannot be discerned with any certainty, even though this was the intended emblem which adorned the ship's prow.[41]

Our dating of this series is based on the craftsmanship shown in the execution of the die cutting, and on a comparative study of the Aradian coins with those of the other Phoenician mints. The lack of inscriptions is characteristic of early issues, as we have seen at the other mints.[42] As the cities developed similar types, with the extended use of the galley for instance, marks of identification were needed to differentiate the issues of the different mints. This need became apparent by ca. 410 B.C.E., when the first inscriptions were used by the Phoenician mints.

The Second Aradian Series
ca. 410-400 B.C.E.

3. OBV: 𐤌𐤀(𐤌𐤀), above. Figure of marine deity to r., as on 1; lower part of body decorated with lines; fishes held by the tail in each hand; border off flan.

    REV: Galley to r., as on 1; eye in prow; aphlaston on poop obscure; all in shallow incuse square (dotted).

AR Tetrobol (flatter fabric), London.

4. OBV: Same as 3 above.
    REV: Galley to r., as on 3; eye in prow; poop off flan;
          two fish below to r.; all in cable-pattern square.

    AR Stater, Paris.

5. OBV: Same as 3 above, except with cable border.
    REV: Galley, to r., as on 3; below, two fish; all
          within cable-pattern square.

    AR Diobol (flatter fabric), New York.

The second Aradus series includes a number of transitional types.[43] The major difference between this series
and the preceding one is the addition of an inscription.
Other than this, the eye on the prow of the galley is engraved
more clearly, and the fabric of the coins is flatter,
suggesting a later minting with slightly more refined
techniques in use.[44]

The addition of the inscription is worthy of comment.
It consists very simply of two Phoenician letters, ✗ℋ.[45]
The traditional interpretation for the letters is the
abbreviation for *mi-'Arvad* — Babelon's *ex Arado*.[46] The
ethnic upon the coins of Aradus in the Hellenistic period
was simply Å, the city's initials in Greek or an abbreviation for *Aradou*, "of (belonging to) Aradus." This led
Babelon and others to interpret the Phoenician inscription
in the same manner.[47] Several other theories have been
suggested concerning the inscription: (1) that the letters
are the first letters of the cities Marathus and Aradus;
(2) that the letters are an abbreviation for *milk 'Arvad*,
"king of Aradus."[48] Evidence is lacking, however, which
might lend support to these readings for the inscription.[49]
The particle in Phoenician means "of" or, more often, "from"
in a locative — not a genitive — sense.[50] Therefore, we
propose the following reading, as that for which the abbreviation stood: ממלכת ארוד, *mamlakt 'arvad*, "the kingdom
(or government) of Aradus."[51] Such usage is known in
Phoenician and Punic of this period and earlier ones, in
contradistinction to the rather far-fetched readings
proposed some years ago.[52] The *lam-melek* jar handles from
Judah of the seventh/sixth centuries are a similar usage,

indicating governmental authority as the agent of issuance.[53]

The script of the abbreviation is similar to that found upon the coins of Byblos, discussed below. It is striking that the *mem* is similar to forms known from the early fifth century *Šipṭibaʿl* inscription;[54] while the *ʾalep* is similar to those found in the Byblian *Yehawmilk* inscription.[55] The ethnic is written in archaic, formal characters. The upper cross bar of the *ʾalep* and the middle bar of the *mem* are diagnostic signs for the script. A precise dating is, regretfully, impossible due to the paucity of data from Aradus.[56] Given the sometimes archaizing scripts used on coin types, we might suspect letter forms a bit older than the coins themselves.

Of further interest is the change in the method used to show the scales on the lower half of the deity's body. The speckled dot pattern was replaced with a line pattern, which may have been easier for the engravers to cut into the dies.[57] The fish, often called dolphins,[58] are present as either the deity's attendants or symbolic of his dominance over the entire sea and all that dwells therein. On the stater and diobol the borders have been misinterpreted: Hill, describing the above-mentioned diobol, wrote "below, two dolphins r. over line of waves represented by line of cable-pattern."[59] The "line of waves," however, was merely a part of the square cable-pattern. There is no evidence of waves on the coinage; the drawing in Babelon's *Traité* (no. 807) clearly shows the use of this border pattern on the reverse of the stater.[60] The same situation is evident on the diobol.

The general dating of these coins is dependent upon the dating of the Sidonian series. Undoubtedly the example of the Athenian tetradrachms with their characteristic ΑΘΕ played an important role in the Phoenician adaptation of this Greek usage. When applied to practical situations in Phoenicia the inscriptions made it possible to keep similar types, depicting galleys, separate from one another. The addition of the inscription may have signalled a change in the minting authority of the coins, although we have no means to verify this assertion. Someday the names of the kings of Aradus may come to light, enabling us to correct this situation.

The Third Aradian Series
ca. 400-380 B.C.E.

6. OBV: 𐤌𐤌(מם), above; type similar to 3.

REV: Galley to r., as on 3; eye in prow; row of shields along bulwark; below, winged seahorses to r.; the whole in dotted or cable-bordered incuse square.

AR Tetrobol, New York.

7. OBV: Similar to 6, but with smooth body.

REV: Similar to 6, with dotted or cabled border.

AR Diobol, New York. Plate 6.

8. OBV: 𐤌𐤌(מם), above; half-figure of marine deity, frontal, head to r.; bearded, hair in plaits; fish held in both hands by the tails; dotted border.

REV: Prow of galley to r., with eye; row of shields along bulwark; below, fish, to r.; whole in dotted incuse square.

AR Obol, New York. Plate 6.

The major feature of the third series of Aradian coins is the addition of the seahorse to the reverse types below the galley. The fish which appeared on some of the earlier types was deleted in this series.[61] The seahorse must be the creature attendant upon the god pictured on the obverse. On smaller denominations, the fish continued to be used, perhaps for the purpose of more facile engraving.[62]

Six, writing in 1877, supposed that the seahorse and the fish were to be derived from Tyre.[63] Both motifs appear on the Tyrian coins of the fourth century. Whether the seahorse was understood as a means of locomotion for the marine deity or not, remains unclear.[64] We seriously doubt Babelon's contention that the seahorse was a deity;[65] nor is it to be construed as the serpentine "Tannin" as suggested by Dussaud.[66] If we may interpret the evidence from the Tyrian series, the seahorse and fish (dolphin) are probably no more than attendants to the marine deity or mere symbols of Phoenician maritime activity.[67] More specific identification of these creatures is impossible.[68]

Three silver denominations are known in this series.
It is surprising that no staters are extant from this
series, since only one example is known from our second
grouping.[69] Aradus must not have been issuing coins which
were intended for use in commerce outside the city-state
at this time. The increase in the volume of the output of
the city's mint occurred in the fourth century as trade
burgeoned. This development was coupled with the slow
decline of Persian authority in the outlying provinces.[70]

The smaller coins did not have a standard border
design; cabled and dotted borders were used interchangeably.[71]
On the obol, a new type — with just the upper torso of the
marine deity — appeared. This use of half the god's body
may have been due to the size of the coin. The iconography
remained similar, however, to that which was used on the
larger denominations, including the fish, as a symbol for
the sea.[72] The reverse has just the prow of the galley,
which again was a victim of space limitations.[73] A fish
(probably a dolphin) below the galley substituted for the
winged seahorse. The dolphin's special relationship with
mariners and ships is well known; here, however, the
quality of the die cutting makes a positive identification
of the fish impossible.[74] The stater and diobol of the
second series, both with fish below the galley, are exemplary
of the full-blown development of this type. The tetrobol
was a more transitional piece.[75]

The minting authority changed at least once during the
period 400-380 B.C.E. No clear stabilization of types
occurred. From the data gathered from the other Phoenician
city-states, the decade or two following the minting of
this series was a time of great standardization of coin
types. The types which were adopted as the norms at the
Aradian mint were those of the next series. The third
series, therefore, was a prefatory one in which types were
developed which were used by the Phoenicians in the
greatest period of their commercial activity. This period
fell during the reigns of 'Abd'aštart I of Sidon and his
father, Ba'lšallim II.[76] This series must antedate the types
used in the greatest quantity in this commercially active

period. As before no certain datings from inscriptional
material or royal attributions are available.

The Fourth Aradian Series
ca. 380-351/350 B.C.E.

9.   OBV: Head of marine deity to r.; with laurel wreath
          on head; hair and whiskers dotted; beard shown
          in lines; eye full; border of dots.

    REV: Galley to r., without any oars; eye on prow; row
          of shields along bulwark; below, winged seahorse,
          to r.; inscription off flan.

    AR Tetrobol, London.[77]

10. OBV: Head of marine deity to r.; with laurel wreath
          on head; hair and beard as on 9; border of dots.

    REV: **ᕼᖾ**(מא), above. Galley to r., without any oars;
          eye on prow; row of shields along bulwark;
          ornament and standard on poop; below, three wavy
          lines representing the sea; all in incuse square,
          with border of dots above, and occasionally at
          sides; below, bounded by crescent-shaped depression.
          Aphlaston sometimes visible on prow.

    AR Stater, New York. Plate 6.

11. OBV: Similar to 10.
    REV: Similar to 10.
    AR Tetrobol, New York. Plate 6.

12. OBV: Similar to 10, but facing l.
    REV: Similar to 10.
    AR Tetrobol, London.[78]

13. OBV: Similar to 10.
    REV: **ᕼᖾ**(מא), above. Galley to r. above two lines of
          waves, in incuse square.
    AR Obol, New York. Plate 7.

14. OBV: Same as 10.
    REV: Similar to 10, except the **ᖾ** (מ) is off flan.
    AR Tetradrachm (Attic standard), de Luynes Collection.[79]

15. OBV: Same as 10.
    REV: Similar to 10, except with date, ‖‖ — (prb. 14).
    AR Stater, London and Paris.[80] Plate 7.

The issues of this series comprise the major denominations of the Aradian pre-Alexandrine coinage. The obverse
type has been altered, with the half-human, half-fish

representation of the marine deity being replaced with a
Hellenized depiction of the deity's head. The deity is
shown bearded in an Oriental,[81] though thoroughly anthro-
pomorphic, style. This is interestingly compared to the
former type with the serpentine lower body.[82] Although Hill
refused to name this deity, Babelon referred to him as
"Baal-Arvad."[83] Others have called him 'Melqarth.'[84]
There is no logical reason to assume that a different
deity is shown on this series from that which was shown on
the previous coins. The style in which the head is engraved
is similar to the manner in which Athena was represented on
the coins of Athens of the fifth and early fourth centuries.[85]
Imitations of the Athenian tetradrachms were in use in
Syria-Palestine, and were certainly known in Phoenicia.[86]
The deity is best described merely as a "marine" divinity.

The new type with the head of the deity appeared upon
each of the coins of this series — the stater, the tetrobol,
and the obol. The tetrobol (no. 9) is a transitional issue
which did not use the inscription. It was moved from the
obverse, where it no longer fit, and was placed on the reverse
with the galley below it.[87] No oars were shown on the galley,
although the shields, the eye on the prow, and the battering
ram were retained. The aphlaston over the prow is not a
new development, although the fine, careful die cutting
used here made such a detail more visible.[88] The winged
seahorse on the tetrobol (no. 9) was replaced with the simple
line of waves, reminiscent of the Sidonian coinage in use
in this same period.[89] It is probable that Sidonian
influences were being felt in Aradus.[90]

After a few years of transitional types, the new
series was standardized and became the coinage of Aradus
during the peak of fourth century Phoenician power. Peaceful,
productive contacts with Greece were increasingly frequent.

Escaping the problems of the revolt of ʿAbdʿaštart of
Sidon in the late 360's, Aradus displayed its true colors
as a member of the Phoenician league in the general revolt
instigated by Tennes. First, it adopted a dating system
similar to that in use at Sidon. The examples which are
extant bear the date "14," although attempts have been made

to read these dates in other ways.[91]   The coins date to
ca. 352/351 B.C.E. — the time of the Tennes rebellion.
These coins were followed, secondly, by an Aradian attempt
to completely abandon the Persic standard; it was at this
time that the stater was minted on the Attic standard.[92]
Only one example survived from this attempt, indicating
that it was short-lived in the face of the massive military
action undertaken by the Persian king against the revolting
satrapies in 351/350 B.C.E.[93]   The use of the Attic
standard would have greatly facilitated the wealthy trade
with the Greek West.

A series of small denominations were developed to
supplement the larger coins. Being a period when great
liberties were taken by the Phoenician mints and when
commercial development reached new and greater heights,
ample supplies of small change, minted in both silver and
bronze, were required in the market place.

16. OBV: Head of marine deity to r., with pointed beard and
           short hair; border of dots.
     REV: Prow of galley to r., with eye in prow, and row
           of shields along bulwark; below, fish to r.;
           whole in incuse square.
     AR 1/8 obol, New York.

17. OBV: Same as 16.
     REV: Tortoise.
     AR 1/8 obol, New York.

18. OBV: (obscure)
     REV: Head of satyr facing; in incuse square.
     AR 1/16 obol, London.

19. OBV: Same as 16.
     REV: Conical headdress (of Ba'l Sapōn ?).
     AR 1/16 obol, London.

20. OBV: Same as 16.
     REV: Same as obverse; concave field.
     AR 1/16 obol.

21. OBV: Same as 16.
     REV: Scorpion, between two branches (?).
     AR 1/16 obol, de Luynes.

22. OBV: Same as 16.
     REV: Scorpion; concave field.
     AR   1/16 obol, de Luynes.

23. OBV: Head of satyr.
     REV: Two fish, to 1.
     AR   1/16 obol, de Luynes.

24. OBV: Figure of marine deity to 1.; lower part of body
           fish-like; wreath held in r. hand; fish held in
           1. hand; border of dots.
     REV: ✗⅄(אמ), above. Galley to r., above two lines of
           waves; figurehead on prow; standard and curved
           ornament on poop.
     AE   2.51 grams, New York. Plate 7.

25. OBV: Same as 23.
     REV: Same as 23.
     AE   0.80 grams, Paris.

Great variation is exhibited in the types of the 1/8 and
1/16 obols. The reversion to the earlier silver types — with
the serpentine marine deity — on the bronze coins is not unusual.[94] Being a new venture in coinage, proven types would be
accepted more quickly and easily by those using the coinage.
There can be little question that a great deal of imitation of
types circulating in northern Phoenicia may be seen in these
small silver fractions. The use of such types as the tortoise
or the scorpion is characteristic of this borrowing.[95] The
satyr, for example, is known on the coinage of Sidon.[96] The
object depicted on no. 19 is cultic.[97] The varying types seem
to have little relation to one another.[98]

The obverse type is the reason why these coins are
generally attributed to Aradus, and why we have included
them in this survey. This type is the same as that which
appears on the larger silver denominations of this series.
Many of these examples were found in or around the Syrian
town of Ruâd — ancient Aradus and its coastal holdings.[99]
As supplementary coinage for the larger denominations, the
small silver and bronze coins filled a gap in a growing
economy's needs. After the military action of ca. 350 B.C.E.,
however, only larger coins were minted, their use (at least
in part) being to pay for the mercenary fleet raised from

the Phoenician cities by the Persian government to fight
the rising menace of Macedonia.

This is the largest series minted at Aradus. It is
dated to the period in which the greatest standardization
of coinage took place in the Sidonian coinage, which is
more precisely datable. As at Sidon, no coins were minted
by local authorities immediately following the revolt; such
action awaited the outcome of the military ventures in
progress in Phoenicia, Egypt, and Palestine. Only in
ca. 348/347 did the mint resume operations, as daily life
returned to normal.

The Fifth Aradian Series
ca. 348/347-339/338 B.C.E.

26. OBV: Similar to 10, except border usually off flan.

    REV: 𐤀𐤌(אמ), and an additional varying letter,
        above; galley to r., over three lines of waves;
        figurehead on prow; eye in prow; row of shields
        along bulwark; aphlaston on poop; border as on 10.

    AR Stater, New York. Plate 7.

27. OBV: Similar to 10, except border of dots.

    REV: 𐤌𐤀𐤌(ממא) above, similar type to 10.

    AR Tetrobol, New York. Plate 7.

28. OBV: Similar to 10, except border of dots.

    REV: 𐤌𐤀𐤌(ממא) above; similar type to 10.

    AR Obol, London.[100]

Following the great revolt of the Phoenician city-states
in the middle of the fourth century B.C.E., a Persian
effort was made to stimulate the then stagnate Phoenician
economy. Commercial ties in the eastern Mediterranean
had been drastically disrupted by the military campaigns of
351-348 B.C.E. As the Persians, under Artaxerxes III,
slowly regained control of the Levant, commercial activities
were permitted to resume.[101] Aradus appears to have fallen
before Sidon and Egypt, perhaps as early as 350 B.C.E.
The independence of the city-state from Persian control
was short in duration as the attempt to change to the
Attic standard has shown, lasting no more than several
months.[102] So few (only one) of these coins have survived
that probably only a few were struck. Even so, the Persians

doubtless confiscated as many of these coins as possible,
re-melting and re-striking them on their own standard.

With the resumption of Persian control, Mazday, the
satrap of Cilicia, was given charge of the area. To back
the economy of Aradus and its satellite towns, the satrap
authorized the issue of silver coinage. As a port city
for the Persian court, the Persic standard was reinstituted
with the same types used as were in use before the revolt.
Only larger denominations were minted at this time; two
denominations are extant, the stater and the obol.[103]
The new ingredient in the types of this series was a varying
letter added to the two-letter inscription which we have
identified as the ethnic. These letters are problematic
and may have been abbreviations for the names of the
governors appointed by Mazday and his Persian overlords to
rule Aradus. As governors, these people would have had
the authority to mint coins under the strictures imposed
from Persia. Nine different letters are known, only one
of which is coupled with a dating system.[104] The years
covered by this series are the nine years in the middle of
Mazday's reign, ca. 348/347 through 339/338 B.C.E., when
Gir'aštart's reign as governor began. The dating of these
coins is dependent upon the dating of this governor's reign.
There may have been a period of a year or two when no coins
were struck in Aradus following the cessation of hostilities
in the 350 B.C.E. rebellion.

Gir'aštart
ca. 339/338-332 B.C.E.

29. OBV: Similar to 10; border of dots.
     REV: Λ𐤊𐤔(מאב) and dates (1-7) above; similar to 26.
     AR   Stater, New York. Plate 7.

The final issues struck by the mint of Aradus before
the conquest of Alexander the Great were those of Gir'aštart
— who was known as Gerostratus in the Greek sources.[105] The
types are identical to those of the preceding series, except
for the addition of the dates, or years, of the governor's
reign. Following Gir'aštart's monogram, we have the same
dating system used at Sidon, with one mark equalling each

year of his reign.[106] Gir'aštart began his reign in
339/338 B.C.E. The Persian government must have had a
great deal of confidence in him, because all of the other
post-revolt governors ruled for a year or less, if we have
correctly interpreted the lack of markings on those issues.

Gir'aštart was the ruler of Aradus when the armies of
Alexander the Great entered Phoenicia. His government was
deposed by Alexander with no violence.[107]

The pre-Alexandrine coinage of Aradus has presented a
number of complex problems. Owing to the lack of archaeological data with which to work, the king list for the city
is all but nonexistent. Typological studies, therefore,
have been our only tool in establishing the chronological
sequence in which the coins were struck. These data, when
compared with those of the other Phoenician mints, have
enabled us to propose a new chronology for this earliest
coinage of Aradus.

We have seen the Aradian coinage develop from its
origins in the fifth century B.C.E. through several series
to the reign of Gir'aštart, in the 330's. Typological
changes paralleled developments in the three southern mints
in Phoenicia as well as the political/military realities of
the fifth/fourth century Levantine coast.

1. The island is now called *Ruâd*, and lies only 3 km off the Syrian coast. The city was mentioned in Ezekiel's *qînāh* over Tyre, in 27:8; Sidon and Aradus were the "rowers" of Tyre. The island measures a mere 800 m x 500 m, and evidence exists that it was surrounded by a sizable defensive wall. See E. Renan, *Mission de Phénicie* (Paris: Imprimérie national, 1864), p. 20. Aradus was the first Phoenician city encountered on the coast as one travelled from the north. Kurt Galling quoted Pseudo-Skylax in his "Die syrisch-palästinische Küste nach der Beschreibung bei Pseudo-Skylax," *Studien zur Geschichte Israels im persischen Zeitalters* (Tübingen: J.C. Mohr, 1964) 190: Ἀπὸ δὲ Θαψάκου ποταμοῦ ἐστι πρώτη πόλις Φοινίκων Ἄραδος κτλ; "Vom Thapakus-Fluss ist die erste Stadt der Phöniker Aradus usw." Galling went on to note that given the central location of Aradus, the lack of good ports near it, the city was important as a center for trade to and from Phoenicia and Cyrpus. "Man darf vermuten, dass der Gewährsmann des Skylax ein kyprischer oder phönikischer Kauffahrer war, für den der Hafen von Aradus als Handelszentrum eine grössere Bedeutung hatte als vielleicht der eine oder andere der an sich auch nennenswerten Küstenorte" (p. 190).

2. Strabo, 16. 753. Strabo and Pliny differ in their measurement of the distance which the island lies off the coast; see Pliny, *Naturalis historia*, 5.78.

3. Strabo (16. 753), lists the following:
Πάλτος καὶ Βαλαναία καὶ Κάρνος, τὸ ἐπίνειον τῆς Ἀράδου λιμένιον ἔχον· εἶτ' Ἔνυδρα καὶ Μάραθος, πόλις Φοινίκων ἀρχαία κατεσπασμένη. τὴν δὲ χώραν Ἀράδιοι κατεκληρούχησαν καὶ τὰ Σίμυρα τὸ ἐφεξῆς χωρίον.
Of course, these towns come from a list compiled at a somewhat later time; but clearly, Aradus' history has always been bound up in that of the neighboring mainland. Whether or not there was a mainland quarter of the town is not clear: Harden, in *The Phoenicians* (p. 25) has argued that it may have spread off the island onto the mainland as did Tyre to the south and Motya on Sicily. Pliny and Strabo list the same group of cities. Dussaud has postulated that the city's control over such towns as Mariamme and Sigon did not come about until Hellenistic times [*Revue archéologique* 3rd ser., 31 (1897) 316, 336; see Arrian, *Anabasis*, 2.13.8]. If so, then Diodorus Siculus also made this error; however, the actual towns controlled by Aradus are of secondary importance to the fact that the town's sway vastly exceeded its walls. R. Peitschmann, in his *Geschichte der Phönizier* (Berlin: G. Grote'sche, 1889), p. 39, refers to Aradus as the "Mittelpunkt eines Staatswesens." On Aradus' influence on the mainland see J.-P. Rey-Coquais, *Arados et sa pérée aux époques grecque, romaines, et byzantine* (Paris: Librairie orientaliste Paul Geuthner, 1974), pp. 97-99.

4.   Strabo, 16. 753.

5.   The reference is found in the so-called "Table of Nations," which is a J document, edited and reworked with supplementation by the Priestly writer.   The formula, for example, which heads Genesis 10:1, "these are the generations of the sons of Noah," is typical of those P used to frame the major sections of the primordial history recorded in Genesis.   See *CMHE*, pp. 302-303.   E. Speiser notes that this is a section primarily concerned with ethnographic classification; *Genesis, The Anchor Bible*, vol. 1 (Garden City, NY: Doubleday and Co., 1964), p. 71. From the list, it is clear that Aradus was a city of some repute when the Yahwist wrote, antedating Strabo by at least 500 years.

6.   Strabo, 16. 766.   This is probably a local tradition which grew up within the Persian Gulf.   Hill (*BMC Phoenicia*, p. xiii) notes a similar story concerning the founding of Tyre; both stories fall into the same category.

7.   Diodorus Siculus, 16.45.6; Arrian, *Anabasis*, 2.13.7f. Six, in his "Observations sur les monnaies phéniciennes," *NC* 17 (1877) 189, quoted Skylax, who termed Aradus a Βασιλεια Τύρου in this time period.   Perhaps Aradus was convenanted with Tyre in the fourth century.   This may have been the result of the Phoenician revolts of the era.   Without such arrangements, Skylax would have no reason to place Aradus in any sort of formal relationship, politically, with Tyre.

8.   See in particular Babelon, *Traité*, II, 2, pp. 511ff.; and Hill, *BMC Phoenicia*, pp. 1-12.   See also J.G. Milne, "The Coinage of Aradus in the Hellenistic Period," *Iraq* 5 (1938) 12-22.

9.   See J.P. Six, "Observations," 183ff.; J. Rouvier, "Numismatique des villes de la Phénicie," *Journal international d'archéologie numismatique* (1900) and his article "Repartition chronologique du monnayage des rois phéniciens d'Arvad," in the same journal of 1898; J. Babelon, *Traité*, II, 2, pp. 501-531, and pl. 116; Hill, *BMC Phoenicia*, pp. 1-12, and plates 1-2.

10.   Cf. Babelon, *Traité*, II, 2, pp. 505, 509-510; Hill, *BMC Phoenicia*, pp. xxii-xxiii.   Byblos, Sidon, and Tyre used the Phoenician standard, while the Palestinian mints in Jerusalem and the Gaza area employed the Attic standard.   The weight standards may be compared as follows:

a Phoenician šeqel	=	13.90 grams
a Persic stater	=	10.65 grams
an Attic didrachm	=	8.70 grams

These are only average weights, since the weights of the individual specimens vary considerably.

The usual Phoenician standard, when minted in a double šeqel, and reduced, as occurred at Sidon, equalled roughly 1½ Athenian tetradrachms (about 26.30 grams, since the reduced šeqel was 13.10 grams).   No such easy conversion

is possible, however, with the Persic standard. No effort
was made to convert the coinage into the Athenian standard
which predominated in the commercial life of the late fifth
and early fourth century Levantine trading world. No evidence exists that a reduction or increase in the Aradian
weight standard took place as at Sidon. An Aradian stater
of 16.70 grams is a unique problem to which we will return.

In general, the weights of the Aradian coinage were
based on the Persic standard. The examples cited herein
fall within these guidelines:

Stater	9.99-10.80 g.	(= 2 Persian sigloi of
Tetrobol	2.75-3.50 g.	5.35 g.)
Diobol	1.40-1.70 g.	
Obol	0.55-0.90 g.	

All denominations cited were struck in silver

11. Aradus' location made its city-state's domain
important, linking it, via the Euphrates Valley, to northern
and central Mesopotamia. Several large trading centers,
such as Hamat and Kadeš, were just inland on the Orontes
about 40 miles from Aradus. These links with the overland
trade routes made Aradus' commercial port thrive. They
also inexorably linked it to the heart of the Persian empire,
necessitating certain restrictions on her mercantile policy,
including the use of the Persic standard. With sufficient
trade going into the hinterlands, this standard would be
the logical choice to facilitate business dealings.

12. This is Hill's position; *BMC Phoenicia*, p. xxii.

13. Hill leaves us a hint of this theory (*BMC
Phoenicia*, p. xxii). B.V. Head, in his *Historia nummorum*
(p. 665), suggested that the Persic standard was chosen at
Aradus because of the city's close mercantile relations with
Cyprus, where the standard was also in use. There is no
evidence to support this claim, however, because we know too
little about Aradus' history to fill in such gaps as
the development of trade with Cyprus.

14. Sadly, we are lacking the inscriptional and/or
literary evidence which might give us these much needed data.

15. This is an intriguing idea; cf. *BMC Phoenicia*,
p. xxiii. It seems evident that Aradus was pressured to
maintain the Persic standard, thus facilitating Persian
trade. The ratio of the Athenian tetradrachm, at 17.40
grams, is a bit lighter than five Aradian tetrobols of 3.55
grams each, or 17.75 grams. Such a ratio is satisfactory
only if we assume that Athenian coins were in use in the
region of Aradus in this period. There is no simple exchange
rate between the Persic and Athenian or Persic and Phoenician
standards. It is baffling that a differing standard would
have been used by a Phoenician city closely allied with three
neighboring cities to the south.

16. Note the later issues on which a Hellenized likeness of the deity's head replaced the more archaic likeness
with the serpentine torso. The new die was complete with a

laureated headdress, reminiscent of the imitations of the
Athenian tetradrachms found in Palestine and inland Syria.

17.   See the chapters on the coinages of Sidon and
Tyre.

18.   As the Aradian series developed, more and more
Hellenic influence may be seen in the coin types, along
with more numerous similarities with the types of the
other Phoenician mints. Two points may be stressed: (1)
The striking of the coins is consistently off flan, showing
that the craftsmen lacked a degree of skill in their art.
(2) The style of the engraving moved Babelon (*Traité*, II, 2,
pp. 511f.) to place these coins early in the series.
Certainly the Hellenic influences seen in the later representations of the deity's head were innovations in local
die cutting. Indeed, the similarities with mid- and late-
fifth century Athenian tetradrachms are striking. It was
not until a later period, however, that these were imitated
in volume in Syria-Palestine. The smallness of the galley
on the reverse types was exchanged for a more expressive,
larger likeness on later issues. The impact of the artful
engraving on the Sidonian galley is probably to be seen here.

19.   Babelon, *Traité*, II, 2, p. 511 f. In his discussion of Dagon, Babelon went into lengthy descriptions
of the coiffure of the god's head. This typified the
"monstre marin" adored in Gaza, 'Ašqelōn, and 'Ašdōd, where
"Philistines" held sway (pp. 517-520). To Babelon, it was
from the Philistines that the cult of Dagon spread northward
to Phoenicia and the coast of Crete. He, predictably,
derived this name from the Northwest Semitic *dag*, "fish."

20.   Hill wisely recognized that Dagon might not be
a "fish-god"; he preferred to. discuss the deity without a
proper name, skirting the problems at hand (*BMC Phoenicia*,
p. xx).

21.   See Alfred Maury, "Recherches sur le nom et le
caractère du Neptune phénicien," *Revue archéologique* 5
(1848) 545-556, especially 548-556.

22.   Maury, p. 556.

23.   Maury, p. 551.

24.   Babelon, *Traité*, II, 2, p. 509.

25.   Six is merely following Brandis; *NC* 17 (1877)
183-184.

26.   J. Rouvier, "Baal-Arvad, d'après la numismatique
des rois phéniciens d'Arvad durant la period préalexandrine
(450 à 332 avant J.C.)," *Journal asiatique*, 9th series, 16
(1900) 347-359. Babelon was attracted to Rouvier's article
because of some excavations which took place at the temple
complex of Husn Suleiman (ancient Baetocaece), which is
"une trentaine de kilometres de la côte syrienne" (*Traité*,
II, 2, p. 509). Two deities were worshipped there —

Derceto and Ba'l; this Ba'l Babelon supposed to have been the Ba'l 'Arvad of Rouvier's thesis.

27. Rouvier, "Baal-Arvad, d'après la numismatique," pp. 352-356. Six and Babelon distinguished this sea monster/deity from the head depicted on later issues, which they termed "Melqarth." Rouvier challenged this opinion arguing that "Melqarth" made no sense, since he would have been replaced in Hellenistic types by Heracles and not Poseidon (cf. *BMC Phoenicia*, pp. xx-xxi). At that point, Hill cautioned that even though an argument could not be made for differentiation of the two deities on the basis of their coiffure, neither could the argument be made without reservation that they were one and the same. Moreover, he wrote, the gods worshipped at Baetocaece could not be identified with too much accuracy. Dussaud's publication of the dedicatory inscriptions from the site describe the deity (or deities) as Ζεὺς; θε[οῦ οὐρανίου Δ]ιὸς Βαιτοκαίκης ἁγίου οὐρανίου Διός; and θεῷ Βαιτοχείχει, θεῷ Μ[εγίστῳ?], [θε]ῷ,...θεῷ 'Ασκαλωνίαι(?). (*Revue archéologique*, 3rd Ser., 31 [1897] 319-325; and *CIL*, iii, 184). The celestial nature of the deity is illustrated by reliefs from Ḥuṣn Suleiman, upon which an eagle holds a caduceus between two figures representing, according to Hill, the morning and evening stars (*BMC Phoenicia*, p. xxi, n. 2; and Dussaud, p. 328). This, however, brings little to bear on the marine nature of the deity with which we are concerned. Cumont has suggested that the Zeus of Ḥuṣn Suleiman may have been connected with Ba'l of Apamea; this is alluded to in *CIL*, iii, 184. Hill sees the pairing of a celestial and a marine deity as the solution to the problem. "The god of Baetocaece would thus be the celestial counterpart of the marine god of Aradus" (*BMC Phoenicia*, p. xxi, n. 2). In his article "Adonis, Baal, and Astarte," *The Church Quarterly Review* 66 (1908) 138-139, Hill gives us his concluding remarks on the topic: "It is best to call the laurel-crowned deity Baal-Arvad and to reserve our opinion as to the question of his complete identity with the fish-god. But this much is certain, that a deity of great importance to the Aradians was a fishy monster" (p. 139).

28. W.F. Albright, *YGC*, p. 124. Sargon of Akkad paid homage to Dagon in the twenty-third century B.C.E. In the Ugaritic pantheon lists, *Dagnu* is third on the lists after *'ilu* and *ba'lu*; cf. *CTA* 29; J. Nougayrol, *et al.*, *Ugaritica V* (Paris: Imprimerie nationale et Librarie orientaliste Paul Geuthner, 1968), no. 18, pp. 42-64; and Cross, *CMHE*, pp. 63f. Perhaps the most useful summary of the material on Dagon may be found in F.J. Montalbano, "Canaanite Dagon: Origin, Nature," *CBQ* 13 (1951) 381-397; see now also Giovanni Pettinato, "The Royal Archives of Tell Mardikh-Ebla," *BA* 39 (1976) 48-49. The cult of Dagon (*Dagnu*) was an active one at third millennium Ebla.

29. Montalbano, p. 381.

30. Cross, *CMHE*, p. 14; Ugaritic *Dagnu* became Hebrew *dagān* and Phoenician *dagōn*. This derivation is based simply on the Semitic root meaning grain.

31. Albright, *YGC*, p. 243. Albright bases his conclusion upon Milqart's later identification with Heracles,
who was basically a chthonic deity.

32. This occurred in Hellenistic times. Cf. *YGC*,
pp. 243-244; R. Dussaud, "Melqart d'après de recents
travaux," *Revue de l'histoire des religions* 151 (1957)
10-15; Dussaud, "Melqart," *Syria* 25 (1946-1948) 205-207.

33. Neither the Aradian nor the Tyrian marine
deities may be identified as yet. Suggestions concerning
the god *Sid* have been made by F.M. Cross, although so
little is yet known of him, no firm conclusion may be reached.

34. Dussaud, "Melqart," p. 206; and Dussaud, "Astarté,
Pontos et Ba'al," *Comptes rendus de l'Academie des inscriptions et belles-lettres* (1947) 212-214. He came to the
conclusion that the Greeks transformed Yamm into Poseidon,
"ce que Philon de Byblos exprime en disant que Pontos (Yam)
eut pour fils Poseidon."

35. Ba'l remained distinct from Milqart, and there is
no evidence which would support the notion that Yamm and
Ba'l coalesced into Milqart. In this period, Milqart and
Ba'l both had active cults which were distinct from each
other. Yamm's cult had apparently been otiose for centuries.
Some YMM names are known from the onomastica of Mari and
from the Murašû texts; their antiquity, however, lends no
support to a theory regarding a functioning cult of Yamm
in the late fifth and early fourth centuries, B.C.E.. The
evidence surrounding Yamm comes almost completely from
Ugarit. See texts CTA 3.3.36, 4.7.4, and 4.6.12, in which
Yamm is called "the beloved of 'Ēl"; or texts 2.3.21, 2.4.16,
2.4.14, 2.4.22, 2.4.25, 2.3.23, 2.4.29, 2.3.16, 2.3.8. Cf.
R.E. Whitaker, *A Concordance of the Ugaritic Literature*
(Cambridge, MA: Harvard University Press, 1972), pp. 306-
310. The phrases employed are construct phrases and usually
appear in parallel in the Ba'l/'Anat Cycle: They are
zubul yammi and *ṯāpiṭu nahari*, meaning "Prince Sea" and
"Judge River." Ū. Oldenberg has also argued this point in
his *The Conflict of El and Ba'l in Canaanite Religion*
(Leiden: E.J. Brill, 1969), p. 32. Cf. Eusebius, *Praep.
evang.* I 10, 27. In short, no functioning cult of Yamm is
known, and the names are uncertain at best.

36. Of the Phoenician deities associated with the sea,
Ba'l Haddu/Ba'l Ṣapōn appears to have the strongest connections. He defeated Sea in the Ugaritic myths and established
his kingship over heaven and earth. In his victory he
received a palace as his terrestrial home on Mount Cassius,
or Mount Ṣapōn. Cf. *YGC*, pp. 124-125; and O. Eissfeldt,
*Baal Zaphon, Zeus Kasios und der Durchzug der Israeliten
durchs Meer* (Halle: Max Niemeyer Verlag, 1932), pp. 23-30.
The maritime side of Ba'l Ṣapōn is discussed by Albright in
his article "Baal-Zephon," *Festschrift für Alfred Bertholet*,
W. Baumgartner, *et al.*, eds. (Tübingen: J.C.B. Mohr [P.
Siebeck], 1950), pp. 8-9. Albright discusses, among other
things, a papyrus from Egypt (Papyrus Sallier No. IV), in
which the phrase "'*i-na-ya(t) B-'-al* (det. *Sth*, divinity)

da-pu-na (det. throw-stick, divinity)" occurs; this trans-
lates "to the bark of *Baʿl Ṣapon*" (p. 7). This comes from
a listing of deities worshipped at Memphis; the associations
with the sea of this deity are clear if Albright's translation is correct. There is other evidence, such as the vassal
treaty between Baʿl of Tyre and Esarhaddon, and the like.
Albright wrote that "Hadad was himself in a general way the
storm-god, but Baal-ṣaphon was the marine storm-god *par
excellence*, like Greek Poseidon. As such, he was also the
protector of mariners against storms." *YGC*, pp. 127-128.
Temples in his honor sprung up all over the eastern
Mediterranean, even so far south as Tahpanhes and Memphis
in Egypt.

37. It is significant that this type appears wholly
or in part on all pre-Alexandrine coins of Aradus. Its
use as a standard for the city is certain.

38. The development of two revolts in Phoenicia in
the fourth century may indicate that Phoenicia's several
powerful city-states were in some way covenanted into a
league. Tyre and Sidon were the strongest members of the
group with their commercial power. Although Aradus was
not included in the list of cities participating in the
Tennes rebellion, according to Diodorus Siculus, the city
must have had some role in the subversive activities undertaken by the Phoenicians against Persia. Cf. Diodorus
Siculus, 16.45.6. Under Persian hegemony the cities were
encouraged to act alone — not in concert, so that political
and military activities might be controlled and uprisings
thwarted. The usual Persian policy was the shrewd use of
"divide and conquer." The revolts of ʿAbdʿaštart I and
of Tennes, which were orchestrated with Egyptian and
Palestinian support, were examples of the power which
Phoenicia could muster when acting in a unified league.
We are reminded of the note in Ezekiel 27:8: "The inhabi-
tants of Sidon and Aradus are your rowers; your wise men,
O Tyre, that are in you, are your pilots." The cities did
work together. We may compare this league to such ancient
coalitions as the five-city Philistine league; militarily
and economically the cities were inexorably linked into one.

39. Herodotus, 7.98.

40. This is a typical problem found in the early
Phoenician series. With the smaller denominations,
craftsmanship of a high quality was difficult to maintain.

41. This is the pataecus which Herodotus (3.37) described; it was placed by the Phoenicians on the prows of
their galleys. The aphlaston, a combination rudder and
standard, was commonly imbued with apotropaic powers. It
was a common feature on Phoenician galleys. See chapter 1.

42. The use of inscriptions at Sidon began around
410 B.C.E. As the leading Phoenician mint, it probably
provided the example which the smaller mints followed. The
forms of the inscriptions varied from abbreviations of kings'
or cities' names to fully written royal names, as at Byblos.

43. The types of the second series are very similar to those of the first. However, some small changes have occurred, the most important of which is the addition of the abbreviation of the ethnic. In the third series these small variants gave birth to a completely new type, on which the reverse was greatly altered and smaller denominations were struck for the first time. Development of the mint was slow.

44. Similar developments may be traced in each of the Phoenician mints.

45. This inscription, with additions, will appear on the rest of the pre-Alexandrine coinage of Aradus.

46. Babelon, *Traité*, II, 2, p. 506. Hill accepts this proposal as being "doubtless right"; *BMC Phoenicia*, p. xxiii. Six's proposal that the 𐤀𐤔 referred to a king of Aradus is untenable, given the standard usage of abbreviations in the Phoenician language. More specificity was required than this, as we may see from the example of the Sidonian coins. Cf. *NC* 17 (1877) 183. An example of this usage in the Hebrew Bible may be found in Isaiah 11:11, in which we read *mēʾaššur*, although the rendering is clearly locative, "from ʾAššur." The meaning in Phoenician is the same, and clearly impossible in this case.

47. The Greek use of the genitive is not the same as the abbreviation for the preposition *min*, "from." The only evidence cited for such usage is this coin series. See Z. Harris, *A Grammar of the Phoenician Language* (New Haven: American Oriental Society, 1936), p. 120.

48. Babelon, *Traité*, II, 2, p. 506.

49. Babelon (*Traité*, II, 2, pp. 505-506) cited several examples from Phoenician and Punic colonies in Sicily, Spain, and North Africa which used a longer formula with *min*, meaning "of the citizens of PN"; no examples are known, however, which parallel this supposed use, "of PN." It is unlikely that we have an abbreviation for a longer phrase, such as *min-baʿl ʾarvad*, for which מבא might be used as an abbreviation. The Hellenistic evidence would not back this suggestion. The particle -מ is most often used with a person, rather than a city. The usual rendering of a phrase like "belonging to PN" is with -ל; cf. Harris, *A Grammar*, p. 113.

50. See n. 49 above.

51. Harris, *A Grammar*, p. 118; J. Friedrich and W. Röllig, *Phönizisch-Punische Grammatik*, Analecta Orientalia 46 (Rome: Pontifical Biblical Institute, 1970), p. 99, #207, where a meaning is cited "Königtum, Königswurde." The word is a noun with the feminine abstract ending, from the very common root *m-l-k*, "to rule."

52. Note the examples cited by Harris (n. 51 above); also note the numerous examples of such a usage in Biblical Hebrew. S. Mandelkern, in his *Veteris Testamenti Concordantiae* (Jerusalem, Tel-Aviv: Schoken Books, 1971), p. 689, notes many examples, including a number of singular construct forms with specific place and personal names, found in Exodus 19:6, Numbers 32:33, Deuteronomy 3:4, 10, 13, 1 Samuel 24:21, etc.

53. The similarity is in the indication of the authority behind issuance. The use of *lamed* is different, of course. On the *lam-melek* handles note that examples have been found all over Judah; consequently, numerous publications on these inscriptions exist. See F.M. Cross, "Judean Stamps," *EI* 9 (Jerusalem: IES, 1969), pp. 20-27, for extensive bibliography on these handles, and Cross, "Jar Inscriptions from Shiqmona," *IEJ* 18 (1968) 226-233.

54. See Peckham, *DLPS*, p. 44, lines 1-2, and p. 60. Some letter forms resemble those of the Cypriote mainland; this we will examine below.

55. Peckham, *DLPS*, p. 45, lines 3-4, and pp. 54-55.

56. Peckham, *DLPS*, p. 63. Few inscriptions are known from Aradus, so that it has been impossible to closely analyze the development of the script of Aradus on its own. It resembles the general Phoenician series.

57. As the Phoenician series develop, we seldom see types becoming more complex; generally, the opposite is the case.

58. All of the older works refer to the fish as "dolphins"; see *BMC Phoenicia*, pp. 1-3; and Babelon, *Traité*, II, 2, pp. 511-512. Such specificity is difficult to support. See K. Shepard, *The Fish-Tailed Monster in Greek and Etruscan Art* (New York: privately printed, 1940), p. 113. Many minute engravings of dolphins are known, although most are more recognizably done than are these.

59. *BMC Phoenicia*, p. 2, no. 4 (reverse).

60. Babelon, *Traité*, II, 2, pp. 511-512.

61. See nos. 4 and 5 from the second series.

62. Cf. no. 8 in this series. The fish was associated with the cult of Atargatis and may here be associated as an attendant with the cult of 'Ašerah. See R.A. Oden, Jr., *Studies in Lucian's* De Syria Dea, Harvard Semitic Monographs 15 (Missoula: Scholars Press, 1977), pp. 99-100. Oden quoted Lucian concerning the sacred fish ponds which were part of the worship of Atargatis, as follows: "There is also a lake not very far from the temple, in which are reared many holy fish of different kinds" (ἔστι δὲ καὶ λίμνη αὐτόθι, οὐ πολλὸν ἑκὰς τοῦ ἱροῦ, ἐν τῇ ἰχθύες ἱροὶ τρέφονται πολλοὶ καὶ πολυειδέυς, p. 99). Within 'Ašerah's cult, we remember her divine fisherman,

daggay, and her relationship with Tannit. In *KAI* 81, we read the phrase *lrbt l ʿštrt wltnt*. This dates from the third or second century B.C.E. and provides additional evidence linking fish and the sea to Atargatis. Linkage of 'Ašerah to Tannit and of 'Ašerah/Derketo all indicate the same conclusion, with regard to the goddess' marine nature. Cf. *CMHE*, p. 33; F.M. Cross, "Origin and Early Evolution of the Alphabet," *EI* 8 (1967) 12*, n. 27; and R.B. Coote, "The Serpent and Sacred Marriage in Northwest Semitic Tradition" (Ph.D. dissertation, Harvard University, 1972), p. 118.

    63. Cf. *NC* 17 (1877) 189. Both cities used this iconography. It is quite impossible, however, to argue that one city borrowed the motifs from the other. All of Phoenicia depended upon the sea; the common use of such things as the galley, the fish, or the seahorse, therefore, is to have been expected.

    64. In the Israelite appropriation of the Canaanite myth, in which Yahweh turned his anger against Leviathan, appearing "against them with his chariots (the clouds of heaven), he rode on a cherub and flew, and rode on *ʿărăḇōt* and came swiftly upon the wings of the wind," U. Cassuto, *The Goddess Anath*, I. Abrahams, trans. (Jerusalem: Magnes Press and the Hebrew University, 1971), pp. 73-75. The imagery of Yahweh as the divine warrior is well documented. For example, in Psalm 68:34-35, Yahweh rides the clouds, bringing to mind Baʿl's epithet in *CTA* 4.7.28ff. See P.D. Miller, Jr., *The Divine Warrior in Early Israel*, Harvard Semitic Monographs 5 (Cambridge, MA: Harvard University Press, 1973), pp. 102-113.

    65. Babelon, *Traité*, II, 2, pp. 519-520. "L'hippocampe du revers est évidemment lui aussi, un dieu marin de la Phénicie, dont le nom nous échappe....Peut-être, à Arados, est-il le symbole de la source d'eau douce qui, pareille à la fontaine Ortygie de Syracuse, jaillissait au milieu des flots de l'Océan, dans le detroit qui séparait l'île du continent; cette source alimentait au temps de guerre la ville qui n'avait d'eau potable que celle de ses citernes et celle que les habitants allaient quérir à la côte." This is a rather farfetched interpretation of the iconography colored by Hellenistic subversion from sources such as Strabo. Such subversion is purely anachronistic and can bear no weight in a discussion of the motifs present on these coins.

    66. Cf. Dussaud, "Astarté, Pontos et Baʿal," pp. 213-214. See also Hassine Fantar, "Le cavalier marin de Kerkouane," *Africa* 1 (1966) 29.

    67. The seahorse and dolphins cannot be deities, as Babelon has postulated, in the Tyrian series. There is no reason why the fish or dolphins should be deities at Aradus either.

    68. Dussaud and Babelon have only clouded the picture with unsubstantiated theories.

69. See coin no. 4 (Babelon's no. 807).

70. By the early fourth century, as Hermann Bengston put it, "the Achaemenid Empire, still imposing to the outward eyes, was by now a colossus with feet of clay. The empire's ruling race, the Persians, had long since lost the energies that had won them a world under Cyrus and Darius I. Their original character had been weakened by affluence, by the influence of Oriental, especially Babylonian, civilization; power was slipping from their grasp." See *The Greeks and the Persians from the Sixth to the Fourth Centuries*, Delacorte World History (New York: Delacorte Press, 1968), p. 307. In this absence of direct Persian control, with palace intrigues and border problems, the Phoenicians found themselves ignored and managed to exercise a certain amount of independence. Their trade increased and their coinage spread throughout the Levant, Egypt, Syria, and Asia Minor.

71. Compare examples 7 (with cable border) and 8 (with a dotted border) in *BMC Phoenicia*, or Babelon's nos. 812 and 813. The use of two differing border designs is characteristic of the idiosyncracies of the die cutters who made the coins. No standardization had yet occurred, allowing the craftsmen a degree of liberty.

72. Occasionally the fish were left off flan, when the coins were struck off-center.

73. The shields along the bulwark and the prow's battering ram are indicative of the military nature of these galleys. See Rey-Coquais, p. 145.

74. E.B. Stebbins, *The Dolphin in the Literature and Art of Greece and Rome* (Menasha, WI: George Banta Publishing Company, 1929), pp. 86-90. Dolphins were often considered sacred and played an important role in the cultic lives of cities near the sea. In the Greek tradition, Poseidon was considered the lord of the dolphins (p. 84); cf. Aristophanes, *Knights*, 551-560. These fish would help fishermen in distress and were even known to converse with mariners. In Phoenicia we have no texts which discuss the special relationship of dolphins to humans, as we have in Greece. Many dolphins are known from the Greek coinages: see the coins of Tarentum discussed in C. Seltman, *Greek Coins* (London: Methuen and Company, 1955), 2nd ed., pp. 119-120, pls. 19-20; F. Imhoof-Blumer and O. Keller, *Tier- und Pflanzenbilder auf Münzen und Gemmen des klassichen Altertums* (Leipzig: B.G. Teubner, 1889), pl. 20, nos. 15-34; and S.C. Langher, *Contributo ala Storia della Antica Moneta Bronzea in Sicilia* (Milan: Giuffre Editore, 1964), pp. 293-297. Therein several coins are described which are attributed to Dionysios of Syracuse, ca. 382 B.C.E., on which dolphins and seahorses appear interchangeably, but not together. His no. 450 has a reverse with "stella di mare fra due delfini"; no. 462 has "delfini e stella" on the reverse. Each of these coins has the same obverse as no. 465, which has an "ippocampo" on the reverse. See pp. 293 and 296. The forms of a dolphin are fairly consistent and easily recognized. F.J. Dölger has identified the

fish in the hands of the marine deity as dolphins ("Meist hält der Gott in jeder Hand einen Delphin am Schwanz"). See his IXΘYC, *Der heilige Fisch in den antiken Religionen und im Christentum*, vol. 2 (Münster in Westf.: Verlag der Aschendorffschen, 1922), pp. 262-263. Dölger, however, also made it clear that many different kinds of fish were known in the eastern Mediterranean (pp. 262-269). For this reason, and because N. Glueck, in his *Deities and Dolphins* (New York: Farrar, Straus and Giroux, 1965), pp. 315-356, has erred in just discussing dolphins and their relationship to the cult of Atargatis/Hadad, we believe it is safer to say that the marine deity is merely holding fish; they may be dolphins. Too often the quality of the engraving of the dies was not such that any certain identifications of species could be made. See also the review of Glueck's book by J. Starcky, "Le temple nabatéen de Khirbet Tannur. A propos d'un livre récent," *RB* 75 (1968) 228.

75. The tetrobol was earlier than the stater and the diobol. It lacked the fish below the galley, which was a development reflected in the next series and altered into the winged seahorse of the larger denominations.

76. We know that Phoenicia, as a whole, prospered while kings Ba'lšallim II and 'Abd'aštart I of Sidon were on the throne (from ca. 386 until 363 B.C.E.) In the Classical sources, 'Abd'aštart I was known as Straton, the Philhellene. He had a special entente with Athens, facilitating the passage of an Athenian embassy through Sidon's gates to the Persian court. These peaceful relations between Greece and Phoenicia's strongest city-state led to increased wealth and opulence in all four major Phoenician cities. Cf. W. Judeich, *Kleinasiatische Studien* (Marburg: N.G. Elwertsche Verlagsbuchhandlung, 1892), pp. 166 and 209.

77. This coin was acquired by the British Museum in 1909. It is a transitional issue, which undoubtedly had the inscription on the reverse, had it not been so poorly struck.

78. This coin is an anomaly, and probably represents a mistake by a disoriented die cutter. It is in the British Museum, and was acquired from C.L. Woolley in 1913.

79. E. Babelon, *Catalogue de la collection de Luynes*, vol. 3 (Paris: J. Florange and L. Ciani, 1930), p. 129, no. 3054, pl. 111.

80. The London example is Hill's no. 55; the Paris coins are Babelon (*Traité*, II, 2), nos. 849 and 851; the de Luynes coin is identical to no. 849.

81. The shape of the beard compares favorably with the usual depiction of Syrians on the reliefs from Persepolis. Cf. Pritchard, *ANEP*, no. 61. The date of that relief is close to the date of our coin's issue. The eye and the laureated head are reminiscent of the Attic tetradrachms of the mid-fifth century, which were imitated for years

following in the Levant.   See C.G. Starr, *Athenian Coinage 480-449 B.C.* (Oxford: Clarendon Press, 1970), pls. 25-26, which are enlargements of the several coin types under discussion.   Note also the so-called "Philisto-Arabian" imitations in Hill, *BMC Palestine*, pp. 178 and 181, nos. 14 and 28.

82.   With the coinage of Alexander, the Classical-style head became the norm in the Near East.   This type is a forerunner of advancing Hellenism in the Orient.   Such clear anthropomorphism was new in Syria-Palestine.   Cf. *ANEP*, pp. 166-170; the marine deity of Aradus is more Classical in style, differing greatly from the usual bronzes, terra cottas, and sculpted (or carved) deities.

83.   Hill, *BMC Phoenicia*, pp. 4ff.; Babelon, *Traité*, II, 2, pp. 510-511.

84.   Six, for example, has argued that this is a "Melqarth-Heracles" figure; cf. "Observations sur les monnaies phéniciennes," *NC* 17 (1877) 184.

85.   See n. 81 above.

86.   Trade invariably moved up and down the Levantine coast.   Imitations from Gaza/'Ašdōd/'Ašqelōn reached Phoenicia and circulated farther inland along the trade routes.   Cf. M. Thompson, O. Mørkholm, and C.M. Kraay, *An Inventory of Greek Coin Hoards* (New York: ANS, 1973), hoards 1752, 1753, 1830 (from the far east, Afghanistan), 1484, 1485, 1487, 1488, 1490, and 1504, for example: these imitations have been found from Al-Mina, to Nablus, to Babylon, to the far reaches of Afghanistan.   The Attic types were known and accepted everywhere as legal tender.

87.   See our stater, no. 10.   Baramki considered this to be the head of a male deity such as "possibly Baal Yamm ("Lord of the Sea") equivalent of the Greek Poseidon or Roman Neptune" (*Phoenicia and the Phoenicians* [Beirut: Khayats Press, 1961], pp. 80-81).

88.   The use of the aphlaston above the poop was begun on the preceding series, although the die cutting was not of sufficient quality to make this feature visible.

89.   See the chapter on Sidon.   The seahorse's connections with this marine deity are transparent.   Cf. G. Wissowa, *Paulys Real-Encyclopädie der classischen Altertumswissenschaft* (Stuttgart: J.B. Metzler, 1913), vol. 8, 1748-1749.

90.   Sidon's mint was the foremost center of the production of Phoenician coins in this period.   As the leader of the fourth century trading community in the eastern Mediterranean, it set standards for the other mints.   The galley on the Aradus reverses probably paralleled the Sidonian use of the galley as a symbol for Phoenicia.   Using this symbol, the coinage was given a mark of identification which could be recognized all over the eastern Mediterranean

and inland, as well. Indeed, some of the Aradian coins
may have been re-used by other mints, since countermarks
appear on a number of the extant examples. In the series
of tetrobols like our no. 11, note the following examples:

a. $\wedge\!\wedge$ (נ׳); BM no. 38.

b. $\vee$ (ש); BM no. 43.

Two staters, Babelon's nos. 837-838, have countermarks of O
(ע) or 90(עב); these may have been countermarked by
'Abd 'aštart I of Sidon. No. 837 also is marked with an $\maltese$
(א) — the usual mark for Aradus. There was definitely a
close association between Aradus and Sidon. Whether formal
agreements regarding a Phoenician league were ever drafted
is irrelevant; a union of mercantile, political and military
horizons was effected by the four major Phoenician city-states
(at least — other minor cities were doubtless involved in
this also) in the first half of the fourth century B.C.E.

91. Babelon's no. 849 was previously read as year
10 (-4ש); however, as his illustration (pl. 117, no. 5)
shows, it is clearly to be read as year 14 (ווו—4ש).

92. We have coins from Sidon and Tyre minted on the
Attic standard. Like Sidon, however, Aradus' attempt ended
in failure. 'Abd 'aštart I minted a tetradrachm with his
own likeness on the obverse; only one example of this issue
is extant. Tyre's change to the Attic standard proved
successful. The Persians could not allow Aradus to change
standards, however, and provoke grave problems for the
overland trade which went inland from Aradus around the
Fertile Crescent to Persia. The rulers of Aradus attempted
the change while in revolt. Closer and closer ties with the
Greeks and East Greeks made such a change appear attractive,
given the ease with which trade could then have been con-
ducted. The mints of the southern Palestinian coast and
Jerusalem had used the Attic standard since before 400 B.C.E.
The mint's monetary coup was not allowed by Persian officials.
Mazday, the satrap of Cilicia, took control of the mint with
the surrender of Aradus following the Tennes rebellion.

93. Sidon may have escaped the Persian sword in this
first attack by the armies of Artaxerxes III; Aradus, more
than likely, did not escape, since it lacked the wealth
and power which Sidon controlled. See A.F. Rainey, "The
Satrapy 'Beyond the River'," *Australian Journal of Biblical
Archaeology* 1 (1968-1971) 70-71.

94. There is great similarity between the symbolism
of the marine deity and a sealing found in Sardinia,
published by Harden in *The Phoenicians,* pl. 109h. The Greek
influence is tangibly felt in this example. The motif is
taken up in an article by Bernard Goldman, "A Luristan
Water-Goddess," *Antike Kunst* 3 (1960) 53-57. The double-
tailed fish deity, often resembling a serpent, is known
from various parts of Asia, including Susa, Tell Halaf, and
other areas of Mesopotamia (see pp. 56-57 especially).
Extraordinarily similar depictions of a sea god come from
Greece; specifically, see the South Italian pyxis from
Würzburg, pl. 12, no. 78a in K. Shepard, *The Fish-Tailed
Monster in Greek and Etruscan Art.* Note also the gem from

Berlin (pl. 10, no. 67), and the various examples shown on
pls. 8 and 9, especially the Attic red-figured vase from
London (no. 54) and the coins from Kyzikos, Campanian Cymae,
and Itanos (Crete). In Sidon we also see the conservative
maintenance of old types in the bronze issues after new
types have been struck in silver. Note an unpublished coin
in the collection of the Bibliothèque nationale, Paris, no.
1964, Y.28883,2, on which the obverse has the countermark
ς; the coin is the same as our no. 25 (Babelon, no. 918).
We may only conjecture that this was some authority's
attestation that the coin was legal tender.

95. Aegina issued coins with a sea tortoise on the
obverse type; see G.K. Jenkins, *Ancient Greek Coins* (London:
Barrie and Jenkins, 1972), p. 84, no. 164. These staters
date from 480 to 400 B.C.E. The earliest Aeginetan use of
the tortoise dates to the seventh/sixth century B.C.E. The
scorpion is a bit rarer, although it is known on seals and
other works of art from Syria, Mesopotamia, and Egypt. Cf.
Keller, *Die antike Tierwelt*, vol. 2, pp. 474-475. In Syria
the scorpion was used as a heraldic animal (Keller's
Wappentier); "Für heisse Länder wie Afrika und Syrien war
der Skorpion ein natürliches Emblem" (p. 475).

96. See our discussion of the satyr and his role in
the cult and *marziḥ* of Sidon. Hill's suggestion that this
may not be "Bes" but instead the "pataecus which adorned
the prows of the Aradian ships" (*BMC Phoenicia*, p. xxv) is
doubly mistaken. The face is neither Bes nor the pataecus.

97. The object is some sort of headdress worn by the
Canaanitic storm god, presumably Ba'l Ṣapōn, in Aradus.
The conical hat is well known from numerous portraits of
the storm god; cf. *ANEP*, nos. 481, 484, and 490, from Ras
Shamra, which depict Ba'l (Haddu), the god of lightning.
Similar hats were worn by royalty in Syria; a relief now in
Berlin from Zinjirli shows King Kilamuwa with such a hat.
Cf. *ANEP*, no. 455, and p. 302.

98. There is no apparent connection, for example,
between a satyr and a fish, or a scorpion and the head of
the marine deity. The cults in which these symbols had
their special meanings probably existed side by side
within the walls of Aradus. On all of the coins, at least
one type involves the sea — the factor which unites all
known examples.

99. Cf. Hill, *BMC Phoenicia*, p. xxv; Babelon, *Traité*,
II, 2, p. 520; and Babelon, *Les Perses achéménides*, intro.,
p. clvi.

100. A tetrobol from the British Museum, no. 64, has
similar types, but a different inscription — ϙϞ. The *mem*
of the Aradian ethnic is lacking, with the first two letters
of the name of the city Gaza having been substituted. The
poor quality of the engraving and the inscription may point
towards an imitation, struck in Gaza. This imitation may
have occurred in the decade following 345, when these issues

were in circulation. Of course, the inscription may relate
to an unknown ruler of Aradus.

101.   The Persian economy was nearly wrecked by the
Phoenicians' participation in the general revolt of 351.
It was imperative for Persepolis to insure the peaceful
growth of commercial activities in the eastern Mediterranean.
The threat from Macedonia also required the preparedness of
naval forces to protect Persian interests along the
Levantine coast.

102.   From all available data, the re-institution of
satrapal control occurred no later than 349/348 B.C.E.
Sidon held out longer than any other city, but also fell
by 347 B.C.E.

103.   No smaller denominations are known from this
period.   The bronze and small silver issues may have still
been in use as small change, although the probable inflation
which accompanied the war may have made their use obsolete.
As prices rose, only larger denominations were in demand in
the market place.   The conscious imitation of Greek types,
such as those of Aegina, was officially frowned upon, as
was the nationalistic use of the coin types for propagandistic purposes.

104.   Hill (*BMC Phoenicia*, p. xxiv) suggested that these
letters represented dates, ranking them in order, according
to the data then in his possession. He postulated that
the series was issued "at different mints or for different
parts of the Aradian territory." As dates, however, the
sequence of letters is incomplete, and reaches dates too
high for the years available. Beginning with *yōd*, "10,"
we go up to *pē*, "80," and possibly even *qōp*, "100." Dates
on Phoenician coins were always shown by slash marks —
not letters; letters were used in Hellenistic times, but
not earlier. The possibility that these letters represented
dates in an era of Aradus (pre-Alexandrine) cannot be
proven. The types are post-375 B.C.E., and the numbering
system would take us much earlier. The series of letters
may represent governors, perhaps military governors, who
ruled Aradus after the revolt until the reign of Gir'aštart —
the only king's name we know from Aradus. A *gimel* following
the ethnic with dates 1 to 7 comprise his coinage, discussed
below. Our readings for the letters which followed the
ethnic, in addition to the *gimel*, are as follows (note that
our readings differ occasionally from the readings proposed
by Hill, Babelon, and Rouvier):

a. ﬩ (ʾ); Rouvier, no. 6
b. ﬩ (כ); BM, no. 56; Babelon, no. 907.
c. ﬩ (ל); BM, no. 58; Rouvier, no. 5.
d. ﬩ (מ); BM, no. 57. This issue may be of
          Mazday himself.
e. ﬩ (ס); BM, nos. 59 and 60.
f. ﬩ (ע); BM, nos. 61-63.
g. ﬩ (פ); BM, no. 65.
h. ﬩ (ק); BM, no. 54.

The forms of the letters are sometimes difficult to read on

the small flans. This led to some misreadings and false
interpretations. *Yōd* is formed much like examples from
Byblos of the late fifth/early fourth century; the stance
is rotating from vertical to the left by 45° (see Peckham,
DLPS, p. 45, 1.5). *Kap* is from the same period. *Lamed*
was often mistaken for *nun*; this form is similar to those
known from the Batno'am inscription of the early fourth
century,although a bit transitional from these towards
later forms, with a longer down stroke (*DLPS*, p. 45, 1.5).
Mem is identical to that of the ethnic. *Samek* was confused
with *'alep* (cf. Imhoof's two examples noted in *NC* 17 [1877]
186); the form differs from those of Byblos and more closely
parallels Cypriote forms of Milkyaton (ca. 386) or Pumiyaton
(ca. 328). See *DLPS*, p. 9, 1.1 and 6. *'Ayin* is closed,
like forms in the Byblian Sidonian coin scripts (*DLPS*, pp.
44 and 66). *Pē* is more rounded than usual; engraving in
such limited space, however, may have dictated certain
alterations in the usual form. It is not unlike fifth/
fourth century examples from Sidon, although the stance has
rotated approx. 10° clockwise. *Qōp* is not well preserved.
It appears to have been made in two strokes: 〉 , and then 𐤒 ,
the cross stroke (*DLPS*, p. 66, 1.7). No lists of names for
the governors behind these abbreviations exist. The *mem*
is probably for Mazday; he put his initials on types from
Sidon in two separate instances of satrapal usurpation of
the minting authority. Including Mazday and Gir'aštart,
nine different governors apparently ruled Aradus in this
period after the revolt, up to 332 B.C.E. Initials indicative of local rule appear on Cilician coins of Mazday
also: note the use of the letters ע, מ, ש, י, ז, ר, and א
(Babelon, *Traité*, II, 2, pp. 443ff.). Babelon, p. 453,
suggests that "les lettres...représentent sans doute un nom
de magistrat monétaire comme les autres lettres que nous
rencontrons sur les pièces de la même série."

    105. From Arrian's *Anabasis*, 2.13.7f., we learn that
Aradus and several other towns of the πρόσοικοι were surren-
dered to Alexander by Straton, son of Gerostratus, the king.
Gir'aštart, as was his Phoenician name, was a vassal of the
Persian government charged with the surrender of Aradus.
The name, גרעשתרת, is well known in the Phoenician sources
and is a construct-phrase name, using the participial form
of the root *g(w)r*, meaning "client of (the goddess) 'Aštart."
Cf. *PNPPI*, pp. 106 and 298. A similar name, *Girmilqart*, is
now known from Sarepta; see J.B. Pritchard, *Sarepta: A
Preliminary Report on the Iron Age* (Philadelphia: The
University Museum, 1975), pp. 99-100, figs. 30:2 and 54:2.

    106. The initial ג is a good abbreviation for the
full name. The years on his coins are shown, with the
inscription, as follows:

year 1 =			⌐	or	339/338 B.C.E.
year 3 =		|||	⌐	or	337/336 B.C.E.
year 5 =	||	|||	⌐	or	335/334 B.C.E.
year 6 =	|||	|||	⌐	or	334/333 B.C.E.
year 7 = |	|||	|||	⌐	or	333/332 B.C.E.

107. Gir'aštart was apparently away from Aradus serving with the navy under Autophradates. In his absence, Straton, or 'Abd'astart, his son, "met Alexander with a golden crown and surrendered the island city as well as the mainland cities of Marathus, Sigon, and Mariamne." Cf. A.T. Olmstead, *History of the Persian Empire* (Chicago: University of Chicago Press, 1948), p. 505. Cf. A.R. Bellinger, *Essays on the Coinage of Alexander the Great*, Numismatic Studies, No. 11 (New York: The American Numismatic Society, 1963), pp. 52-53; Aradus was probably the first mint allowed to re-open following the conquest of Alexander in the Levant, striking Alexander's royal types. See the article by Milne, "The Coinage of Aradus in the Hellenistic Period," cited above in note 8.

Chapter 4

BYBLOS

Byblos was a small city during the Persian period, and was located on the central Phoenician coast between Tripolis and Berytus. The city claimed great antiquity, having been founded by Kronos, according to the cosmogonies of Sakkunyaton.[1] Historically, documents dating back at least as far as the sixth dynasty of Egypt mention the city.[2] However, little is known of the history of Byblos during the Persian period, when only a few isolated bits of information are available to us from the extant epigraphic and numismatic evidence.[3] Excavations during the last thirty years have shed some light on fifth and fourth century Byblos, but the stratigraphic control needed to confirm the value of such data was lacking.[4]

Using the Phoenician standard, a mint began striking coins at Byblos in the last years of the fifth century B.C.E. Although the city did not rival Aradus, Sidon, or Tyre in importance as a commercial center,[5] a number of coin types are known. From the existing denominations we may assume that the Byblian mint was a secondary one, the coinage of which was probably intended solely for local use.[6] The coins may have supplemented the coinages of the larger, regional trading cities.

The First Series
Ca. 425-410 B.C.E.

1. OBV: Sphinx, seated to l., wearing the double crown of Egypt.

    REV: Lightning bolt of Ba'l Hadad; dotted border; all in incuse square.

    AR Attic Didrachm, London and New York.[7] Plate 8.

2. OBV: (Obliterated).

    REV: Same as 1.

    AR 1/4 Šeqel, London.[8] Plate 8.

3. OBV: Sphinx, seated to l., wearing double crown of Egypt, as above.

REV: Lion; dotted border.
AR 1/16 Šeqel, Rouvier.[9] Plate 8.

4. OBV: As 1, above.
    REV: As 3, above.
    AR 1/32 Šeqel, Rouvier.[10]

    The types used in this first series are totally unlike
the types which appeared in the later series from the mint
of Byblos. Rouvier originally suggested that these types
were struck at Byblos due to their provenance.[11] Indeed
Dunand's recent excavations have unearthed several examples
of these types.[12] The coins bear great resemblances to
Greek coins of the period, and are typical of early issues
in Phoenicia, which combined local types with some imitation
of Greek or East Greek types.[13] The didrachm is one of
the earliest coins struck in Byblos; the use of the Attic
standard may indicate the influence of Athens in the trade
and coinage in use at the time.[14] The mint, however, was
quick to adopt the Phoenician standard, complying with the
other Phoenician mints at Sidon and Tyre. All of the
smaller denominations of this series were struck on this
standard.

    All of the obverses depict a sphinx, crouched to the
left, wearing the double crown of Egypt. A similar representation of the sphinx is known from Aradus and is typical
of the Egyptian heritage which pervaded this part of
Phoenicia.[15] The significance of the type is not clear.
There are slight differences between the engraving of the
didrachm's dies and those of the smaller coins: the larger
coin is less cramped stylistically, whereas the smaller
ones depict the sphinx as crouched rather than truly seated.
Most likely the sphinx represented the cherubim, such as
those known from the 'Aḥiram sarcophagus.[16] As a support
for the divine throne, the sphinx was directly paralleled
at Megiddo on an ivory panel illustrating the victorious
homecoming for a ruler in the Egyptian style.[17] These
sphinxes may have supported the throne of Ba'l Samēm, known
from the Yaḥīmilk inscription; this was one of the chief
deities of Byblos.[18] The lightning bolt compares favorably

with those known from reliefs and seals of the Near East.[19]
In terms of style, this coin (no. 1) is more clearly Greek;
the lightning bolts are almost identical to those which
appeared on Elian coins of the fifth century B.C.E.[20] As
part of the equipment of the storm god, lightning bolts are
common. Numerous representations of Ba'l Hadad are known
in this pose.[21]

The depiction of the lion on the reverse of the small
denomination is not entirely clear. The condition of the
extant examples of this type makes a certain description
of this reverse impossible. As such, however, the lion
was associated with the cult of 'Ašerah, who by this time
was probably known in Byblos as the *Ba'lat-Gubl*. Certain
representations of 'Ašerah (as Qudšu in Egypt) show her
mounted upon the backs of lions.[22]

The dating of this series is dependent upon the dating
of the use of the incuse method, which was used in the
production of the second series in ca. 410 through the
early fourth century.[23] The types in this first series
are dissimilar from the rest of the Byblian series and are
to be classed by themselves early in the chronological
scheme of the mint. The use of the Attic standard betrays
the early date, when controls upon the mint were minimal:
also, the crude technology apparent in the striking of these
coins is indicative of an early date.[24] We have no clue as
to the identity of the minting authority or authorities,
since inscriptions were not yet in use in the Phoenician
mints. The historical sources are equally as mute concerning
this phase in Byblian history.

The Second Series
ca. 410-375 B.C.E.

5. OBV: Galley, to l.; prow terminating in head of a
           horse; inside, three warriors with shields,
           facing l.; below, winged seahorse to l.; border
           of dots.

    REV: Vulture, with wings outstretched, to l.; it
           stands over body of a ram (in incuse) to l.,
           with head looking back to r. over body; border
           of dots; whole in incuse square.

    AR Šeqel, Athens and Vienna.[25]

6. OBV: Same as 5.
    REV: Same as 5.
    AR 1/4 Seqel, London. Plate 8.

7. OBV: Similar to 5, except only one warrior in galley.
    REV: Same as 5.
    AR 1/16 Seqel, Paris (Six).[26] Plate 8.

8. OBV: Same as 7.
    REV: Similar to 5, except without winged seahorse.
    AR 1/32 Seqel, Berlin.[27]

Although inscriptions began to appear on coins in the other mints in this time period, no inscriptions were yet employed at Byblos.[28] The types used in this series, however, were unique and became the standard ones used for many years at Byblos. Four denominations are known; no double Seqels have been discovered as yet.

The galley played an important role in the Byblian coinage, just as it did in the other three pre-Alexandrine Phoenician mints. The Byblian galley has a battering ram, a prow with the head of a horse, shields along the bulwark, and three (less on the smaller denominations) soldiers with crested helmets riding in the ship.[29] The style of the armor worn by the marines is Hellenic, suggesting an influence of Greek or East Greek technology.[30] The winged seahorse is similar to the one already seen at Aradus. Its role in the cult of the marine deity is beyond doubt.[31]

The reverse of these coins presents an unusual scene of the vulture overlooking or standing upon a ram. The scene is slightly varied upon the small denominations where limited space forced different adaptations of the type.[32] The meaning of the motif remains obscure, unfortunately. Babelon interpreted it as an allusion to Euagoras I of Salamis, who reigned at this time and whose power was felt over the entire Levant.[33] Pietschmann believed the type to be religious, with the bird of prey representing some destructive divinity.[34] There may be some correlation between the vulture and the lion, however, since the lion replaced the bird on later types. It is not clear if this is evidence for syncretism between 'Ašerah (with her lions)

and the violent goddess 'Anat.[35] The Ba'lat-Gubl may have
been a syncretistic goddess made up of aspects of these two
goddesses.[36] The Egyptian vulture goddess, $n\underline{h}bt$, was sometimes presented in this manner; as the patron deity of the
pre-dynastic kings of Upper Egypt, she (represented icono-
graphically by the vulture) was a symbol for regal power.[37]
In the crown of Tutankhamun, for example, the cobra and
vulture symbolically represent the pharoah's rule over both
Lower and Upper Egypt. To be sure, the scene of the animal
combat is not new; the use of the vulture, on the contrary,
is altogether unique. The similarity to certain issues
from southeastern Anatolia and Cyprus is striking; however,
no positive identification or explanation of the Byblian
types is possible.[38]

The ram upon which the vulture is standing is engraved
in incuse. This technique "des revers partiellement incus"
was probably adopted from Magna Graecia, according to Naster,
although no specific dates are suggested.[39] The period
from ca. 430 until 385 B.C.E. witnessed considerable use
of this method in the four Phoenician mints, especially in
Sidon and Tyre. The data from these two mints have aided
us in dating this Byblian series to the late fifth and early
fourth centuries B.C.E.

The sequence of denominations was unbroken from the
quarter šeqel to the thirty-second. No double šeqels, šeqels,
or half šeqels are extant. Moreover, only one double šeqel
is known from Byblos in all of the series minted before
Alexander the Great.[40] Large denominations were probably
not struck in Byblos because of the use of Sidonian and
Tyrian double šeqels and šeqels in the coastal trade. Many
coins of these two mints were found within the walls of
Byblos by archaeological excavations, further suggesting
the supplementary nature of the small local denominations.[41]

The dating of this series is in keeping with the comparative typology of the series. The appearance on this series'
types of the galley and its later standardization further
correlates with the issues from other mints in this time
period. In all cases, standardized types were developed
prior to 390 B.C.E. when the coin types appear to have become

standard throughout the four mints.

The Third Series
'Elpaʻol, King of Byblos
ca. 375-365 B.C.E.

9. OBV: Galley to l., over zigzag line of waves;
          winged seahorse below; all as on 5 above;
          murex shell below seahorse; border of dots.

    REV: **Ⴑɡ∧ɣⴑɣⴑoɔⴑⴕ**(אלפעל מלך גבל), above; lion
          standing l. on body of bull, l., head facing
          (bull in incuse); border of dots.

    AR Šeqel, Paris.[42]

10. OBV: Same as 9.

    REV: **ⴑoɔⴑⴕ**(אלפעל) above, and **ɣ**(מ), below; other-
          wise same as 9; in incuse square.

    AR 1/2 Šeqel, New York. Plate 8.

11. OBV: Same as 9.

    REV: **ⴑoɔⴑⴕ**(אלפעל), above; otherwise same as 9.

    AR 1/2 Šeqel, New York.

12. OBV: Same as 9.

    REV: Similar to 9, except no inscription.

    AR 1/16 Šeqel, London.[43]

13. OBV: Similar to 9, except no murex shell.

    REV: Winged griffin, seated to l.

    AR 1/32 Šeqel, Paris.[44] Plate 8.

The third Byblian series was struck under the authority
of a king named 'Ēlpaʻol. His reign extended for a number
of years during the early fourth century B.C.E., although
specific dates can be only speculative and approximate.
'Ēlpaʻol's types closely resemble those of the vulture
series, although there are three significant differences:
(1) on the obverse, a zigzag line of waves and a murex shell
were added; (2) on the reverse, the scene with the vulture
and ram was replaced with that of a lion and a bull; and
(3) also on the reverse, an inscription was added.

The depiction of the waves is similar to that found
upon the coins of Sidon and Aradus. The murex shell was
the symbol of the Phoenician trade in purple dye; the shell
appeared also on the obverse types of Tyre.[45] These motifs
were shared with other Phoenician mints.

The scene of the animal combat, with its new partici-
pants, has here taken on an appearance commonly known in
the Levant.[46]   In this same period, types like these appeared
for the first time in Cilicia, from the mint of Tarsus.
Some borrowing may have occurred, although the scene was a
very common one throughout the eastern Mediterranean.[47]

The inscription is very clear; it reads: 'Ēlpaʿol
milk Gubl — "'Ēlpaʿol, King of Byblos."   The same pattern,
with the personal name followed by the official title, is
used on the larger denominations throughout the rest of the
pre-Alexandrine coinage of Byblos.   The pattern appears to
have been borrowed from the Cilician satraps.   A shortened
version of the inscription occurs on the smaller denominations.   The name of the king is given, sometimes with a *mem*,
which probably is an abbreviation for the phrase *milk Gubl*.[48]
The smallest coins delete the inscription altogether.[49]
This name is known only from this coin series, and is a
verbal sentence name meaning "'Ēl has made (done)."[50]   The
theophoric element is the chief god of the Phoenician
pantheon, 'Ēl; the verbal element is the common verb "to
make, do," *p-ʿ-l*.[51]

Paleographically, the coin script cannot be dated with
too much accuracy, except that it is clearly of the fourth
century B.C.E.[52]   The script falls chronologically between
the Yeḥawmilk and Batnoʿam inscriptions, which are datable
to the late fifth and first half of the fourth centuries
respectively.[53]   A date, therefore, in the period 375 to
365 B.C.E. is most probable and is in keeping with the
numismatic evidence.

No double šeqels of this king are known.   The small
denominations show slight variations typologically.   The
winged griffin, for example, is unique upon the thirty-
second šeqel.   Stylistically, it is in keeping with
numerous Syrian examples.[54]   Whatever function the griffin
may have played in the cult is unknown, if indeed there was
such a function.

The Fourth Series
'Uzziba'l, King of Byblos
ca. 365-350 B.C.E.

14. OBV: Galley to l., prow terminating in head of lion;
           three warriors inside, with shields, to l.;
           below, zigzag line of waves and a winged seahorse,
           to l.; below seahorse, murex; border of dots.

     REV: ⌐9ʌy⌐ʎⴽog⌐o(עזבעל מלך גבל), above; lion, to l.,
           bringing down bull, l.; border of dots; slight
           incuse circle.

     AR Seqel, New York. Plate 8.

15. OBV: ⌐o(עז), above seahorse's tail. Galley to l.,
           prow, with eye, terminating in head of lion; two
           warriors inside with shields, to l.; below, winged
           seahorse, l.; border of dots.

     REV: ⌐9ʌy⌐ʎⴽog⌐o(עזבעל מלך גבל), above; lion to l.,
           bringing down bull; slight circular incuse;
           border of dots.

     AR 1/16 Seqel, New York. Plate 8.

     The fourth series may be attributed to another king,
'Uzziba'l, son of Batno'am. The changes in the types are
insignificant, ranging from the prow's termination in a
lion's head rather than in a horse's head, to a slightly
differing portrayal of the animal combat scene. No longer
is the lion on top of the bull; in this series, the lion is
depicted bringing down the bull in a fight.[55]

     In the Batno'am inscription, the mother of 'Uzziba'l
dedicated a sarcophagus; the date of the script is the
first half of the fourth century.[56] 'Uzziba'l is a nominal
sentence name meaning "Ba'l is my strength (or protection)."[57]
The Greek vocalization is from Herodotus, 'Αζβαλος; other
sources read a-zi-ba-'-al.[58] The non-theophoric element is
a common appelative of divinity, occurring in various forms
with divine names such as b'l, tnt, mlqrt, and mlk.[59]

     In this series the types were standardized using types
from the previous series. Several coins, however, have
presented exceptions to this rule.

16. OBV: Similar to 15, except lacking inscription.
     REV: ⌐ʌ(גל), above; lion, to l., bringing down bull,
           to l.; incuse circle; border of dots.
     AR 1/16 Seqel, New York. Plate 9.

17. OBV: Similar to 14, except illegible inscription above.
     REV: Similar to 14, except lacking inscription.
     AR Šeqel, Byblian hoard.[60]

The sixteenth šeqel appears to have been struck under
'Uzziba'l, although the two-letter inscription does not
prove this. Typologically it is part of this series; the
gimel-lamed reading for the inscription is probably an
abbreviation for *Gubl*, "Byblos." The coin is a transitional
issue from early in 'Uzziba'l's reign when his types were
being altered. The placement of the inscription on the
reverse paralleled that of the king's name, although the
size of the flan limited the length of the inscription.
From the other examples of the sixteenth šeqels, we see that
the two-letter abbreviations for his name were used,
although in this coin such usage was not yet developed and
had not been changed over to the obverse.

     The šeqel is unusual because it has an inscription on
the obverse where it would usually appear on the reverse.
Unfortunately, the inscription is illegible. Only *zayin*
is visible, which may have been part of this king's name.
The coin appears to have been struck by the last ruler to
have governed Byblos before Phoenicia's fall in the revolt
ca. 351/350 B.C.E. The coin, and all of those like it, is
heavily worn and has visible die breaks, indicating the
heavy use of the coin dies.[61] Such a situation may have
occurred in the time of the Tennes rebellion, due to military
action and the difficulties in maintaining a functioning
mint in wartime. Partially visible on this coin are the
first two letters of "Gubl"; thus the pattern "PN, king of
Gubl" was probably in use. Although no names of kings
except 'Uzziba'l survive from this period, this appears to
be the best candidate for this coinage.[62]

     This šeqel brings us to the mid-point of the fourth
century. No historical data concerning Byblos in this era
are available, although we may assume that it played an
active part in the revolt since it was the center of
Phoenicia's production and shipping of cedar wood. The dating
of this series is coincident with the coinage of Mazday,
satrap of Cilicia, whose types are almost identical to those

of ʿUzzibaʿl.

The Fifth Series
ʾAddirmilk and ʿIyyēnʾēl, kings of Byblos
ca. 348-332 B.C.E.

18. OBV: 𐤉𐤊(𐤀𐤍) over tail of seahorse; otherwise similar
            to 14; four warriors in galley.
     REV: 𐤋𐤂𐤍𐤕𐤋𐤊𐤋𐤌𐤊𐤋𐤌𐤓𐤃𐤀(אדרמלך מלך גבל), above; otherwise
            similar to 14.
     AR Šeqel, London.[63]

19. OBV: 𐤉𐤊(𐤀𐤍), over tail of seahorse; otherwise similar
            to 15.
     REV: Same as 18.
     AR 1/16 Šeqel, New York.

20. OBV: Similar to 14, except no visible inscription
            (badly worn).
     REV: 𐤋𐤂𐤍𐤕𐤊𐤋𐤌𐤊𐤋𐤍𐤏(עינאל מלך גבל), above; otherwise
            similar to 14.
     AR Šeqel, London.[64] Plate 9.

21. OBV: [𐤉] 𐤊 ([𐤍]𐤀) above seahorse's tail; otherwise
            similar to 15.
     REV: Same as 20.
     AR 1/16 Šeqel, New York.[65] Plate 9.

The last of the pre-Alexandrine series from Byblos
continued the types already discussed. No changes were
incorporated into these types except the use of two new
minting authorities' names, ʾAddirmilk and ʿIyyēnʾēl —
probably the Enylus of the Greek histories who surrendered
Byblos to Alexander in 332 B.C.E.[66]

The abbreviations of the names were formed in the
usual manner, with the first and last letters of the name.
No two-letter abbreviations of ʿIyyēnʾēl are extant and none
may have been used, due to this ruler's continued use of
the obverse dies of ʾAddirmilk. The full name is a verbal
sentence name meaning "ʾĒl views intently."[67] A variant
spelling occurs on a coin; Babelon described a reverse type
which lacked the ʾalep.[68] This spelling is probably an
engraver's mistake. The second name, ʾAddirmilk, is a
nominal sentence name meaning "the king (Baʿl ?) is mighty
(or glorious)."[69] ʾAddir is an appellative which usually
occurs in Punic texts with reference to Baʿl.[70]

Hill persisted in placing 'Addirmilk following
'Iyyēn'ēl; thus it appeared that Alexander allowed Byblos
to continue striking coins on its Persian independent types
after it was officially annexed to Alexander's empire.[71]
This is not possible. The sixteenth šeqel from London of
'Iyyēn'ēl used the obverse dye of 'Addirmilk's sixteenth;
'alep is clearly read, not 'ayin. The coin was misinterpreted by Hill. It is a transitional issue of 'Iyyēn'ēl,
struck soon after his succession to the throne. Specific
dates for this change in minting authority are impossible,
although it would appear to have been well after 340 and
was probably ca. 334/333 B.C.E.

On the coins of 'Iyyēn'ēl the sign of Tannit was used
on several obverse types in place of the abbreviation of
the king's name. From the Paris collection note the
following: (1) on šeqels, the sign was under the lion (on
one example it was on the bull itself);[72] (2) on sixteenth
šeqels, there are several variations, including the reverse
type inscriptions ⅄𝐲o(עמנ) and ⅄o(עב).[73] These are
abbreviations for 'Iyyēn'ēl milk Gubl and 'Iyyēn'ēl Gubl.[74]
The sign of Tannit appeared on both of these coins. The
sign is similar to the symbol which was used on the coins
of Demonicus of Citium.[75] Its purpose on the coins remains
unknown. However, recent evidence from Sarepta has shown
that the cult of Tannit or at least Tannit-'Aštart, was not
unknown on the Phoenician mainland.[76]

The next coins issued by the Byblian mint were struck
under the authority of Alexander in the late fourth century
B.C.E.[77]

In summation, coins were struck in Byblos by a number of
rulers from the mid- to late-fifth century until the coming
of Alexander the Great. Never reaching the prominence of
Sidon or Tyre in the Persian period, Byblos remained an old,
established port city of general importance to the commercial
activity of the Phoenician city-states. The Byblian mint
issued coins which supplemented the Levantine coast's major
Phoenician currencies, increasing the ease with which trade
could function. Religious motifs were most commonly employed

on the coin types, as we have seen elsewhere. The mint
remained functional under Alexander, who authorized coin
series on his own types.

Notes

1. Karl Mras, ed., *Eusebius Werke*, Vol. 8, part 1, *Die Praeparatio evangelica* (Berlin: Academie Verlag, 1954), I 10, 19:

Ἐπὶ τούτοις ὁ Κρόνος τεῖχος περιβάλλει τῇ
ἑαυτοῦ οἰκήσει, καὶ πόλιν πρώτην κτίζει τὴν
ἐπὶ Φοινίκης βύβλον.

2. From Byblos have come artifacts dating as early as 3000 B.C.E. Texts from Egypt's fourth dynasty record trade with Byblos for such commodities as cedar wood. Military expeditions against Byblos are noted for the fifth and sixth dynasties. See CAH^3, vol. 1, part 2, pp. 345-346; and Harden, *The Phoenicians*, p. 40, n. 33.

3. Several inscriptions provide us with some information on the Byblian Persian period. The Yeḥawmilk and Šipṭiba'l inscriptions (*KAI* 10 and 9) are the primary sources, although several others are known. The inscriptions' content, regretfully, is banal. A few names have been gleaned from them giving us a limited onomastica with which to work. See also F.M. Cross, "A Recently Published Phoenician Inscription of the Persian Period from Byblos," *IEJ* 29 (1979) 40-44.

4. Cf. M. Dunand, *Fouilles de Byblos*, vols. 1-2 (Paris: Librairie d'amérique et d'orient Adrien Maisonneuve, 1939-1958), *passim*. Dunand's methods were architectural, rather than stratigraphic. The reports themselves must be re-excavated to glean whatever data are needed.

5. The number of times that Aradus, Sidon, and Tyre are mentioned in the historical sources is proof enough of this point. Byblos' heyday was in the second millennium B.C.E. This was a time when Wenamun, the Egyptian emissary, was sent to Byblos by Ramesses XI around 1100 B.C.E. See R.D. Barnett, "Early Shipping in the Near East," *Antiquity* 32 (1958) 226-227; and Hans Goedicke, *The Report of Wenamun* (Baltimore: The Johns Hopkins University Press, 1975), pp. 6-9. Wenamun. in his negotiations with Zikrba'l, the Byblian king, recorded the necessity to recount trading deals of previous kings in order to establish credit for the Egyptian throne with the Byblian merchants (pp. 76, 84, 91, 94, and 98). Such commercial prosperity for Byblos ceased with the Babylonian and Persian conquests. The once-great supplier of timber to King Solomon was then reduced to a small city-state vastly overshadowed by Sidon and Tyre. See chapter 1 for a summary of the denominational metrology.

6. Very few large coins are known from the mint. In the hoards from the Levant, Asia Minor, Egypt, and inland Syria and Mesopotamia, few Byblian coins have been found. Cf. *IGCH* nos. 1256, 1259, 1263, 1481-1504, 1506-1507, 1639, 1650-1651, 1653, 1747, and 1790; with coins from Aradus,

123

Tyre, and Sidon found from Cilicia to western Iran and even to the delta of the Nile, the coins of Byblos are found only in the central part of Phoenicia and the bordering sections of Syria. These coins did not circulate as did the more commercially oriented issues of the larger city-states.

7. *BMC Phoenicia*, p. lxv; Babelon, *Traité*, II, 2, nos. 882-883. A coin of this type was unearthed by Dunand; cf. *Fouilles de Byblos*, 2 (texte), pp. 67-68, no. 7114. Other examples of this type are in New York (ANS) and London; the London coin is numbered "1957, 12-4-1," and is not yet published.

8. The coin is unpublished and is presently in the British Museum, no. "1960, 9-7-1." Newell (see n. 21 below) has argued that these coins are light examples "due to the very serious corrosion" of coins struck on the Persic standard (pp. 12-13). The coins are not badly corroded, however, as the writer observed in London on 18 June 1976. The standard is more precisely that of Athens.

9. J. Rouvier, "Numismatique des villes de la Phénicie: Gebal-Byblos," *JIAN* 4 (1901) 38, no. 628.

10. Rouvier, "Numismatique," p. 38, no. 629.

11. See Hill's remarks, *BMC Phoenicia* p. lxv. Rouvier, commenting on these coins, wrote that each was "trouvé dans l'ancien port de Gebail (anc. Gebal)"; *JIAN* 4 (1901) 38.

12. See Dunand, *Fouilles de Byblos*, 2 (texte), pp. 67-68.

13. Interestingly a relief from Aradus depicts the same scene used on the obverse of these coins. The relief is made of alabaster (0.61 m high) with a freize of palmettes above the winged sphinx. Harden (*The Phoenicians*, p. 182, fig. 57) has dated it to the eighth/seventh century B.C.E. Another close parallel is the sphinx from Megiddo first published in 1939 and discussed in R. Dussaud, *L'art phénicien du IIᵉ millénaire* (Paris: Librairie orientaliste Paul Geuthner, 1949), p. 93, fig. 56. Thus, the obverse is paralleled within Syria-Phoenicia. The reverse type, however, is more Greek in style, reflecting the lightning bolts of Zeus as represented on the coins of Olympia: see A.B. Cook, *Zeus: A Study in Ancient Religion* (New York: Biblo and Tannen reprint, 1965), Vol. 2, Part 1, p. 780, pl. 36, nos. 1, 4, 6, and 8, averaging in date to 450-440 B.C.E. The lightning bolt on our coin is closer to these examples in style than to the usual Near Eastern examples. See Cook, pp. 740-766, for a useful summary of the evidence.

14. In the Persian realm no restrictions were placed upon coinage by the government except in the case of gold coinage. No gold issues were permitted except from the king himself; however, silver coins were permitted to circulate and to be struck in the names of local satraps and other rulers. Cf. A.F. Bellinger, *Essays on the Coinage of*

Alexander the Great, p. 40. Daniel Schlumberger has made
the same point in his important monograph *L'argent grec
dans l'empire achéménide* (Paris: Imprimerie nationale,
1953), pp. 24-27. With so many differing types in circulation, Alexander chose to present a unified monetary system
to the East, making types the same in each area, to facilitate the acceptance of specie in all parts of his vast
kingdom. Schlumberger wrote "[Alexandre] a voulu doter
d'une monnaie d'argent partout acceptable comme telle un
empire qui n'en avait pas, et, ce faisant, étendre l'usage
de la monnaie d'argent comme tell (et non comme lingot) au
territoire entier de cet empire" (p. 27). In many cases
the coinage of Athens provided the impetus which got local
mints into operation. The Attic standard was used in the
southern part of Palestine and in trading operations along
the Levantine coast. Attic coins were known from a number
of sites along the coast (*IGCH*, pp. 202-204). At Byblos we
have only the didrachm which was struck on this standard.
The smaller denominations were minted on the usual Phoenician
standard.

15. Cf. H.T. Bossert, *Altsyrien* (Tübingen: E. Wasmuth,
1951), pp. 35 and 157, no. 510; the sphinx of Aradus was
dated to the "Persische Epoche."

16. *ANEP*, no. 456-458. Nos. 456 and 458 show the
sphinx throne on which King 'Aḥiram was seated. The cherubim
were the beasts which held up the throne. This situation
is known in several biblical texts, ranging from Psalm 80:1
to Isaiah 37:16. Yahweh was even depicted as flying across
the heavens on the back of a cherub in Psalm 18:11 (Hebrew).
Cf. S.A. Cook, *The Religion of Ancient Palestine in the
Light of Archaeology* (London: The British Academy, 1930),
pp. 34-35.

17. See the excellent article by R.D. Barnett,
"Phoenician and Syrian Ivory Carving," *PEQ* (1939) 16-17,
in which sphinxes are discussed. Barnett emphasizes the
point that this Egyptian religious paraphernalia does not
mean that Egyptian cults had replaced Phoenician ones.
Rather, we see Egyptian symbols in use for Phoenician
religious accouterments. See Barnett's pl. 3.1 and pl. 5.1.
From the report of the early excavations of Byblos, in
Pierre Montet, *Byblos et l'Égypte* (Paris: Librairie
orientaliste Paul Geuthner, 1928), Texte, p. 292, we read,
for example, that Montet was arguing that Byblian art was
Syrian and, as such, it influenced Egyptian art forms.
Occasionally, however, as with our sphinx, the Byblian
artisans "se sont assez...contentés de copier plus ou moins
fidelement des modèles égyptiens...pour leur seule valeur
décorative" (pp. 291-292). This was probably the case with
the sphinx on our coins. In addition, see Dussaud, *L'art
phénicien,* pp. 89-90, 95; and H. Frankfort, *The Art and
Architecture of the Ancient Orient,* the Pelican History of
Art (Baltimore: Penguin Books, 1970), pp. 270-271, figs.
316-317. The likeness between the 'Aḥiram and Megiddo
sphinxes is striking. Cf. A.S. Kapelrud, *The Violent
Goddess Anat in the Ras Shamra Texts* (Oslo: Scandinavian
Books, 1969), pp. 106-107.

18.   *KAI* 4, line 3 and following: יארך·בעלשמם
ובעלת<גבל·ומפחרת·אל·גבל·קדשם·יתן·יחמלך·ושנתו·עלגבל·
That is, "May Ba'l Šamēm and Ba'lat-Gubl, and the assembly
of all the holy gods of Byblos prolong the days of Yaḥimilk
and his years over Byblos...." Ba'l Šamēm and Ba'lat-Gubl
are paired here and probably represent the principle
deities of the Byblian pantheon. Just as the throne of 'Ēl
and that of Yahweh were supported by cherubim, so too we
may assume that the throne of Ba'l Šamēm was supported in
such a way. See R.J. Clifford, *The Cosmic Mountain in
Canaan and the Old Testament* (Cambridge, MA: Harvard
University Press, 1972), pp. 44-46. All of the assembly of
the gods, according to Sakkunyaton, were given wings, so
that they could "fly with Kronos": τοῖς δὲ λοιποῖς θεοῖς
δύο ἑκάστῳ πτερώματα ἐπὶ τῶν ὤμων, ὡς"οτι δὴ συνέπταντο τῷ
Κρόνῳ. (from Eusebius, *Praep. evang.*, I.10.37). See P.D.
Miller, Jr., *The Divine Warrior in Early Israel*, pp. 42-
53; and *CMHE*, pp. 35-36 and 69. F.M. Cross has shown how
the iconography of Punic Ba'l Ḥammon derived directly from
that of Ugaritic *'ilu*; the throne with cherubim were all
part of this portrayal. Examples are known from Ugarit;
see C.F.A. Schaeffer, "Les fouilles de Ras-Shamra-Ugarit.
Huitième campagne," *Syria* 18 (1937) pl. 17; *CMHE*, p. 35,
n. 137. Other examples have been discovered at Sousse and
in Sardinia; see P. Cintas, "Le sanctuaire punique de Sousse,"
Revue africaine 91 (1947) 1-80, pl. 49, fig. 48; and A.M.
Bisi, *Le stele puniche* (Rome: Universita di Roma, 1967),
figs. 57-58. The cult of Ba'l Šamēm, as "lord of the
heavens," could easily have borrowed some of this iconography in this late period; in no way, however, may Ba'l
Šamēm and Ba'l Ḥammon/'Ēl be equated or considered merged
by some syncretistic occurrence.

19.   Cf. *ANEP*, nos. 490, 500-501, 531-532, and 537-538.
The lightning was not done in the Egyptian style as was
the sphinx. Note R.D. Barnett, *A Catalogue of the Nimrud
Ivories* (London: British Museum, 1957): "The Phoenicians
used Egyptian symbolism for their own purposes and gave it
meaning of their own. Their artistic viewpoint was much
the same as that of the Egyptians" (p. 62).

20.   A monograph on these coins, struck by the temple
authorities of Olympia, was written by C.T. Seltman,
entitled "The Temple Coins of Olympia," *Nomisma* 8 (1913),
9 (1914), and 11 (1921). The development of the Greek
form of the lightning bolt need not concern us here. The
form used in Byblos most resembles the reverse of a coin
dated to ca. 510-ca. 471 B.C.E. (Cook, *Zeus*, Vol. 2, Part
1, pl. 36.1). Although such coins may never have circulated
in or near Byblos, the symbolism of the bolt was known;
Greek and/or East Greek sources may have been responsible.
Cf. L. Anson, *Numismata graeca* (London: L. Anson, 1910),
pls. 9-13. C.M. Kraay, *Archaic and Classical Greek Coins*
(Berkeley and Los Angeles: University of California Press,
1976), p. 288). Kraay calls the lightning bolt a
"stylized lotus." The late Assyrian seals cited, however,
provide no evidence to corroborate this assertion. Kraay
adds, however, that "its meaning remains obscure." This,
regretfully, is very true.

21. E.T. Newell was the first writer to suggest the bolt's use on this coin. See E.T. Newell, "Some Unpublished Coins of Eastern Dynasts," *ANSNNM* 30 (1926) 10-11. Newell dated the coin to the "early fifth century B.C." No evidence from Phoenicia would permit us to date any coins before 450-440 B.C.E. Undoubtedly, this coin was early in the series from Byblos, as Newell realized; however, we doubt that it was so early as he guessed. The Elian coins with the lightning bolts were earlier but over and over again, such apparent borrowings from the West were not instantaneous, but took some years to be used in Phoenicia.

22. See n. 35 below.

23. The incuse method was used in all four Phoenician mints. See P. Naster, "La technique des revers partiellement incus de monnaies phéniciennes," ANS *Centennial Publication*, N. Ingholt ed. (New York: ANS, 1948) 503-511, especially 506ff. The method was used between 410 and 380 B.C.E. It seemingly originated in southern Italy: "la technique pratiquée par les villes de Tyre, Arados, Byblos et Sidon est au fond chaque fois la même et est une simple variante de la technique habituelle ou, si l'on veut, elle est la somme de la technique habituelle de gravure en creux et de la gravure de coins pour incuses telle qu'elle se pratiquait en Grande-Grece." See Naster, p. 510.

We wish to note an interesting specimen unearthed at Byblos by Dunand between 1933 and 1938: see Dunand, *Fouilles de Byblos*, 2, no. 7117. The coin is unique and may have been minted by the Byblian mint, in the same series as our seated, Egyptianized sphinxes.

    OBV: Winged seahorse, to l. (forepart of seahorse only).
    REV: Sun disc with three bending rays, counter-clock-
          wise; in dotted square.
    AR Unknown denomination, from the surface of the tell
          of Byblos.

Regretfully, we have no indication as to the size or weight of this coin; from the drawing supplied by Dunand, we may speculate that it was a Phoenician šeqel. It was probably struck in ca. 420 B.C.E. The seahorse was common along the coast as types from Aradus, Byblos, and Tyre have shown. The sun disc, sometimes called the "Lycian symbol," is more difficult. Cook (*Zeus*, Vol. 1, pp. 300ff.) agrees with Babelon (*Les Perses achéménides*, p. xc f.) that the symbol must have something to do with the god of the heavens. The disc is known with two, three, or four rays, although three (such as we see on this coin) are the most common. Examples from Lycia date from the fifth and fourth centuries (on coins) and may have provided the model on which this coin was made; cf. *BMC Lycia*, pp. 9-23.

24. Some coins in this series were struck off flan, while others were otherwise misshapen. The people entrusted with the coining of the money were inexperienced. As we may see from later issues, the technology was mastered as they were struck more successfully.

25. Babelon, *Traité*, II, 2, no. 858. The British Museum recently acquired a similar coin, although it is badly worn and broken; the coin is numbered "1972, 6-29-1."

26. Babelon, *Traité*, II, 2, no. 861; and Rouvier, "Numismatique," no. 632.

27. Babelon, *Traité*, II, 2, no. 862.

28. See P. Naster, "Le developpement des monnayages phéniciens avant Alexandre," *INCJ*, p. 13: of the Byblian coinage, "pour l'ensemble il parait que le numéraire de Byblos n'ait eu qu'une aire réduite de circulation et qu'il n'a pas été très abondant." The subsidiary nature of the coinage is emphasized by the fact that there are so few extant coins, and all of them are of smaller denominations.

29. The warriors are a feature of the Byblian galleys which we do not see in the other three mints. The horse's head on the prow was typical of Phoenician merchant vessels which the Greeks called ἵπποι. Such ships were used until about the end of the first century B.C.E., according to Strabo. See R.D. Barnett, "Early Shipping in the Near East," pp. 227-228. A single bank of oars is now shown on the coins, so that the specific type of ship depicted here is impossible to discern. On the Phoenician ships, see J.-G. Février, "L'ancienne marine phénicienne et les découvertes récentes," *La nouvelle clio* 2 (1950) 128-143.

30. There were probably Greeks and East Greeks living in the Levant in this period as representatives of various trading concerns. From such first-hand sources and from the various instances when Persian and Greek armies clashed, such military technology was known in Byblos. Hellenic-style helmets, with crests, were well known and correspond to those depicted upon these coins. See the black-figure vase from Chalcidice and the bronze vase from Vix, illustrated in J. Boardman, *The Greeks Overseas* (Baltimore: Penguin Books, 1973), 2nd ed., pls. 16a and 16b-17. See also R.M. Cook, *Greek Painted Pottery* (London: Methuen and Co., 1972), 2nd ed., pl. 12a, a Corinthian kotyle of ca. 580 B.C.E., pl. 24b, an Attic black-figure siana cup of 570-560. The helmets on the cup are the same as those worn by the soldiers on our coins; it is unusual that the armor is Greek in style rather than Syrian. On helmets, see A.M. Snodgrass, *Early Greek Armour and Weapons* (Edinburgh: Edinburgh University Press, 1964), pp. 31-32. The helmets resemble "Ionian" helmets, first known from the seventh century B.C.E. in East Greek contexts.

31. Numerous instances in ancient art depict the sea-horse as an acolyte of various deities. See for example the British Museum vase illustrated by S. Reinach in *Répertoire des vases peints*, Vol. 2 (Paris: E. Leroux, 1900), p. 89, in which the seahorse serves Thetis; also see the plates in H. Heydemann, *Nereiden mit den Waffen des Achill* (Halle: Max Niemeyer, 1897), pls. 3-4; and K. Shephard, *The Fish-Tailed Monster in Greek and Estruscan Art*, pp. 97-102,

and pl. 7, all of which detail the animal's relationship
to various deities.

32. Usually the vulture's right wing is extended
over the ram's body. Hill (*BMC Phoenicia*, pl. lxv) has
noted a variation on the obverse type on a small denomination
from Berlin; cf. F. Imhoof-Blumer, *Monnaies grecques*
(Leipzig: K.F. Koehler, 1883), p. 441. On this coin a
ram's head covers part of the obverse type. It is not
clear if this same usage occurred on the thirty-second šeqel
(Imhoof-Blumer, p. 441, no. 9). No illustrations were
provided of these coins, however, so that precise charac-
teristics cannot be ascertained.

33. Babelon, *Les Perses achéménides*, p. clxvi. Such
an interpretation was inspired by the aforementioned ram,
which was commonly used by Euagoras I on his coin types.
Such an interpretation is doubtful, however, since the
animal combat scene is a common, variable one throughout
all of the Near East. Harden (*The Phoenicians*, pl. 109a)
illustrated a seal from the Ashmolean Museum of Oxford (of
the ninth-eighth century from Aleppo, Syria) which depicts
a vulture standing over another animal, in the same style
as our coin type. The animal on the bottom appears to be
an ibex or a stag. Importantly, however, the motif is
clear and it was known throughout Phoenicia in the fourth
century. Its overtones must have been either religious
or decorative; they could not have been political.

34. Pietschmann, *Geschichte der Phönizier*, p. 173.
This notion may be more plausible, but not provable. Cf.
Babelon, *Traité*, II, 2, pl. 111.

35. The use of the iconography of 'Ašerah cannot be
denied. At Ugarit, she was called *'atiratu yammi*, "she who
treads upon the sea." Her marine connections are clear.
W.F. Albright (*YGC*, p. 122) has further noted her title in
the Amarna letters, specifically from Zapon in the middle
Jordan Valley: there 'Ašerah, as the "lion lady" (*labi'tu*)
was equated with *tannittu*, "the dragon lady," **Tannit*.
F.M. Cross (*CMHE*, pp. 32-33) has drawn attention to the
parallel epithets *rabbat 'atiratu yammi*, "the lady who
treads upon the sea (dragon)" from Ugarit, and *dat batni*,
"lady of the serpent" from the Proto-Sinaitic texts.
Another epithet of 'Ašerah, known from Ugarit (*CTA* 14.4.197,
16.1, 16.11, 16.22, etc.) and from Egypt, was *Qudšu*,
"holiness." See I.E.S. Edwards, "A Relief of Qudshu-Astarte-
Anath in the Winchester College Collection," *JNES* 14 (1955)
49-51; and *YGC*, pp. 121-122. Edwards described the goddess'
headdress as depicted upon the reliefs (where she stands
nude on a lion holding one or more serpents) as follows:

> The goddess...is represented on the Berlin stela
> wearing on her head the wig of Ḥathor surmounted by
> a naos with volutes and at the top of the naos are
> the disk and crescent.... Such an elaborate headdress
> is, however, exceptional; as a rule, the naos is
> omitted and the wig is surmounted either by a simple

disk and crescent or by a member which, in the
Hathor capital, forms the abacus. In some cases
this member is surmounted by the disk and crescent.
(Edwards, pp. 49-50)

The three goddesses, Astarte, 'Ašerah, and ʿAnat, were
confused on this relief, so that they appear to have
syncretistically merged into one. On the Yeḥawmilk stela
(*ANEP*, no. 477) the Baʿlat-Gubl is also represented as
Ḥathor, with the characteristic headdress. Thus, the
Baʿlat-Gubl may have been some kind of a syncretistic
product of a merger of these three other goddesses, or
some combination of them. Cf. John Boardman, "Pyramidal
Stamp Seals in the Persian Empire," *Iran* 8 (1970) 26, 29,
pls. 2-3; scenes with a bird of prey tearing a carcass
have been found from Greece to Syria (their origin?).

36. We have already alluded to this syncretism or
merger. To base an argument, however, on the violence
depicted in the vulture scene, as Pietschmann would like,
is very speculative. With the confusion between the
goddesses, almost any interpretation may be suggested.
Cf. W. Helck, *Die Beziehungen Ägyptens zu Vorderasien im 3.
und 2. Jahrtausend v. Chr.* (Wiesbaden: O. Harrassowitz,
1962), p. 500; and R. Stadelmann, *Syrisch-palästinensische
Gottheiten in Ägypten, Probleme der Ägyptologie*, W. Helck,
ed. (Leiden: E.J. Brill, 1967), p. 98: "Die Astarte-
Darstellungen sind geprägt durch das Vorbild der ägyptischen
Hathor." On the "lion lady," see H.T. Bossert, *Ein
hethitisches Königssiegel* (Berlin: Archäologischen
Instituts des deutschen Reiches, 1944), pp. 260-261.

37. A. Gardiner, *Egyptian Grammar*, 3rd ed. (London:
Oxford University Press, 1969), p. 469. See also E.F. Wente,
"Tutankhamun and his World," *Treasurers of Tutankhamun*,
K.S. Gilbert, ed. (New York: Metropolitan Museum of Art,
1976), p. 133.

38. The Egyptian mother goddess, *mwt*, was also known
as, or depicted with, a vulture. See O. Keller, *Die antike
Tierwelt*, Vol. 2, p. 32. In the Persian period, the
vulture had some significance to the Persians; perhaps as
a borrowed symbol from Egypt or from Babylon, the vulture
appears to have been a symbol for kingship. As the eagle
came to dominate in later times, "vorher in der babylonisch-
assyrischen Welt der Geier dominierte....Das persische
Siegs- und Königszeichen,...auf dem Siegelzylinder des Darius
war ein grosser Geier mit ausgebreiteten Schwingen und wie
so vieles andere eine Schöpfung der Ägypter." (Keller, pp.
35-36. Evidence to back this point, unfortunately, is meager.
Cf. Babelon, *Traité*, II, 2, pl. 111; Babelon, *Catalogue de
la collection de Luynes*, vol. 3, pls. 105-106. Variation
on the scene is evident in the coins struck by Mazday in
Tarsus, where a lion fights either a bull or a ram in issues
from the same mint. See G.F. Hill, *Catalogue of the Greek
Coins of Lycaonia, Isauria, and Cilicia* (London: The Trustees
of the British Museum, 1900), Catalogue of the Greek Coins in
the British Museum, Vol. 21, pls. 30-31. Fernande Hölscher,

in *Die Bedeutung archaischer Tierkampfbilder* (Würzburg:
Konrad Triltsch, 1972), pp. 63-67, has argued that these
scenes began as early as the eighth and seventh centuries
in monumental grave architectural situations, wherein the
lion functioned as a watcher over the burial. From this
function there developed the use of animals to watch over
sacred areas architecturally (pp. 75-82). The slaying of
steers or stags emphasized the *Wildheit* (p. 98) of the lions
as guardians of the shrines. There could, therefore, be
some connection with the Byblian cult and these combat
scenes. John Boardman has classified these combat scenes
in his *Archaic Greek Gems* (London: Thames and Hudson, 1968),
pp. 122-135; he notes that the use of the lion, rather than
the panther, usually denotes the "Egyptian-Phoenician"
type (p. 129). This is the case of Byblos.

39. Naster, "La technique des revers partiellement
incus de monnaies phéniciennes," p. 510. The incuse
technique was used in the sixth century (ca. 550-510 B.C.E.)
in southern Italy: see C.M. Kraay, *Archaic and Classical
Greek Coins*, pp. 163-164. Phoenician colonists may have
known these coins and introduced them into the mainland.
Our thanks to Dr. Margaret Thompson for this suggestion.

40. The British Museum has a double šeqel of 'Addirmilk,
numbered "CG Addenda 7, 10-8-9." The coin is, as yet,
unpublished, and will be discussed below.

41. *IGCH*, no. 1515; and Dunand, *Fouilles de Byblos*,
Vol. 2, p. 68; Vol. 1, pp. 408ff.

42. Babelon, *Traité*, II, 2, no. 863.

43. This coin is unpublished, and is numbered "1974,
4-16-1" in the collections of the British Museum.

44. Babelon, *Catalogue de la collection de Luynes*,
Vol. 3, no. 3155.

45. A brief discussion of the murex shell appears
in chapter 2 above.

46. According to Edith Porada, this scene, in which
lions kill either a bull or a goat, is "one of the stock
motifs of Mesopotamian art, the theme became stereotyped
after the Middle Assyrian period." E. Porada, *The Collection
of the Pierpont Morgan Library* (New York: Pantheon Books,
1968), Corpus of Ancient Near Eastern Seals in North
American Collections, nos. 842-843, and p. 105. Cf. G.
Perrot and C. Chipiez, *History of Art in Phoenicia and its
Dependencies*, W. Armstrong, trans. (London: Chapman and
Hall, 1885), Vol. 2, pp. 405 and 421, figs. 348-349; a
shield, an engraved ornament, and an engraved ostrich egg
bear witness to our type. G.M.A. Richter, in *Engraved Gems
of the Greeks and Etruscans* (London: Phaidon, 1968), has
catalogued examples of this animal combat dating from the
seventh through the fifth centuries. See her examples
nos. 16-17, 194-197, and 379-380.

47. The motifs are very old and complex, defying precise categorization. Thus, "borrowing" becomes a most imprecise concept, especially when dealing with cross-cultural, iconographic motifs. Of greater importance, however, is the form of the inscription used by 'Ēlpaʿol, for it parallels one used by Mazday in Cilicia, which read in Aramaic, "Mazday, who is over ''Abernahara'' and Cilicia." These coins date to the period following 361/360 B.C.E. and may aid us in dating these Byblian coins. See Hill, *BMC Lycaonia, Isauria, and Cilicia*, p. 170.

48. Cf. *PNPPI*, p. 236. An example like this one is in the Berlin cabinet; see Imhoof-Blumer, *Monnaies grecques*, p. 441, no. 10, pl. H.16; and Babelon, *Traité*, II, 2, no. 866. The form of the abbreviation is in keeping with the rules of the Phoenician language.

49. On the sixteenth šeqels, the flan was too small for the engraver to add the inscription to the type. Cf. Babelon, *Traité*, II, 2, no. 876.

50. *PNPPI*, p. 61; and G.A. Cook, *A Textbook of North-Semitic Inscriptions* (Oxford: Oxford University Press, 1903), p. 149, B9. The verb is to be vocalized as *paʿol*, in the 3rd masculine singular, Qal perfect form. Predicate elements in the perfect are discussed by Benz, *PNPPI*, pp. 210ff.

51. *PNPPI*, pp. 266 and 393.

52. A paucity of paleographical material has rendered a closer dating of the script impossible. See Peckham's discussions in *DLPS*, chapter 2, "Byblos."

53. *DLPS*, p. 53.

54. The griffin is a very common motif from Mesopotamian and Syrian art; see Harden, *The Phoenicians*, pp. 183 and 206, pl. 109d. Recent discoveries in the Wâdî ed-Dâliyeh have shed additional light on this type. On several bullae associated with the Dâliyeh papyri, the griffin is seen with wings, lion's head, and ox horn, much like the griffin on our thirty-second šeqel. See F.M. Cross, "The Papyri and their Historical Implications," *Discoveries in the Wâdî ed-Dâliyeh* (AASOR 41 [1974]), P.W. and N.L. Lapp, eds. (Cambridge, MA: ASOR, 1974), pp. 28-29, pls. 62-63. The griffin on seal no. 4 is fighting the Persian king (or hero) in a scene known from the coinage of Sidon. Seals 3A, 11B, and 12 (all on pl. 63) appear to have representations of griffins also. Importantly, these sealings may be dated from their context and the Aramaic script of the papyri to ca. 354-335 B.C.E. This date is close to that of our coins. See G.F. Hill, "Alexander the Great and the Persian Lion-Gryphon," *Journal of Hellenic Studies* 43 (1923) 156-161

55. R. Dussaud, *Les découvertes de Ras Shamra (Ugarit) et l'ancien testament* (Paris: Librairie orientaliste Paul Geuthner, 1937), p. 40: "Il est difficile de pousser plus loin les identifications, mais on peut présumer que les

luttes d'animaux, dans lesquelles semblent intervenir des
êtres mythiques à forme humaine, se rapportent aux concep-
tions des Phéniciens, qui envisageaient la succession des
saisons comme la conséquence de combats d'où les dieux
sortaient vainquers tour à tour." See Boardman, "Pyramidal
Stamp Seals," pp. 26-29, pls. 1-3; and Barnett, "Phoenician
and Syrian Ivory Carving," p. 11, pl. 10.

56. *KAI* 11; M. Dunand, *Fouilles de Byblos*, Vol. 1,
no. 1142, pl. 33; also Dunand, "Inscription phénicienne de
Byblos," *Kêmi* 4 (1931) 151-156, pl. 10; and J. Friedrich's
remarks in "Eine phönizische Inschrift späterer Zeit aus
Byblos," *Orientalistische Literaturzeitung* 6 (1935) 348-350.
The sarcophagus was not found *in situ*, with probable secondary usage. We agree with Peckham (*DLPS*, p. 54), however,
that there is little doubt that this 'Uzziba'l is to be
equated with the minting authority of the same name. The
date of the inscription — the first half of the fourth
century — is in perfect agreement.

57. The name is in the predicate-subject form of the
usual Phoenician nominal sentence name; '*z*, although known
in both positions, is in the predicate here. *PNPPI*, p. 222.
A variant vocalization might be 'Ozba'l.

58. *PNPPI*, p. 374; Assurbanipal, ii. 82.

59. 'Αζβαλος is known from Herodotus 7.98; Arrian
(2.24.5) mentions a similar name, spelling it 'Αζεμιλκος.
The first person singular possessive appears warranted by
these vocalizations. See *PNPPI*, p. 374.

60. Dunand, *Fouilles de Byblos*, Vol. 1, p. 407, nos.
6292-6307; *DLPS*, p. 49. Over two hundred silver šeqels of
kings 'Uzziba'l, 'Addirmilk, and 'Iyyēn'ēl were found in
Dunand's excavations.

Note also several small coins mentioned by Hill (*BMC
Phoenicia*, p. lxviii), which were originally published in
O. Blau, "'Azubal König von Byblos," *Numismatische Zeitschrift*
8 (1876) 231. The coins may be described as follows:
   a. OBV: Bearded head, to r.
       REV: ᴧо above; forepart of seahorse, below.
   b. OBV: Murex shell.
       REV: (ᴎ) о, below; forepart of seahorse, above.
Both coins are apparently from Byblos. They are probably
small denominations issued under 'Uzziba'l in the years
ca. 365-363 B.C.E. when parts of Phoenicia were in revolt.
The bearded head, by analogy with the coins of 'Abd'aštart I
of Sidon, was the head of the local king. No other examples
of these types are known.

61. Sixteen šeqels like this one were found in Dunand's
hoard (n. 60 above); all of them were extensively worn.

62. Peckham (*DLPS*, p. 50) has suggested the possibility
of a king whose name began with *zayin*, since this letter is
visible. His conjecture is for a name such as *ZKR* given the

space limitations of the flan. The coin was struck
slightly off-center, however, so that reading of 'Uzziba'l
is probably to be preferred.

63. The coin is numbered "CG Addenda 7, 10-8-9" and
is in London. Hill did not know the coin when the catalogue
was published.

64. The writer examined a coin like this one in the
de Luynes collection (no. 3148), housed in the Bibliothèque
nationale, Paris. Two more examples are now in the British
Museum, both weighing 13.10 grams: one is from the 1947
Byblian hoard and the other is merely numbered "1951, 10-7-9."
The latter was struck from very badly worn dies, with
numerous die breaks visible on the obverse. No inscriptions
appear on the obverse, and the bull is *not* shown in incuse.

65. We have reconstructed the abbreviation as אך for
'Addirmilk. It is clear the 'Iyyēn'ēl reused the obverse
dies of his predecessor without altering them in any way.
The inscription of 'Addirmilk is partially off flan. Only
reverse dies were made for the sixteenth šeqels. On the
šeqel dies, the obverse inscription was probably rubbed out
by the die cutters; the wear exhibited by the coins accounts
for this action. Hill (*BMC Phoenicia*, p. 96) studied the
die links between the obverse dies. The *'alep* is the most
persuasive piece of evidence.

66. Arrian, *Anabasis*, 2.20.1.

67. No examples of the abbreviation על are known; the
reuse of the obverse dies made this highly improbable. The
name combines the theophoric element *'ēl* with a D-stem
perfect form denominative from *'-y-n*, being an intensive
of "to see." *PNPPI*, pp. 171 and 377.

68. Babelon, *Traité*, II, 2, no. 873; עינל.

69. *PNPPI*, p. 261. A common phrase was *b'l 'dr*
(pp. 261-262); see 2 Kings 17:31.

70. Cf. J.-G. Février, "À propos de Ba'al Addir,"
Semitica 2 (1949) 21-28; and T. Klauser, ed., *Reallexikon
für Antike und Christentum*, Vol. 1 (Stuttgart: Hiersemann,
1950), p. 1084; cf. H.W. Haussig, ed., *Wörterbuch der
Mythologie, Götter und Mythen im Vorderen Orient* (Stuttgart:
E. Klett, 1965), p. 270.

71. *BMC Phoenicia*, pp. lxii and 96; Babelon, *Traité*,
II, 2, pp. 539-542, in which Babelon completely rearranged
the order, with 'Addirmilk before 'Uzziba'l and 'Iyyēn'ēl.

72. These coins were struck from new dies. The sign
of Tannit was this king's addition, and may have meant that
her cult was active in Byblos in the fourth century. Cf.
Babelon, *Traité*, II, 2, nos. 874-875.

73. Babelon, *Traité*, II, 2, no. 877-878.

74. The first letter of each word was used in the abbreviations.

75. G.F. Hill, *Catalogue of the Greek Coins of Cyprus*, Catalogue of the Greek Coins in the British Museum, Vol. 24 (London: Trustees of the British Museum, 1904), p. xxxix and pl. 19.9. Tannit's cult, however, was practiced on the Phoenician mainland, and not just in the western colonies. See, for example, M. Dothan, "A Sign of Tanit from Tel ʿAkko," *IEJ* 24 (1974) 44-49; this example was found on a sherd of a "large pottery vessel" in a stratum dating to the Hellenistic period (second century B.C.E.). The sign of Tannit was also recently found upon a lead weight at ʾAšdōd-Yam and on a piece of glass from the Phoenician harbor town of Sarepta: see E. Linder, "A Cargo of Phoenicio-Punic Figurines," *Archaeology* 26 (1973) 184-185 (several figurines had the sign on them); J.B. Pritchard, "Sarepta," *Bible et terre sainte* 157 (1974) 4-14; Pritchard, *Sarepta: A Preliminary Report on the Iron Age* (Philadelphia: The University Museum, University of Pennsylvania, 1975), fig. 59.2. An excellent study on the origin of the sign of Tannit and its various forms is in Ronzevalle, "Notes et études d'archéologie orientale," *MUSJ* 16 (1932) 33-48, pl. 5.

76. F.M. Cross has argued for the derivation of the name *Tannit* from *tannin*, "serpent." It is a very old name, "surviving only on the fringes of the Canaanite realm (Ugarit, Šamʾāl, Sinai, Carthage, and the western Mediterranean." (*CMHE*, pp. 32-33). Now, however, Pritchard has found an inscription on an ivory plaque in Sarepta, dedicating an image, or statue, to Tannit-ʿAštart — *ltnt ʿštrt*. See J.B. Pritchard, *Recovering Sarepta, A Phoenician City* (Princeton: Princeton University Press, 1978), pp. 104-107. This additional datum parallels an inscription from Carthage: *lrbt l ʿštrt wltnt blbnn*, "to the ladies, ʿAštart and Tannit in Lebanon" (*CMHE*, p. 30). The two deities are paired, with temples of their own, strongly suggesting, for example, that at Tas Silg the temples were originally dedicated to both Tannit and ʿAštart, and perhaps to the triad, ʾĒl and his wives (*CMHE*, p. 30, n. 104). Our thanks to F.M. Cross for the information concerning the new inscription from Sarepta. In short, the evidence for a cult of Tannit on the mainland is increasing year by year. It is no longer surprising, therefore, to have found the sign of Tannit on these coins. For an example from Sidon, see J.E. Reinach, *Mission de Phénicie* (Paris: Imprimerie impériale, 1864), p. 431.

77. See Bellinger, *Essays on the Coinage of Alexander the Great*, pp. 54-55 and 84. Within a few years of the conquest by Alexander, the mint began issuing coins on his types.

Conclusions

Coins struck in the Levant before Alexander the Great have been ignored by Classicists and have tended to remain numismatic mysteries through the years. Recent archaeological discoveries have made it possible to undertake a new study of these coins and their mints.

Four mints struck coins in pre-Alexandrine Phoenicia — Sidon, Tyre, Aradus, and Byblos. These mints were dependent upon each other and other Levantine, Syrian, and Palestinian cities for their general economic well-being, trade, and communications. Complex series of coins were issued in the fifth and fourth centuries B.C.E. which have historical as well as artistic and religious import for the study of the ancient Near East.

The most important Phoenician city of the period was Sidon, which served as the political and military leader of the Phoenician city-states. Recent epigraphical finds have greatly increased the precision with which the earliest coins of Sidon may be dated and typologically organized. Beginning with the coins struck under the last kings of the dynasty of 'Ešmun'azor, Sidonian kings struck coins until the coming of Alexander in 332/331 B.C.E. By ca. 435 the Sidonian types were standardized with a galley over waves on the obverse and a chariot drawn by horses with a driver and the King of Persia riding inside on the reverse. Numerous parallels for this scene are known from the glyptic art of Achaemenian Persia.

Beginning with King Ba'lšallim I in ca. 420, royal names were abbreviated on the coin flans using the appropriate conventions of the Phoenician language. Complete series from double šeqels through the minute thirty-second and sixty-fourth šeqels are extant in some cases. The reverse types were altered to include the supplicant king of Sidon following the Persian king's chariot: The cult of the Great King played an increasingly important role in Sidon.

With the reign of 'Abd'aštart I, in about 372 B.C.E., however, rebellion broke out. As Persian power waned the

Phoenician cities joined together into a loosely confederated
league bent on gaining independence from Persepolis. The
types which had consistently been struck in Sidon were
altered to depict the head of the rebellious local monarch.
These coins are dated to the period 364-361 when the revolt
led by Sidon was at its peak. The Sidonians also changed
the weight standard for their coinage from the Phoenician
to the Attic. This commercial maneuver would greatly
enhance Sidon's foreign trade with Greece and East Greece,
if allowed to stand.

Persian retribution was swift and harsh. Sidon's mint
was seized by the Persian government; from 361 until 358
B.C.E. all coins were struck in the name of Mazday, the
Persian satrap of Cilicia and "Abernahara." Under yet
another local king in the late 350's, Sidon again revolted.
This time it was joined by Egypt, Cyprus, and most of
Phoenicia and Palestine. The military campaign which
defeated the rebels destroyed many cities and towns in the
Levant. Diodorus Siculus noted the peculiar maliciousness
which colored Sidonian-Persian relations in this era.
With the collapse of the Sidonian economy, Mazday again
issued coins attempting to maintain the commerce which was
so vital to Persian economic stability.

Tyre was relegated to second position behind Sidon in
the Persian period. Her coins emphasized motifs such as
the dolphin and the murex shell — symbolic of the city's
famed purple dye industry. The owl, with crook and flail
(Egyptian symbols of kingship and authority), became the
standard reverse motif on most denominations. On the
obverse a bearded deity, shooting a bow, and riding on a
winged seahorse above the sea was standardized. The iconographic detail of this representation of divinity is difficult
to identify with precision. The deity's association with
Tyre's maritime interests is clear, however.

The Tyrian shift from the Phoenician to the Attic
standard occurred in the mid-fourth century; this change
has attracted some attention from numismatists and historians
in recent years. Some have claimed that the alteration must
have coincided with the forced introduction of Alexander's

own standard. Others have argued that this shift occurred
before the Macedonian conquest. The evidence concerning
Alexander's monetary policies in conquered lands as well
as the available epigraphic and archaeological data
indicate that the pre-Alexandrine date for the shift is to
be preferred. Phoenician eyes were definitely turning
away from Persia toward the West.

The seaport of Aradus was the northernmost Phoenician
city of prominence in the Persian period. Ancient sources
are regrettably mute, however, concerning its commercial,
political, and military life in this period. A series of
coins was issued late in the fifth century depicting a
marine deity, part man and part fish. The reverse of these
coins bore a war galley with the usual accoutrements. This
mint used the Persian standard, which was lighter than the
usual Phoenician standard which was used at first by the
other coastal mints. The identity of the deity shown on
the Aradian series has been debated for over sixty-five
years. No positive identification is possible given our
present understanding of Canaanite religion in the third
quarter of the first millenium B.C.E.

Inscriptions first appeared at Aradus on the coins
ca. 410 B.C.E.; the two Phoenician letters, 𐤀𐤌, may be
read as an abbreviation for *mamlakt 'arvad* ("the kingdom,
or government, of Aradus"). Thus Aradus alone among the
Phoenician mints sought to identify its coins with an
ethnic. Abbreviations of kings' names were commonly used
in the other cities, especially at Sidon and Byblos.

Byblos was also a small city during the Persian period.
Its coinage was limited in scope and may have served as a
supplement for the larger, regional currencies of Tyre and
Sidon. Beginning before the end of the fifth century, its
coins typically depicted a galley carrying warriors above
a seahorse on the obverse; on the reverse was a lion
standing over the carcass of a bull or stag in the common
scene of animal combat. Lengthy Phoenician inscriptions
giving the name of the king and his title, *milk Gubl*
("king of Byblos"), appear on these and later issues. The
reverse motifs are symbolic of the cult of the Ba'lat-Gubl,

the chief goddess of Byblos at the time. Certain syncretistic elements from her cult indicate influences from both
the cults of 'Ašerah and 'Anat.

The coinages of all these Phoenician cities were used
extensively in the commerce of the period. Persian
economic growth was controlled by the trade and commercial
activity of the Phoenician city-states and the cities on
the trade routes inland from the Mediterranean which the
Phoenician ports served. The coinage provides a historical
and religious backdrop for the developments which trans-
pired in the waning years of Persian hegemony preceding the
conquest of Alexander the Great.

Plate 6: 1. Tyre, coin no. 37   8.79 g.
          2. Tyre, coin no. 37   8.75 g.
          3. Tyre, coin no. 37   8.51 g.
          4. Aradus, coin no. 2   3.22 g.
          5. Aradus, coin no. 7   2.18 g.
          6. Aradus, coin no. 8   0.68 g.
          7. Aradus, coin no. 10   10.35 g.
          8. Aradus, coin no. 11   3.24 g.
          9. Aradus, coin no. 11   3.26 g.

Plate 7: 1. Aradus, coin no. 13   1.18 g.
          2. Aradus, coin no. 15   10.79 g.
          3. Aradus, coin no. 24   0.96 g.
          4. Aradus, coin no. 26   10.31 g.
          5. Aradus, coin no. 26   10.47 g.
          6. Aradus, coin no. 26   10.45 g.
          7. Aradus, coin no. 27   3.35 g.
          8. Aradus, coin no. 29   10.04 g.
          9. Aradus, coin no. 29   10.22 g.

Plate 8: 1. Byblos, coin no. 1   9.31 g.
          2. Byblos, coin no. 2   2.74 g.
          3. Byblos, coin no. 3   1.39 g.
          4. Byblos, coin no. 6   2.86 g.
          5. Byblos, coin no. 7   0.90 g.
          6. Byblos, coin no. 10   3.15 g.
          7. Byblos, coin no. 13   0.54 g.
          8. Byblos, coin no. 14   13.06 g.
          9. Byblos, coin no. 15   0.67 g.

Plate 9: 1. Byblos, coin no. 16   0.67 g.
          2. Byblos, coin no. 20   13.14 g.
          3. Byblos, coin no. 21   0.70 g. (variant)

Figure 1: Sidon, coin no. 32   17.00 g. (approx.)

ILLUSTRATIONS

Plate 1

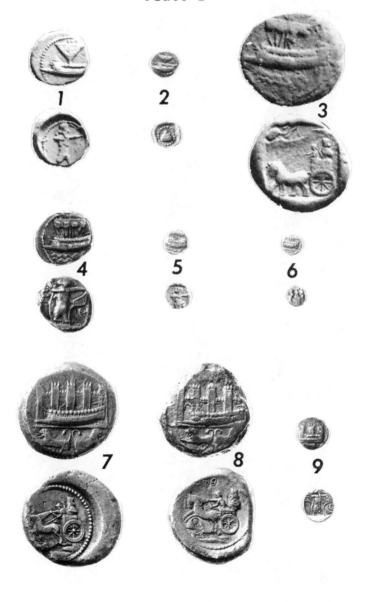

Plate 2

Plate 3

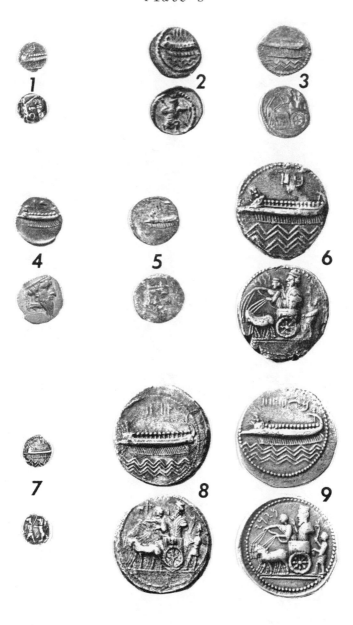

Plate 4

Plate 5

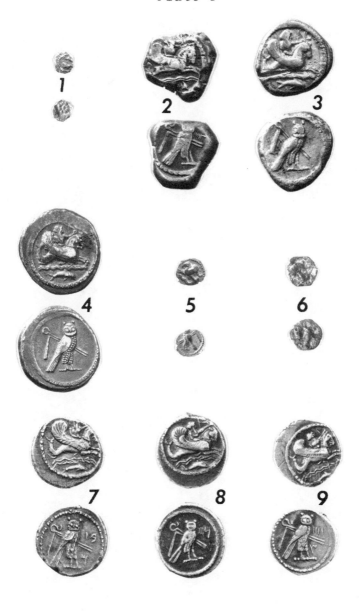

Plate 6

Plate 7

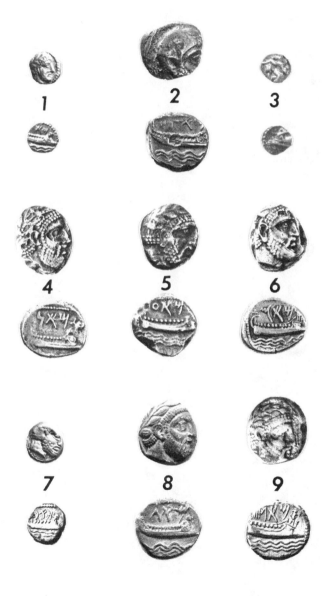

Plate 8

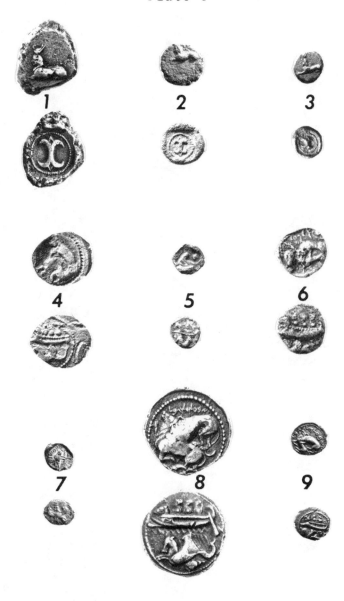

Plate 9

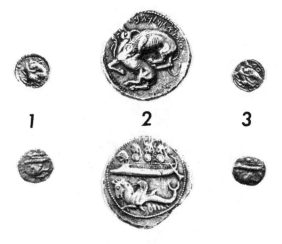

1   2   3

Figure 1

BIBLIOGRAPHY

Bibliography

Aimé-Giron, N. "Un naos phénicien de Sidon," *Bulletin de l'Institut français d'archéologie orientale* 34 (1933) 31-42.

Akurgal, Ekrem. *Die Kunst anatoliens von Homer bis Alexander.* Berlin: Walter de Gruyter and Co., 1961.

Albright, W.F. "A Votive Stele Erected by Ben-Hadad I of Damascus to the God Melcarth," *BASOR* 87 (1942) 23-29.

_____. *Archaeology and the Religion of Israel.* 5th ed. Garden City, NY: Doubleday Anchor Books, 1968.

_____. "Baal-Zephon," in *Festschrift Alfred Bertholet zum 80. Geburtstag.* Edited by W. Baumgartner, *et al.* Tübingen: J.C.B. Mohr (Paul Siebeck), 1950. Pp. 1-14.

_____. *From Stone Age to Christianity.* New York: Doubleday Anchor Books, 1957.

_____. "Light on the Jewish State in Persian Times," *BASOR* 53 (1934) 20-22.

_____. "New Light on the Early History of Phoenician Colonization," *BASOR* 83 (1942) 14-22.

_____. *The Archaeology of Palestine.* Baltimore: Penguin Books, 1949.

_____. "The Babylonian Matter in the Predeuteronomic Primeval History (JE) in Gen 1-11.2," *JBL* 58 (1939) 91-103.

_____. *The Biblical Period from Abraham to Ezra.* New York: Harper and Row, 1963.

_____. "The Evolution of the West Semitic Deity 'An-'Anat-'Atrâ," *The American Journal of Semitic Languages and Literatures* 41 (1925) 73-101. "Further Observations on the Name 'Anat-'Atrah," *American Journal of Semitic Languages and Literatures* 41 (1925) 283-285. "Note on the Goddess 'Anat," *American Journal of Semitic Languages and Literatures* 43 (1927) 233-236.

_____. *Yahweh and the Gods of Canaan.* Garden City, NY: Doubleday and Co., 1969.

al-Salihi, Wathiq. "Hercules-Nergal at Hatra," *Iraq* 33 (1971) 113-115.

Anson, L. *Numismata graeca.* London: L. Anson, 1910.

Astour, M.C. "Some New Divine Names from Ugarit," *JAOS* 86 (1966) 277-284.

_____. "The Origin of the Terms 'Canaan,' 'Phoenician,' and 'Purple,'" *JNES* 24 (1965) 346-350.

Avi-Yonah, M. "Syrian Gods at Ptolemais-Accho," *IEJ* 9 (1959) 1-12.

Babelon, E. *Catalogue de la collection de Luynes*, Vol. 3. Paris: Florange et Ciani, 1930.

_____. *Catalogue des monnaies grecques: Les Perses achéménides, les satrapes et les dynastes de leur empire: Chypre et Phénicie.* Paris: Follin et Feuerdent, 1893.

_____. "Le Cabinet des médailles pendant la guerre. II. Les accroissements et acquisitions. A. Monnaies antiques," *RN* 2nd ser., 23 (1920) 111-115.

_____. *Manuel of Oriental Antiquities.* Revised edition. London: H. Grevel and Company, 1906.

_____. *Traité des monnaies grecques et romaines.* Vol. II, Part 2. Paris: E. Leroux, 1910.

Barag, D., "The Effects of the Tennes Rebellion on Palestine," *BASOR* 183 (1966) 6-12.

Baramki, Dimitri. *Phoenicia and the Phoenicians.* Beirut: Khayats, 1961.

Baramki, J. "Coin Hoards from Palestine, II: 1. A Hoard of Silver Coins of Sidon and Alexander from Khirbet el-Kerak," *QDAP* 11 (1944) 86-90.

Barnett, R.D. *A Catalogue of the Nimrud Ivories.* London: British Museum, 1957.

_____. "Early Shipping in the Near East," *Antiquity* 32 (1958) 220-230.

Baudissin, W.W.G. *Adonis und Esmun.* Leipzig: J.C. Hinrichs'sche Verlag, 1911.

Bellinger, A.R. *Essays on the Coinage of Alexander the Great.* Numismatic Series No. 11. New York: American Numismatic Society, 1963.

Bengston, Hermann. *The Greeks and the Persians from the Sixth to the Fourth Centuries.* Delacorte World History. New York: Delacorte Press, 1968.

Benz, F.L. *Personal Names in the Phoenician and Punic Inscriptions.* Rome: Pontifical Biblical Institute, 1972.

Betlyon, J.W. "A New Chronology for the Pre-Alexandrine Coinage of Sidon," *ANS Museum Notes* 21 (1976) 11-35, pls. 2-4.

Bey, Hamdy and Reinach, T. *Une nécropole royale à Sidon.* Paris: E. Leroux, 1892-1896.

Bisi, A.M. *Le stele puniche.* Rome: Universita di Roma, 1967.

Bivar, A.D.H. "A Hoard of Ingot-currency of the Median Period from Nūsh-i Jān, near Malayir," *Iran* 9 (1971) 97-111.

Blau, O. " Azubal König von Byblos," *Numismatische Zeitschrift* 8 (1876) 229-232.

_____. "Barsine, Gemahlin Alexanders des Grossen," *NZ* 8 (1876) 234-237.

Boardman, J. "Pyramidal Stamp Seals in the Persian Empire," *Iran* 8 (1970) 19-44.

_____. *The Greeks Overseas.* Baltimore: Penguin Books, 1964.

Borger, Riekele. *Die Inschriften Asarhaddons Königs von Assyrien.* Graz: E. Weidner, 1956.

Bossert, Helmut Th. *Altanatolien.* Berlin: Verlag Ernst Wasmuth, 1942.

_____. *Altsyrien.* Tübingen: E. Wasmuth, 1951.

_____. *Ein hethitisches Königssiegel.* Berlin: Archäologischen Instituts des deutschen Reiches, 1944.

Brandis, J. *Das Münz- Mass- und Gewichtswesen in Vorderasien bis auf Alexander den grossen.* Berlin: Verlag von Wilhelm Hertz, 1866.

Cassuto, U. *The Goddess Anath.* Trans. I. Abrahams. Jerusalem: Magnes Press and the Hebrew University, 1971.

Clemen, Carl. *Die phönikische Religion nach Philo von Byblos.* In Mitteilungen der vorderasiatisch-aegyptischen Gesellschaft 42. Leipzig: J.C. Hinrichs Verlag, 1939.

Clifford, R.J. *The Cosmic Mountain in Canaan and the Old Testament.* Cambridge, MA: Harvard University Press, 1972.

Contenau, G. *La civilisation phénicienne.* Paris: Payot, 1926.

Cook, A.B. *Zeus: A Study in Ancient Religion.* Vols. 1-2. New York: Biblo and Tannen Reprint (Cambridge: Cambridge University Press, 1914), 1965.

Cook, G.A. *A Textbook of North-Semitic Inscriptions*.
Oxford: Oxford University Press, 1903.

Cook, R.M. *Greek Painted Pottery*. 2nd ed. London:
Methuen and Co., 1972.

Cook, S.A. *The Religion of Ancient Palestine in the Light
of Archaeology*. The Schweich Lectures of the British
Academy, 1925. London: Oxford University Press, 1930.

Corpus inscriptionum semiticarum. Ab Academia inscriptionum
et litterarum humaniorum. Paris: e Republicae
typographeo, 1881-.

Cross, F.M. "A Reconstruction of the Judean Restoration,"
JBL 94 (1975) 4-18.

_____. "Aspects of Samaritan and Jewish History in Late
Persian and Hellenistic Times," *HTR* 59 (1966) 201-211.

_____. *Canaanite Myth and Hebrew Epic*. Cambridge, MA:
Harvard University Press, 1973.

_____. "Jar Inscriptions from Shiqmona," *IEJ* 18 (1968)
226-233.

_____. "Judean Stamps," *EI* 9 (1969), W.F. Albright Volume,
pp. 20-27. Jerusalem, 1969.

_____. "Papyri from the Fourth Century B.C. from Daliyeh,"
New Directions in Biblical Archaeology, ed. D.N.
Freedman and J.C. Greenfield, pp. 45-69. Garden City,
NY: Doubleday Anchor Books, 1969.

_____. "The Discovery of the Samaria Papyri," *BA* 26 (1963)
110-121.

_____. "The Oldest Manuscripts from Qumran," *JBL* 74 (1955)
147-172.

_____. "The Papyri and Their Historical Implications,"
Discoveries in the Wâdî ed-Dâliyeh, ed. Paul and Nancy
Lapp. *AASOR* 41 (1974) 17-29.

Culican, W. "Syrian and Cypriot Cubical Seals," *Levant* 9
(1977) 163-167.

_____. "The Iconography of Some Phoenician Seals and Seal
Impressions," *Australian Journal of Biblical Archaeology*
1 (1968-1971) 50-103.

Cumont, Franz. *Études syriennes*. Paris: August Picarde-
Éditeur, 1917.

Dayton, John. "Money in the Near East before Coinage,"
Berytus 23 (1974) 41-52.

Dolger, J. ΙΧΘΥC, *Der Heilige Fisch in den antiken
Religionen und im Christentum*. Vol. 2. Münster in

Westf.: Verlag der Aschendorffschen, 1922.

Donner, H., and Röllig, W. *Kanaanäische und Aramäische Inschriften.* Vols. 1-3. Wiesbaden: Harrassowitz, 1968-1971.

Dothan, M. "A Sign of Tanit from Tel 'Akko," *IEJ* 24 (1974) 44-49.

Dunand, M. "Byblos, Sidon, Jerusalem. Monuments apparéntes des temps achéménides," *Congress Volume, Rome (Suppl. to VT 17)*, pp. 64-70. Leiden: E.J. Brill, 1969.

_____. *Fouilles de Byblos.* Vols. 1-2. Paris: Librairie d'amérique et d'orient Adrien Maisonneuve, 1939-1958.

_____. "Inscription phénicienne de Byblos," *Kêmi* 4 (1931) 151-156.

_____. "La Defense du front Mediterranéan de l'empire achéménide," *The Role of the Phoenicians in the Interaction of Mediterranean Civilizations*, ed. W.A. Ward, pp. 43-51. Beirut: American University of Beirut, 1968.

_____. "La piscine du trone d'Astarté dans le temple d'Echmoun à Sidon," *BMB* 24 (1971) 19-25.

_____. "Le temple d'Echmoun à Sidon. Essai de Chronologie," *BMB* 26 (1973) 7-25.

_____. "Nouvelles inscriptions phéniciennes du temple d'Echmoun à Bostan ech-Cheikh, près Sidon," *BMB* 18 (1965) 105-109.

_____. "Rapport sur les fouilles de Sidon en 1967-1968," *BMB* 22 (1969) 101-107.

_____. "Sondages archéologiques effectués à Bostan-Ech-Cheikh, près Saida," *Syria* 7 (1926) 1-8.

_____. "Stele araméenne dediée à Melqart," *BMB* 3 (1939) 65-76.

Dussaud, R. "Astarté, Pontos et Ba'al," *Comptes rendus de l'Académie des inscriptions et belles-lettres* (1947) 201-225.

_____. *L'Art phénicien du IIᵉ millénaire.* Paris: Librairie orientaliste Paul Geuthner, 1949.

_____. *Les découvertes de Ras Shamra (Ugarit) et l'ancien testament.* Paris: Librairie orientaliste Paul Geuthner, 1937.

_____. "Melqart," *Syria* 25 (1946-1948) 205-230.

_____. "Melqart, d'après de recents travaux," *Revue de l'histoire des religions* 151 (1957) 10-15.

Edwards, I.E.S. "A Relief of Qudshu-Astarte-Anath in the Winchester College Collection," *JNES* 14 (1955) 49-51, pls. 3-4.

Eiselen, F.C. *Sidon: A Study in Oriental History.* New York: Macmillan, 1907.

Eisen, G.A. *Ancient Oriental Cylinder and Other Seals with a Description of the Collection of Mrs. William H. Moore.* Chicago: University of Chicago Press, 1940.

Eissfeldt, O. "Ba'alšamēm und Jahwe," *ZAW* 16 (1939) 1-31.

_____. *Baal Zaphon, Zeus Kasios und der Durchzug der Israeliten.* Halle: Max Niemeyer Verlag, 1932.

_____. *Sanchunjaton von Beirut und Ilumilku von Ugarit.* Halle: Max Niemeyer Verlag, 1952.

Fantar, Hassine. "Le cavalier marin de Kerkouane," *Africa* 1 (1966) 19-32.

Février, J.-G. "À propos de Ba'al Addir," *Semitica* 2 (1949) 21-28.

_____. "L'ancienne marine phénicienne et les découvertes récentes," *La Nouvelle Clio* 2 (1950) 128-143.

Fick, A. *Die griechischen Personennamen.* Göttingen: Vandenhoeck and Ruprecht, 1874.

Fisher, L.R. *The Claremont Ras Shamra Tablets.* Rome: Pontifical Biblical Institute, 1971.

Fleming, Wallace B. *The History of Tyre.* New York: Columbia University Press, 1915.

Frazer, J.G. *Adonis, Attis, Osiris: Studies in the History of Oriental Religion.* Vol. 1 New York: St. Martin's Press, 1966.

Friedrich, J. "Griechisches und römisches in phönizischen und punischen Gewande," *Festschrift Otto Eissfeldt zum 60. Geburtstage,* ed. J. Fück, pp. 109-124. Halle an der Salle: N. Niemeyer, 1947.

_____, and Röllig, W. *Phönizisch-Punische Grammatik,* Analecta orientalia, vol. 46. Rome: Pontifical Biblical Institute, 1970.

Frothingham, A.L. "Babylonian Origin of Hermes the Snakegod, and of the Caduceus," *AJA* 20 (1916) 175-211.

Frye, R.N. *The Heritage of Persia.* Cleveland: World Publishing, 1963.

Galling, Kurt. "Die syrisch-palästinische Küste nach der Beschreibung bei Pseudo-Skylax," *Studien zur Geschichte Israels im persischen Zeitalters,* pp. 185-209.

Tübingen: J.E. Mohr, 1964.

Gardiner, A. *Egyptian Grammar*. 3rd ed. London: Oxford University Press, 1969.

Gardner, Percy. *A History of Ancient Coinage, 700-300 B.C.* Oxford: Clarendon Press, 1918.

Gaster, Moses. *The Samaritans: Their History, Doctrines and Literature*. The Schweich Lectures of the British Academy, 1923. London: Oxford University Press, 1925.

Gaster, Theodor H. *Thespis: Ritual, Myth and Drama in the Ancient Near East*. Revised edition. New York: Harper Torchbooks, 1966.

Ghirschman, R. *Iran*. Baltimore: Penguin Books, 1954.

_____. *Persia from the Origins to Alexander the Great*, trans. S. Gilbert and J. Emmons. Paris: Thames and Hudson, 1964.

Goedicke, Hans. *The Report of Wenamun*. Baltimore: The Johns Hopkins University Press, 1975.

Goldman, B. "A Luristan Water-Goddess," *Antike Kunst* 3 (1960) 53-57.

Gray, J. "The Canaanite God Horon," *JNES* 8 (1949) 27-34.

Gröndahl, Frauke. *Die Personennamen der Texte aus Ugarit*. Rome: Pontifical Biblical Institute, 1967.

Grose, S.W. *Catalogue of the McClean Collection of Greek Coins*. Vol. 3. Cambridge: Cambridge University Press, 1929.

Halevy, J. *Mélanges d'épigraphie et d'archéologie sémitiques*. Paris: Maisonneuve, 1874.

Harden, Donald. *The Phoenicians*. Baltimore: Pelican Books, 1971.

Harris, Z. *A Grammar of the Phoenician Language*. New Haven: American Oriental Society, 1936.

Head, B.V. *Historia nummorum*. 2nd rev. ed. Oxford: Clarendon Press, 1911.

Helck, W. *Die Beziehungen Ägyptens zu Vorderasien im 3. und 2. Jahrtausend v. Chr.* Wiesbaden: O. Harrassowitz, 1962.

Hemmy, A.S. "The Weight-Standards of Ancient Greece and Persia," *Iraq* 5 (1938) 65-81.

Hill, G. "Adonis, Baal, and Astarte," *The Church Quarterly Review* 66 (1908) 118-141.

164

_____. "Alexander the Great and the Persian Lion-Gryphon," *Journal of Hellenic Studies* 43 (1923) 157-161.

_____. *Catalogue of the Greek Coins of Arabia, Mesopotamia, Persia, Etc.* London: British Museum, 1922.

_____. *Catalogue of the Greek Coins of Cyprus.* London: British Museum, 1904.

_____. *Catalogue of the Greek Coins of Lycaonia, Isauria, and Cilicia.* London: British Museum, 1900.

_____. *Catalogue of the Greek Coins of Palestine.* London: British Museum, 1914.

_____. *Catalogue of the Greek Coins of Phoenicia.* London: British Museum, 1910.

_____. *Historical Greek Coins.* London: Archibald Constable and Company, 1906.

_____. "Notes on the Imperial Persian Coinage," *PEQ* (1919) 116-129.

Howorth, H.H. "The History and Coinage of Artaxerxes III, His Satraps and Dependents," *NC* 4th ser., 3 (1903) 1-46.

Huffmon, H.B. *Amorite Personal Names in the Mari Texts: A Structural and Lexical Study.* Baltimore: The Johns Hopkins University Press, 1965.

Hultsch, Friedrich. *Griechische und Römische Metrologie.* Berlin: Wiedmannsche Buchhandlung, 1882.

Imhoof-Blumer, F. *Kleinasiatische Münzen.* Vol. 2. Vienna: A. Hölder Verlag, 1901-1902.

_____. *Monnaies grecques.* Leipzig: K.F. Koehler, 1883.

Jacobsen, T. *The Treasures of Darkness.* New Haven: Yale University Press, 1976.

Jenkins, G.K. *Ancient Greek Coins.* London: Barrie and Jenkins, 1972.

Jensen, L.B. "Royal Purple of Tyre," *JNES* 22 (1963) 104-113.

Jidejian, N. *Sidon Through the Ages.* Beirut: Dar el-Machreq, 1971.

Judeich, W. *Kleinasiatische Studien.* Marburg: N.G. Elwertsche Verlags-buchhandlung, 1892.

Keller, Otto. *Die Antike Tierwelt.* Leipzig: W. Engelmann Verlag, 1913.

_____. *Tier- und Pflanzenbilder auf Münzen und Gemmen des klassischen Altertums.* Leipzig: B.G. Teuber, 1889.

Kerenyi, C. *Dionysus: Archetypal Image of Indestructible Life*. Princeton: Princeton University Press, 1976.

Kienitz, F.K. *Die politische Geschichte Ägyptens vom 7. bis 4. Jahrhundert vor der Zeitwende*. Berlin: Academie-Verlag, 1953.

Kindler, A. "The Greco-Phoenician Coins Struck in Palestine in the Time of the Persian Empire," *INJ* 2 (1964) 25-27.

_____. "The Mint of Tyre — the Major Source of Silver Coins in Ancient Israel," *EI* 8 (1967) 318-325 (Hebrew).

Klauser, T., ed. *Reallexikon für Antike und Christentum*. Vol. 1. Stuttgart: Hiersemann, 1950.

Kleemann, I. *Der Satrapen-Sarkophag aus Sidon*. Berlin: Gebr. Mann, 1958.

Knight, A.E. *Amentet*. London: Longmans, Green, and Co., 1915.

Kraay, C.M. *Archaic and Classical Greek Coins*. Berkeley and Los Angeles: University of California Press, 1976.

_____. "Hoards, Small Change and the Origin of Coinage," *Journal of Hellenic Studies* 84 (1964) 76-91.

_____. "The Archaic Owls of Athens: Classification and Chronology," *NC* 6th ser., 16 (1956) 43-68.

_____, and Moorey, P.R.S. "Two Fifth Century Hoards from the Near East," *Revue numismatique* 6th ser., 10 (1968) 181-235.

Kraeling, Emil G. *The Brooklyn Museum Aramaic Papyri*. New Haven: Yale University Press for the Brooklyn Museum, 1953.

Langher, S.C. *Contributo alla Storia della Antica Moneta Bronzea in Sicilia*. Milano: Giuffre Editore, 1964.

Lemaire, André. "Le monnayage de Tyr et celui dit d'Akko dans la deuxième moitié du IVe siècle av. J.-C.," *Revue numismatique* 6e series 18 (1976) 11-23.

L'Heureux, C.E. "El and the Rephaim: New Light from *Ugaritica V*." Unpublished Ph.D. dissertation, Harvard University, 1971.

Linder, E. "A Cargo of Phoenicio-Punic Figurines," *Archaeology* 26 (1973) 182-187.

Maury, Alfred. "Recherches sur le nom et le caractère du Neptune phénicien," *Revue archéologique* 5 (1848) 545-556.

Mazar, B. "The Philistines and the Rise of Israel and
   Tyre," *Proceedings of the Israel Academy of Sciences
   and Humanities*. Vol. 1, no. 7, pp. 1-22. Jerusalem,
   1967.

McCarter, K. *The Antiquity of the Greek Alphabet*. Missoula:
   Scholars Press, 1975.

McKeon, J.F.X. "Achaemenian Cloisonné-Inlay Jewelry: An
   Important New Example," *Orient and Occident*, ed.
   H.A. Hoffner, Jr., pp. 109-117. Kevelaer: Butzon
   and Bercker, 1973.

Merker, I.L. "Notes on Abdalonymos and the Dated Alexander
   Coinage of Sidon and Ake," *ANS Museum Notes* 11 (1964)
   13-20.

Meshorer, Y. *Jewish Coins of the Second Temple Period*
   (Hebrew). Tel Aviv: Am Hassefer Publishing, 1966.

_____, and Currier, R.L. *Coins of the Ancient World*.
   Minneapolis: Lerner, 1975.

Miller, P.D., Jr. *The Divine Warrior in Early Israel*.
   Cambridge, MA: Harvard University Press, 1973.

Milne, J.G. "The Coinage of Aradus in the Hellenistic
   Period," *Iraq* 5 (1938) 12-22.

Mionnet, T.E. *Description des médailles antiques, grecques
   et romaines*. Vol. 10, Supplement. Paris: Imprimerie
   de Testu, 1808.

Montalbano, F.J. "Canaanite Dagon: Origin, Nature," *CBQ*
   13 (1951) 381-397.

deMoor, J.C. "Studies in the New Alphabetic Texts from
   Ras Shamra, I," *Ugarit-Forschungen* 1 (1969) 167-175.

Moscati, S. *The World of the Phoenicians*. New York:
   Praeger, 1968.

Mullen, E.T., Jr. "A New Royal Sidonian Inscription,"
   BASOR 216 (1974) 25-30.

Narkiss, M. *Coins of Palestine*. Vol. 2. Jerusalem:
   Jewish Palestine Exploration Society, 1938.   (Hebrew)

Naster, P. "La technique des revers partiellement incus
   de monnaies phéniciennes," *American Numismatic Society
   Centennial Publication*, ed. H. Ingholt, pp. 505-511,
   pl. 28. New York: American Numismatic Society, 1958.

_____. "Le Ba'al de Sidon," *Anadolu Araştirmalari*, pp. 327-
   332. Istanbul: Edebiyat Fakultesi Basimevi, 1965.

_____. "Le developpement des monnayages phéniciens avant
   Alexandre, d'après les trésors," *Proceedings Interna-*

tional Numismatic Convention, Jerusalem, 27-31 December, 1963, pp. 3-24. Tel Aviv: Schocken, 1967.

_____. "Le suivant du char royal sur les doubles statères de Sidon," *RBN* 103 (1957) 1-20.

_____. "Les monnaies phéniciennes: evocation historique d'un grand empire maritime," *Archeologia* 21 (1968) 52-57.

Naveh, J. "The Development of the Aramaic Script," *Proceedings of the Israel Academy of Sciences and Humanities*, Vol. 5, no. 1. Jerusalem: Ahva Press, 1970.

Newell, E.T. "Some Unpublished Coins of Eastern Dynasts," *ANSNNM* 30 (1926) 1ff.

Newell, T. *The Dated Alexander Coinage of Sidon and Ake*. New Haven: Yale University Press, 1916.

Nilsson, M.P. *The Dionysiac Mysteries of the Hellenistic and Roman Age*. Lund: C.W.K. Gleerup, 1957.

Oden, R.A., Jr. "Baʿal Šāmēm and 'Ēl," *CBQ* 39 (1977) 457-473.

_____. *Studies in Lucian's De Syria dea*. Missoula: Scholars Press, 1977.

Oldenberg, U. *The Conflict Between El and Baʿal in Canaanite Religion*. Leiden: E.J. Brill, 1969.

Olmstead, A.T. *History of the Persian Empire*. Chicago: University of Chicago Press, 1948.

Oppenheim, A. Leo. "Essay on Overland Trade in the First Millennium B.C.," *Journal of Cuneiform Studies* 21 (1967) 236-254.

Openheim, M.F. von, *et al. Tell Halaf III: Die Bildwerke*. Berlin: de Gruyter, 1955.

Osten, Hans Henning von der. *Ancient Oriental Seals in the Collection of Mr. Edward T. Newell*. Chicago: University of Chicago Press, 1934.

Peckham, J.B. *The Development of the Late Phoenician Scripts*. Cambridge, MA: Harvard University Press, 1968.

Peitschmann, R. *Geschichte der Phönizier*. G. Grote'sche, 1889.

Perrot, G. and Chipiez, C. *History of Art in Phoenicia and its Dependencies*, trans. W. Armstrong. London: Chapman and Hall, 1885.

Peters, F.E. *The Harvest of Hellenism*. New York: Simon

and Schuster, 1970.

Picard, Colette. "Genèse et évolution des signes de la bouteille et de Tanit à Carthage," *Studi Magrebini* 2 (1968) 77-87, pls. 1-9.

Porada, E. *The Collection of the Pierpont Morgan Library*, in Corpus of Ancient Near Eastern Seals in North American Collections. New York: Pantheon Books, 1968.

Pritchard, J.B. *Sarepta*. *A Preliminary Report on the Iron Age*. Philadelphia: The University Museum, 1975.

_____. "Sarepta," *Bible et Terre Sainte* 157 (1974) 97-104.

Radet, George. "Alexandre en Syrie les offres de paix que lui fit Darius," *Mélanges syriens offerts à Monsieur René Dussaud*, Vol. 1. Bibliothèque archéologique et historique 30 (1939) 235-247.

Rainey, A.F. "The Satrapy 'Beyond the River,'" *Australian Journal of Biblical Archaeology* 1 (1968-1971) 51-78.

Rawlinson, G. *History of Phoenicia*. London: Longmans, Green, and Co., 1889.

Reifenberg, A. "A Hebrew Shekel of the Fifth Century, B.C.," *PEQ* (1943) 100-104.

_____. *Ancient Jewish Coins*. Jerusalem: Rubin Press, 1973.

Renan, E. *Mission de Phénicie*. Paris: Imprimerie nationale, 1864.

Ridgeway, W. *The Origin of Metallic Currency and Weight Standards*. Cambridge: Cambridge University Press, 1892.

Ronzevalle, S. "La couronne (Nemapa?) d'Atargatis à Delos," *MUSJ* 22 (1939) 110-121.

_____. "Les monnaies de la dynastie de 'Abd-Hadad et les cultes de Hiérapolis-Bambycé," *MUSJ* 23 (1940) 1-82.

Rouvier, J. "Baal-Arvad, d'après la numismatique des rois phéniciens d'Arvad durant la periode préalexandrine (450 à 332 avant J.C.)," *Journal asiatique* 9th ser., 16 (1900) 347-359.

_____. "Note sur une trouvaille de doubles statères des rois Phéniciens des Sidon," *Bulletin archéologique du Comité des travaux historiques et scientifique* (1901) 371-373.

_____. "Numismatique des villes de la Phénicie: Gebal-Byblos," *JIAN* 4 (1901) 103-117.

_____. "Numismatique des villes de la Phénicie: Sidon," *JIAN* 5 (1902) 99-116.

Schaeffer, C.F.A. "Nouveaux témoignages de culte de El et de Baal à Ras Shamra-Ugarit et ailleurs en Syria-Palestine," *Syria* 43 (1966) 1-19.

_____. "Une trouvaille de monnaies archaiques grecques à Ras Shamra," *Mélanges syriens offerts à Monsieur René Dussaud*. Bibliothèque archéologique et historique, vol. 30, pp. 461-487. Paris: Paul Geuthner, 1939.

Schlumberger, Daniel. *L'argent grec dans l'empire achéménide*. Paris: Imprimerie nationale, 1953.

Schmidt, E.F. *Persepolis I: Structures, Reliefs, Inscriptions*. Chicago: University of Chicago Press, 1953.

_____. *Persepolis II: Contents of the Treasury and Other Discoveries*. Chicago: University of Chicago Press, 1957.

_____. *Persepolis III: The Royal Tombs and Other Monuments*. Chicago: University of Chicago Press, 1970.

Seltman, C.T. *Athens: Its History and Coinage Before the Persian Invasion*. Cambridge: Cambridge University Press, 1924.

_____. *Greek Coins*. London: Methuen and Co., 1955.

_____. "On the 'Style' of the Early Athenian Coins," *NC* 6th ser., 6 (1946) 97-110.

_____. "The Temple Coins of Olympia," *Nomisma* 8 (1913), 9 (1914), and 11 (1921).

Seyrig, H. "Antiquités syriennes: 40. Sur une idole hiérapolitaine," *Syria* 26 (1949) 17-28.

_____. "Antiquités syriennes: 64. Sur une prétendue ère tyrienne," *Syria* 34 (1957) 93-98.

_____. "Antiquités syriennes: 69. Deux reliquaires," *Syria* 36 (1959) 43-48.

_____. "Antiquités syriennes: 70. Divinités de Sidon," *Syria* 36 (1959) 52-56.

Shepard, K. *The Fish-Tailed Monster in Greek and Etruscan Art*. New York: Privately printed, 1940.

Silverman, M.H. "Aramean Name-Types in the Elephantine Documents," *JAOS* 89 (1969) 691-709.

Six, J.P. "Le satrape Mazaios," *NC* 3rd ser., 4 (1884) 97-159.

_____. "Observations sur les monnaies phéniciennes," *NC* 17 (1877) 177-239.

Solá Solé, J.M. "Miscelanea Punico-Hispana I. 3. HGD 'RŠF y el Panteon Fenicio Punico de España," *Sefarad* 16 (1956) 341-355.

Speiser, E. *Genesis*. The Anchor Bible, Vol. 1. Garden City, NY: Doubleday and Co., 1964.

_____. "The Name Phoinikes," *Oriental and Biblical Studies*, ed. J.J. Finkelstein and M. Greenberg, pp. 324-331. Philadelphia: University of Pennsylvania Press, 1967.

Starr, C.G. *Athenian Coinage 480-449 B.C.* Oxford: Clarendon Press, 1970.

Stebbins, E.B. *The Dolphin in the Literature and Art of Greece and Rome*. Menasha, WI: George Banta Publishing Co., 1929.

Stern, Ephraim. "Achaemenid Lion-Stamps from the Satrapy of Judah," *EI* 10 (1971), Zalman Shazar Volume, 268-273, pls. עא-עב (Hebrew). Jerusalem, 1971.

_____. "Eretz-Israel in the Persian Period," *Qadmoniyyot* 2 (1969) 110-124 (Hebrew).

_____. "Phoenician Masks and Pendants," *PEQ* (1976) 109-118, pls. 9-11.

_____. *The Material Culture of the Land of the Bible in the Persian Period, 538-332 B.C.* Jerusalem: Bialik Institute and the Israel Exploration Society, 1973. (Hebrew)

Tarn, W.W. *Alexander the Great*. Cambridge: Cambridge University Press, 1948.

Thompson, G. "Iranian Dress in the Achaemenian Period," *Iran* 3 (1965) 121-126.

Thompson, M., Mørkholm, O. and Kraay, C. *A Catalogue of Greek Coin Hoards*. New York: American Numismatic Society, 1973.

Vandier, J. "Review of F.K. Kienitz's *Die politische Geschichte Ägyptens vom 7. bis 4. Jahrhundert vor der Zeitwende*," *Bibliotheca Orientalis* 11 (1954) 189-190.

Virolleaud, C. "Les nouveaux textes mythologiques et liturgiques de Ras Shamra," *Ugaritica V*, ed. J. Nougayrol, *et al.*, pp. 545-551. Paris: Imprimerie nationale, 1968.

Weinberg, S.S. "Post Exilic Palestine: An Archaeological Report," *Proceedings, Israel Academy of Sciences and Humanities*. Vol. 4, no. 5, pp. 78-97. Jerusalem, 1969.

Weinfeld, M. "'Rider of the Clouds' and 'Gatherer of the Clouds,'" *Journal of the Ancient Near Eastern Society of Columbia University* 5 (1973) 421-426.

Wente, E.F. "Tutankhamun and His World," *Treasurers of Tutankhamun*, ed. K.S. Gilbert. New York: Metropolitan Museum of Art, 1976.

Whitaker, R.E. *A Concordance of the Ugaritic Literature.* Cambridge, MA: Harvard University Press, 1972.

Widengren, G. *Die Religionen Irans.* Stuttgart: Kohlhammer, 1965.

_____. "The Sacral Kingship of Iran," *The Social Kingship,* 8th International Congress for the History of Religions (Rome, April 1955), pp. 242-257. Leiden: E.J. Brill, 1959.

Woolley, C.L. *Carchemish: Part II The Town Defenses.* London: British Museum, 1921.

_____. *Carchemish: Part III The Excavations in the Inner Town.* London: British Museum, 1952.

Wright, G.E. "Shechem, 'Navel of the Land': Part III. The Archaeology of the City," *BA* 20 (1957) 19-32.

_____. *Shechem: The Biography of a Biblical City.* New York: McGraw Hill and Co., 1964.

_____. "The Samaritans at Shechem," *HTR* 55 (1962) 357-366.

Zeuner, F.E. "Dolphins on Coins of the Classical Period," *Bulletin of the Institute of Classical Studies of the University of London* 10 (1963) 97-103.

John Betlyon is currently Director of the Chapel and a member of the faculty of Religion and Biblical Literature at Smith College in Northampton, Massachusetts.

He holds a Ph.D. in Near Eastern Languages and Civilizations from Harvard University. He has done archaeological work in Tunisia, Cyprus and throughout Syria-Palestine, and is currently numismatist for the excavations at Umm al-Jimal, the Central Limes Arabicus Project and the Wadi el-Ḥasa Survey Project, all in Jordan.